DANSE MACABRE

MEMOIR OF A POLISH GIRL AT THE TIME OF THE RUSSIAN REVOLUTION
(1914/1924)

Aniela Tarnowicz

DANSE MACABRE

MEMOIR OF A POLISH GIRL AT THE TIME OF THE RUSSIAN REVOLUTION (1914/1924)

IRENE ROCHAS

A.M. BENIS
New York

© 2017 A.M. Benis

ISBN 978-0-578-14916-5

Second edition

All rights reserved under International and Pan-American Copyright Conventions. No part of this publication may be reproduced, stored in any information retrieval system, photocopied, recorded, or transmitted by any means whatsoever without the express written consent of the copyright holder.

Tarnowicz, Tarnowiczówna, Aniela (1906-1993)
  Rochas, Irene (pseudonym)

DEDICATION

To Aniela's grandchildren

CONTENTS

Acknowledgements	ix
Preface	xi
Main Characters	xv

Part I — HOME

Chapter One: View from a Window Sill	1
Chapter Two: Mother and Father	7
Chapter Three: Tom	17
Chapter Four: Madame Zariza's Dream Book	21
Chapter Five: A Visit from Aunt Juta	26
Chapter Six: Bed Time	31
Chapter Seven: Christmas	37
Chapter Eight: The New Year, 1914	40
Chapter Nine: Father's "Name Day"	42
Chapter Ten: The Jewish Quarter	46
Chapter Eleven: Stepping Out at Last	50
Chapter Twelve: Easter	54
Chapter Thirteen: Beggar's Soup	57
Chapter Fourteen: Vacation in Russia!	61

Part II — RUSSIA: WAR AND REVOLUTION

Chapter One: Jadwiga	67
Chapter Two: First Days in Russia	69
Chapter Three: Father Makes the Decision	82
Chapter Four: Moscow is Home	85
Chapter Five: Summer, 1915	94
Chapter Six: School and Friends	106
Chapter Seven: Summer, 1916	112
Chapter Eight: Christmas in Tula	120
Chapter Nine: October 1917	123
Chapter Ten: Surviving Winter	130

CONTENTS

Chapter Eleven: Henryk	139
Chapter Twelve: A Sack of Flour	145
Chapter Thirteen: Summer, 1918	152
Chapter Fourteen: Goodbye to Moscow	154
Chapter Fifteen: The Train	156
Chapter Sixteen: Quarantine	160

Part III — BACK HOME

Chapter One: Pauline	169
Chapter Two: A New Home	178
Chapter Three: Sweets	184
Chapter Four: Danse Macabre	188
Chapter Five: Summer, 1919	191
Chapter Six: Goodbye to Father	193
Chapter Seven: Scarlet Fever	197
Chapter Eight: Bolshevik Invasion	200
Chapter Nine: Letter from Lubyanka	208
Chapter Ten: Class Enemies	218
Chapter Eleven: Magdalena	224
Chapter Twelve: The Sleeping Giant	235
Chapter Thirteen: Rachmaninov Concerto	245
Chapter Fourteen: Phlox	250
Chapter Fifteen: Mrs. Teacher	257
Chapter Sixteen: Narcissus	265
Chapter Seventeen: Mrs. Doctor	277
Chapter Eighteen: Do You Remember…?	281
Chapter Nineteen: Who Is Going to…?	287
Chapter Twenty: Silence in the House	290
Endnote	395
Illustrations	299
Sources of Illustrations	320
Bibliography	321

ACKNOWLEDGEMENTS

I should like to thank my siblings, Artur Jacek Benis and Anne Joanne Marshall for their help and interest in tracking down old family records and reconstructing events of the past.

Thanks also to Professor Andrzej Wyrobisz, son of Janka, to Jacek Chmurski, grandson of Stefa, and to Bohdan Wasiljew, grandson of Jadwiga, who provided information and photographs regarding the Tarnowicz family.

Ms. Anna Jędrzejczyk of the Instytut Sztuki of the Polish Academy of Sciences went out of her way to supply information, and photographs, pertaining to Aniela's career as an actress.

Dr. Diana Poskuta-Włodek of the Juliusz Słowacki Theater, Krakow, researched its archives and kindly provided the photograph reproduced within.

And belated thanks to my colleague, Jacob H. Rand, M.D., who read the manuscript — in 1981 — and was kind enough to offer his opinion of the work.

AMB

PREFACE

Irene Rochas is the pseudonym of my mother, *née* Aniela Tarnowicz in Warsaw on August 2, 1906. She was the youngest child in a large, traditional upper middle-class Polish family; her father was an official with the Warsaw-Vienna Railroad. Besides Aniela, her parents had given birth to nine previous children. With the outbreak of the Great War in 1914, the family found itself stranded in Moscow, and with the further outbreak of the October Revolution, they were not able to return to their homeland until the summer of 1918.

Aniela attended the Conservatory of Music in Warsaw, settling in the School of Drama and graduating in 1929. She then started a busy, but abbreviated, career as an actress, appearing on stage at theaters in Vilnius, Warsaw and Krakow. Her last performance was at the majestic Julius Słowacki Theater in Krakow in 1935. Reviewers of the time praised Aniela's performances for her natural stage presence, her clear voice, as well as her freshness, smile and sunny disposition.* During that time she married a fellow actor, but the relationship lasted only three years. She also traveled abroad widely during those years, exploring thirteen countries in Europe, the Mideast and Northern Africa.

In 1936 she married a second time to Antoni August Benis, a member of a prominent family from Krakow. He had recuperated from serious wounds sustained in the Polish-Russian conflict of 1920 and was in the midst of an active career in international finance. By St. Valentine's Day of 1939 Aniela was the mother of two sons.

On September 1, 1939 Germany invaded Poland, the family finding themselves in Łódz, not far from Warsaw. Learning of Antoni's imminent arrest, they immediately began a flight from their homeland. They managed to cross into Romania on September 16th, just a single day before the Soviet invasion of Poland from the east. Next followed an odyssey through five more European countries before the family finally reached New York during the summer of 1940. They intended to stay temporarily, but with the worsening political situation in Poland,

---

* Aniela Tarnowicz, in *Słownik biograficzny teatru polskiego,* Vol. III, Instytut Sztuki, Polish Academy of Sciences, Warsaw, 2016.

they adopted the United States as their home, eventually becoming naturalized citizens. Aniela had two more children and became Angela Benis, just another busy suburban housewife, trying to raise four children on a modest budget. During those years, in the little spare time that she had, she occupied herself with painting, horticulture and driftwood art. She seemed to have lost all interest in the theater. No one who knew her in New York could have guessed that she had been an actress.

I first learned of Angela's manuscript in 1968. I had returned to New York after an absence of four years abroad. Angela's health was failing, and the family home was being disbanded. Into my possession fell some memorabilia: photographs, Angela's wartime diary (written in Polish) and the manuscript — written in English. I was surprised and curious that Angela had written something in English.

It was not until July of 1981 that I finally read Angela's manuscript. I was astonished — perhaps stupefied is a better word — that Angela had written such an interesting, empathetic and extraordinarily rich work — in English! English was not her second language. Not even her third. It was her *fourth*. She was much more at home with Russian and French than she was with English, which had been more or less forced upon her by the family's exodus from Europe. Angela always spoke English slowly — some would even say haltingly — with a measured cadence, as if she were translating from another language. In addition, apart from her wartime diary, nobody had ever known Angela to have written anything besides occasional letters to relatives. Perhaps she was inspired by the example of Józef Korzeniowski, the Polish seaman who perfected English only as an adult and became the great author, Joseph Conrad?

On a visit to Angela — who was alert although not well — I had to ask right away, "Did all those things really happen?"

She said, "Yes, yes. It's all true..."

I must have raised an eyebrow because she went on, saying something like, "Of course, I had to fill things in when I didn't know exactly what happened."

We talked for a while about those times, so long ago. She recalled how the famine in Russia was so severe that "people were eating the bark off the trees." How her sister Helena had become a very distinguished physician; how Stefa had survived the last war in Warsaw

PREFACE

with her son; her sibling rivalry with Janka; how Henryk had stubbornly remained estranged from the family.

"And Sophie, did she really…?" I asked.

"Yes, yes. Poor, poor Sophie. She was such a good person."

"And Magdalena, did she…?"

"Yes. She was such a good pianist… but she could not perform in public because of stage fright."

I told Angela that the manuscript needed to be published and that I would do my best.

Regrettably, nothing would come of it, and the manuscript returned to the drawer with the other memorabilia, where it would stay for nearly thirty more years.

Then, recently I was contacted by Ms. Anna Jędrzejczyk of the Drama Institute of the Polish Academy of Sciences. They were preparing a biographical encyclopedia of Polish actors and actresses: could I give them some information about Angela? They also had some very rich details — and photographs — of Angela's career. Thus, I began to think once more of Angela's work… and decided that I would do my part to ensure that — at long last — Angela's manuscript would see the light of day.

The manuscript: my sister recalls that Angela wrote it 1958 or 1959, pecking it out on our ancient portable typewriter that had French accent marks and Polish characters. Who prepared the final clean copy, nobody knows. The manuscript in my possession appears to be the second carbon copy of the final version. It is intact, except for a single page where the carbon paper apparently had folded on itself in the lower right-hand corner. The resulting missing words, at the end of the last two lines, are labeled [*words missing*] in the text. There were some errors in spelling, syntax, and so on, but in general the manuscript is presented intact with only minor copy editing.

I did make a few additions to the manuscript. First, I added the subtitle, using the word "memoir" in the literal sense of "remembrance." Second, I added chapter titles. Third, I added a list of "Main Characters" and an endnote. Finally, the infrequent foot-notes are mine.

In addition, Angela had anglicized the names of some of her siblings. In particular, her sister Jadwiga was given the unfamiliar name of "Hedwige." I took the liberty of restoring it to her given name. I also restored "Henry" to Henryk, "Tommy" to Tomasz, and "Helen" to Helena where it seemed indicated.

Angela's pseudonym "Irene Rochas" is a name that no one had ever heard before. But her pseudonym, and the title of her work, "Danse Macabre," are not surprising: Angela had always admired all things French.

Angela's work does have some faults. In particular, readers may be offended by some of her views and language, which at times may sound single-minded or elitist, and her description of the Jewish Quarter seems needlessly pejorative. But if one is put off or offended early in Angela's narrative, I would entreat the reader to persist to the end, and give Angela a chance to redeem herself before making any final judgment.

Does Angela's work have historical or literary merit? Well, as Angela would say, "Maybe it does, and maybe it doesn't." To this reader, anyway, it has merit enough to be given the opportunity to let readers decide for themselves. Angela evidently thought that she had a story to tell us, so let us give her the chance to tell it.

In her later years Angela was infirm and did not speak very much. Often she seemed lost in thought. But it is not difficult to imagine that as she sat there, with eyes flickering, that the pages of time were turning back rapidly, that she was once again six years old, sitting on a window sill in Old Warsaw, watching with a discerning eye what her brothers and sisters were doing… wondering what life is all about… and wondering what the future will bring.

A.M. Benis, M.D.
20th November 2018

MAIN CHARACTERS

Adela. Irene's Polish-Jewish playmate in Moscow.

Akulina. The family's maid in Moscow.

Andrzej. Obstetrician colleague of Helena.

Aunt Juta. Jósefa. Youngest of Father's three sisters.

Aunt Helena. Helena Julia. One of Father's three sisters.

Aunt Nathalie. Mother's eldest sister.

Aunt Tota. Teodozja. Father's eldest sister.

Boris. Husband of Maria Eremeyevna.

Bronek. Bronisław. Son of Aunt Nathalie.

Camilla. Zofia Podkowińska. Daughter of Aunt Juta.

Dvornik. The landlord's handyman in Moscow.

Emily. The live-in maid of the family in Warsaw.

Father. Irene's father, Aleksander Tarnowicz.

Halina. Sister of Adela.

Helena. An elder sister of Irene.

Henryk. One of Irene's brothers. Married Magdalena.

Ira. Daughter of Lydia Alekseyevna.

Irene. Aniela Tarnowicz, the youngest child in the family.

Jadwiga. Also, Yadviga, Yadunya. Eldest child in the family. Married Vlodek.

Jagna. A neighbor's maid in Warsaw.

Janka. Janina. Irene's next-elder sister.

Janusz. Helena's suitor.

Kolia. Son of friends of Vlodek and Jadwiga.

Kozelkova. Russian classmate of Irene.

Kuharka. The landlord's cook in Moscow.

Lydia Alekseyevna. Russian friend of Vlodek and Jadwiga.

Magdalena. Music student who became the wife of Henryk.

Maria Eremeyevna. Russian friend of Vlodek and Jadwiga.

MAIN CHARACTERS

Marfa Grigoryevna. Widow who rented a room in the family's flat in Moscow.

Mila. Marychna. Irene's infant sister who died from scarlet fever.

Mother. Irene's mother, *née* Zofia Grochowska.

Niania. Vlodek and Jadwiga's governess.

Nina. Daughter of Lydia Alekseyevna.

Pauline. Wife of Bronek.

Rachela. Paramour of Adela's father.

Sergei. Houseboy of Vlodek and Jadwiga in Russia.

Sophie. Zofia Wanda. A sister of Irene.

Staś. 1. One of two of Irene's siblings who died as infants from scarlet fever. 2. Elder of Aunt Juta's two sons.

Stefa. Stefania. Sister of Irene.

Tadyo. Tadeusz. Son of Jadwiga and Vlodek.

Tomasz. One of Irene's brothers.

Uncle Sigismund. Zygmunt Podkowiński. Aunt Juta's husband, a physician and surgeon.

Ursula. Former live-in maid of the family in Warsaw.

Viera. Russian classmate idolized by Irene for her ballet dancing.

Vlodek (Vladimir). Wladimir Wasiljew (Владимир Васильев). Husband of Jadwiga. (Alphabetized, the surname would be at the back of a list of names in Polish, but near the front in Russian).

Władek (Władysław). Aunt Juta's younger son.

Yura. Irene's playmate at the Revyakino dacha; son of Maria Eremeyevna.

PART ONE: HOME

Warsaw, 1914

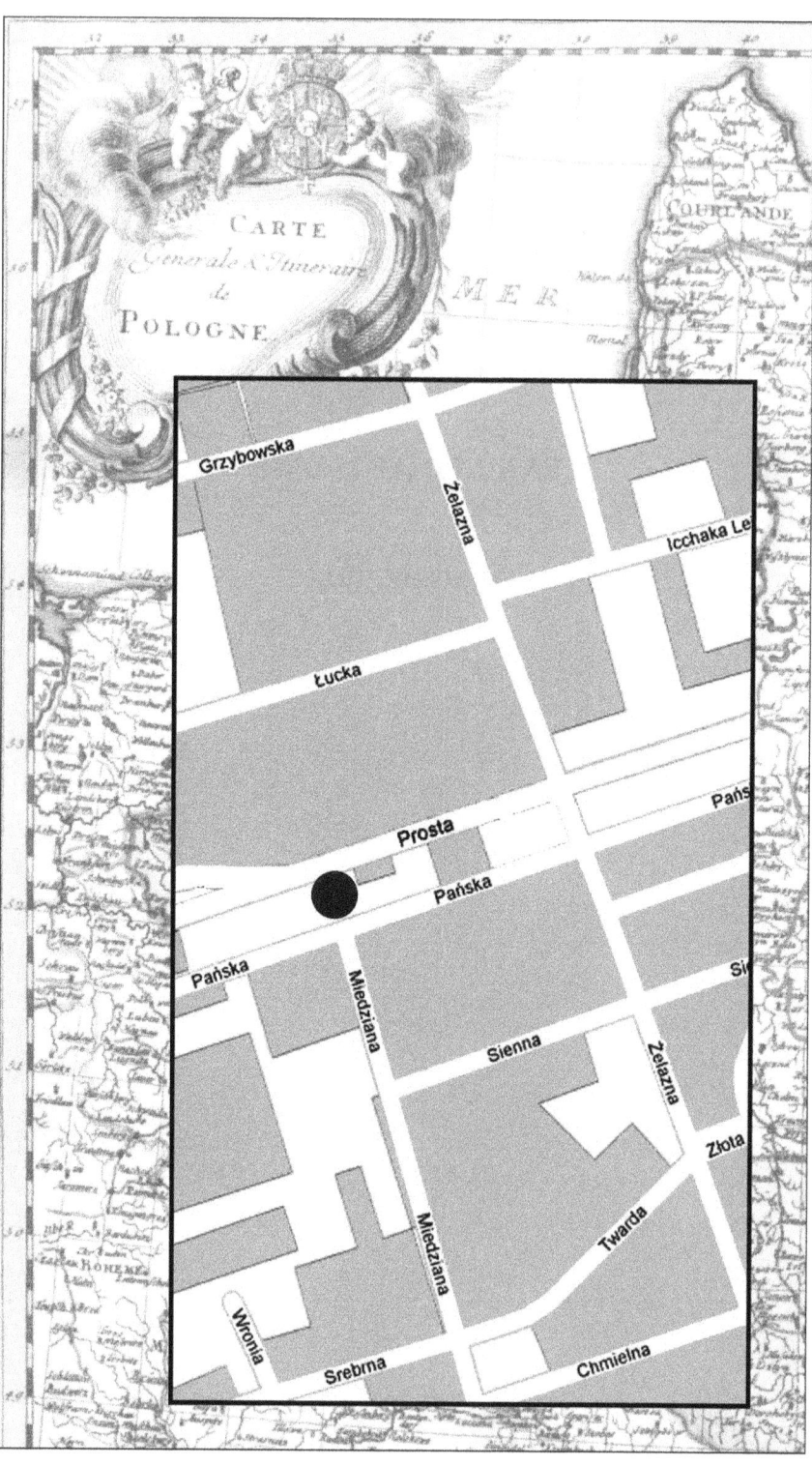

CHAPTER ONE — View from a Window Sill

IRENE was sitting on a window sill in the parlor. The walls were solid brick, about one and a half feet thick, thus making the window sills in the apartment wide and comfortable to sit on. She liked to crawl there, behind the curtains, and pretend it was her own room.

Besides, at this time of the day there was not much else she could do. She was six years old and read large print quite well, but she possessed only two books, both of which had been given to her on her last birthday. She had read and re-read them so many times, and looked so often at the same pictures, that she knew all the stories by heart.

Here, from the window sill, she could see the whole room — called the "salon" — and through the open door, the dining room where her brother and sisters were seated around the long table doing homework.

The girl facing the salon with straight brown hair, gray eyes and thin lips was Helena. She was the eldest. That is, she was the oldest child at home, as Irene had one older sister, Jadwiga, who was already married.

Sitting here alone, Irene liked to pretend she was "talking" to someone, though actually she did not "talk," but "think."

"You see? Jadwiga not only is married, but she *even* has a baby. Her baby was born in this house — in this very room, *as a matter of fact...*" (Irene had just heard Helena use this expression and liked it very much).

PART I — CHAPTER ONE

"Jadwiga's husband is an engineer, but they did not yet have their own home when the baby was about to be born. So, naturally she had it here because her husband had to serve in the army for a while, just like everybody else. A special hospital bed was rented and put in the salon, right here between the piano and the sofa. She had a doctor with her, and a nursemaid who took care of her and the baby as soon as it was born. They all called the nursemaid 'Niania' because that is what they are called. She was hired from a newspaper's advertisement because she was 'willing to travel' — whatever that means. Jadwiga said she would not move one foot without Niania. Her husband was stationed in the southern part of Russia, and that is where she went with Niania and the baby."

"So, you see, Helena is not the oldest, but she is the oldest here. She is fifteen. Right now she is writing something very fast. I wish I could write so fast. Well, anyway, Maman says that I am doing well for my age."

"Henryk is sitting next to Helena; he is awfully smart. Look, he is holding a compass that he uses for drawing circles. Then he draws a straight line between them and measures something and writes lots of numbers. Henryk is fourteen. Doesn't he look funny with so much hair standing straight up on the top of his head? He grows so fast that his school uniform is too tight on him."

"Sophie is sitting on the right side, at the end of the table. Everybody says that Sophie is a most beautiful girl. She has light, curly hair, big blue eyes, and a nose and mouth just right. She and Henryk have very delicate bones. That's what I heard. They have delicate bones because they were born a year apart: Henryk after Helena, and Sophie after Henryk, and Maman did not have enough *calcium* to make their bones. When one listens to grownups, one can hear the strangest things. Who would guess that your bones are made of Maman's calcium before you are born?"

"Naturally, I know *how babies are born*. The night Jadwiga had her baby, she was screaming and yelling so loud that I could not sleep a wink, even with my head under the pillow."

"On the left side, facing Sophie, sits Stefania, called Stefa. She is pretty, too. Her eyes are bluer and her hair lighter than Sophie's, but I heard someone say that she *can't even compare* with Sophie, who has so much 'breeding' in her face and figure. What is breeding? You don't know either? I have to remember to ask Maman about it. Stefa has stronger bones, because she was born almost two years after Sophie, and Maman had enough calcium. Oh, how old is she? She is eleven. She is memorizing some poem, mumbling words half out loud. Sophie is also trying to memorize something; she covers her ears with her hands so as not to be disturbed by noises, and sways back and forth. This makes Henryk nervous. From time to time, he shouts, 'Will you stop swaying!' But Sophie stops only for a minute, then forgets and starts swaying back and forth again."

"On the fourth side of the table, with her back toward me, sits Janka. Like Helena, she has straight, brown hair and hazel-gray eyes, but her nose is not quite the same. Janka has a fleshy, upturned nose. She has a funny habit of wiping her nose with the back of both hands… it makes her look like a squirrel. Actually, her nose does not need any wiping. Janka is more than three years older than me, but everyone says that we grow like twins; we share the same room and dolls, and we play together. This year Janka started school. You have to learn a lot of things at home before you can go to a girl's private school and be admitted to the Preparatory Class. Why does one have to know so many things? If Preparatory Class prepares you for the First Class in the Girls' School, why do you have to prepare for preparing? Oh, everything is so complicated."

It got dark very quickly.

Emily, the maid, came into the dining room, pulled down the lamp that hung on brass chains above the dining room table, took off the glass and lighted the lamp with a match. She blew a few times at the glass, wiped it on her apron, put it back and pulled the chains up in place. The lamp swayed back and forth for a long time after she had left the room, and the shadows of the sitting children danced on the walls around the big circle of light made by the lampshade. None of them paid much attention, or even noticed, Emily's coming and going.

The light from the dining room fell through the open door into the salon in a soft, golden and diffused beam. It fell on the carpet and on the piano, which was still open, a few sheets of music resting on it. It shone on the golden frame of Mozart's miniature — in his white wig with a frilly *jabot* under his chin — and on the two brass candelabra that held half-burned candles. The rest of the room was almost dark. Irene could hardly see the contours of the high coffee table, two sofas, chairs, a side table that held a tall lamp with a glass shade (called an "abat-jour") and a large breakfront, the upper part of which was filled with books and the lower used as a linen closet.

Irene's attention was not concentrated on the room, though, but on the outdoors. Through the window, right across the street, she could see Miedziana Street, or translated "Copper Street." During the warm-weather months, when Irene could play on the wrought iron balcony, she could see — to the right and to the left — Pańska Street on which they lived.

"Some streets have funny names," she thought. "There is Gold Street and Silver Street, Long and Short Streets... you would not believe it, but there is even one called Jump Street because it is so short... and one called Crooked Wheel... another, Crow... and one called Frog Street. There aren't even any frogs on it. I was there because that's where all the ladies buy their hats. You go from one store to another and try on hundreds of hats and look for bargains. That's where Maman bought her big hat with the two white wings, and which she pins on her head with such dreadful, long pins. Each time Maman puts her hat on, I am afraid that the pins will go right through her head, but they don't."

Irene liked to sit here at twilight, when everything outside looked suddenly blue. The street was empty. Far away she could see a man with a torch and a long stick. He stopped at each lamppost, put the torch inside the glass, and presto! — the lamp was on. Then he crossed to the opposite side, lighted the next lamp, and came back in a zigzag path, back and forth, back and forth, until the street had all of its lights on.

For Irene, there was some magic in it all. Even though she knew that there was nothing magic in pulling the chain which opened the flow of gas and lighting it, every night she watched with the same fascination as the small, gray figure of a man carrying a torch moved about. Tonight he looked even more like a magician or a ghost, because it was foggy and one could hardly see him. The light had a big halo, which when Irene squinted her eyes, had all the colors of the rainbow.

Mother came into the room through the door leading from her bedroom. She was holding a lamp, which she put on top of the breakfront. Emily came too, holding a pile of freshly-ironed linen so tall that you could not even see her face. Mother opened the drawers with a key held with others on a ring, and started to put away the linen. Now you could see Emily's face. It was not very pretty, but nice, with a cheerful expression and healthy, pink cheeks. Emily came back twice more with linen from the kitchen until everything had been put away in the drawers. Then mother locked it up and returned the jangling keys to her pocket.

Mother went back to her bedroom where she would mend or sew, or do something like that. Irene remembered that Emily often said:

"With six children in the house there is always something for Madame and for me."

Irene wished that she could go into the kitchen and talk with Emily, but mother wouldn't let anybody stay there because, she said, "Emily puts into children's heads those silly stories about ghosts, devils and witches that make no sense."

"*Everybody* has to mind Maman because she is so smart and works so hard to run the house," thought Irene. "She was brought up in a big, big house in the country, with many servants, but she never complains about having only one maid now. Maman never spanks you or even raises her voice, but everyone is a little afraid of her, which is different from what you feel for Papa."

Father, or as Irene called him, "Papa," was gentle and soft-spoken, and usually didn't say much. Nobody could possibly be afraid of *him*. He would come from the office, eat his dinner, and go out to visit his sisters, or for a "demitasse" at the café where he would meet his friends and read the papers.

Irene always thought that people drank "demitasse" in a café because it was cheaper than a whole cup.

"Papa is terribly handsome," Irene said to her imaginary friend. "Jadwiga and Sophie look very much like him. I look a little like him, too: the same large blue eyes, same nose and mouth, and the same blond, wavy hair. Naturally, *I* don't wear a moustache. Do I love him? I don't know much about love, but I am happy when Papa is home, and I miss him when he leaves. I don't care so much about others. In fact, I am even glad when Maman goes out, because I can sneak into the kitchen and talk to Emily. Papa never tells you to sit up straight, to keep your elbows together, or to eat soup quietly like Maman does."

Sometimes, when in a good mood, father would give Irene a "ride" on his knee, or sit down at the piano and play gay marches, Schubert's songs, and sing. He was never taught how to play the piano, and his voice was nothing much, but to Irene it all sounded marvelous because she felt that on that day papa must have been less sad than usual.

The double windows were weather-stripped for winter, yet the chill of the November night lingered on the window sill. Irene pulled her pleated skirt down over her knees. She decided that there was nothing else to do here; the man with the torch had gone long ago. She would have to wait until tomorrow evening to see him again, though she knew that at dawn he would be there, walking like a ghost among the morning mists and putting out all the lights.

She had seen him only once at such an early hour. It was the night before Jadwiga had her baby, a year ago. Irene could not sleep that night, for Jadwiga was screaming every few minutes in that inhuman voice. This made Irene tremble and afraid that her sister was going to die. She had crawled out of bed, gone to the window in the dining room and pressed her forehead against the cold windowpane.

The bluish mist had been everywhere beyond the window, and in it she had seen the lonely man (this time without a torch) going from one lamppost to another, pulling the chain and extinguishing the lights. Suddenly she had become aware of quiet in the house.

That had been a year ago, but somehow Irene often recalled that night and early morning; maybe the lonely man on a deserted street had something to do with it.

The door from the salon had opened. There stood maman in her flannel petticoat and bed jacket, smiling. Behind her stood Niania holding a little bundle in her arms.

"Don't you want to see your nephew?" maman had asked.

The shivering little girl had gone near and looked at the tiny baby, who in swaddling clothes looked like the Jesus that she had seen in the crèche the Christmas before. It had seemed to her such a miracle — his coming from nonexistence, born out of pain, yet tranquil, contented and asleep.

It had been too much for her to try to hold so many emotions in her heart any longer... the awe, admiration and love for the miracle of birth, of life. She had run to her bed, buried herself under the covers and began to cry.

"She is just jealous," Niania had said.

A year had passed, yet the same man (or maybe it was not the same man?) still came to light and then extinguish the gas lamps...

Irene jumped down from the window sill and sat in the dining room, coloring pictures with crayons until suppertime.

CHAPTER TWO — Mother and Father

"Emily, will you button my coat?" asked Irene.

Emily put the sweeping brush in the corner and helped Irene with her coat, mittens and galoshes.

Father and the children left early in the morning, as usual, and Irene was to go with her mother to do the marketing. On Tuesdays and Fridays, which were big marketing days, Emily went with them to help mother carry things; otherwise she started cleaning as soon as the children left for school. Mother and youngest daughter went to the Halles alone, carrying a milk can and basket.

For Irene it was the only walk of the day during the winter months, but in the spring she and Janka sometimes went to the public park with Emily in the afternoon.

The Halles were only a few minutes' walk from home. One had only to turn right from Miedziana Street and there it was: a huge, domed glass building in which there were hundreds of booths and stalls. Butchers in one place, bakers in another; grocery, vegetable and fruit vendors in still another. Outside, on the cobblestone square behind the Halles, there was a marketplace where peasants came with their horse carts. Here, mother bought milk, butter, sour cream, cheese, eggs, and so on.

She would always ask the peasant if it was fresh, and he would say: "Of course, my lady. It couldn't be fresher." But mother would try a bit of butter or cheese with her nail, put it in her mouth and make a funny sucking noise with her lips before buying it.

In the fall, on market days, there were so many horse carts that it was hard to walk between them. Then, mother would buy potatoes and vegetables for the whole winter, and lots of fruit in large bushel baskets.

She would bargain and squeeze the fruit, hold heads of cabbage to see if they were heavy, and bargain some more.

Then the peasant would follow her home in his horse cart and store everything in the cellar. Mother would pay him, and he would ask for a tip. Naturally, mother would say no, that he had over-charged for everything as it was, and the peasant would whip the horse and drive away looking very mad. But in fact, he was glad that he had sold everything and could go home right away, instead of having to sell little by little to many customers all day long.

That particular day, while Irene was following her mother around the market, it did not take them very long. They just got milk, and soon they were inside the Halles. In spite of the glass roof and walls, it was much darker inside than out. With the ceiling many stories high, there were strange acoustics; people walking and talking made a constant buzzing noise, which to Irene seemed exciting and cheerful.

They bought bread, rolls, and little twisted rolls with raisins from the man in a red fez. Mother called him "Turek," which means Turk.

"Maybe he is, maybe he isn't a Turk, but he is a Moslem, and that's why he always has to wear that funny red hat with the black fuzzy tail," Irene explained to her always present yet invisible friend.

Then they walked to the butcher's section, where mother looked at the meat and showed the butcher what and how much he should cut. He wrapped the meat in brown paper, mother paid him, and they were ready to go home.

At the exit there were stalls where you could buy sweets. Mother bought long, white and red-striped mint candies, and a bag of honey candies called "little bees." You were supposed to keep them in your mouth until they slowly dissolved, leaving a taste of honey. However, Irene always crushed them between her teeth into tiny, golden splinters and swallowed them right away. Thinking of "little bees" reminded Irene that one of her front teeth was wiggling. Mother had said that any day now, she would have to pull it out. Irene took off her mitten and tried the tooth. It wiggled, but not too much.

"Take your hand out of your mouth," mother said severely.

They were back home. Mother left everything in the kitchen, except the candy, of course, and sat in a chair by the large French door leading to the balcony. She usually did her sewing in the dining room during the morning because the light there was the best. Here, she could work. Her eyes were not too good, even though she used glasses for reading and sewing.

Each week mother and daughter stayed in this room for many hours until dinner time. That meant until the children came from school and father from his office. Now and then, of course, mother would get up to see what Emily was doing and tell her about dinner.

Sitting at the dining room table, with an extra pillow on the chair because she was so small, Irene was learning how to write. She considered big *D* and *W* the most difficult, and maybe *F*. She always got mixed up with small *b* and *d*. Which was which?

"Remember — *b* has a stomach up front," mother would say, "and *d* has a seat in the back to sit on." But Irene got mixed up from time to time, just the same.

When Irene got tired of writing, mother would tell her many stories, always true. Mother never wasted time on fairy tales or any such nonsense. Anyway, there were so many interesting true stories to be heard that Irene could listen all day.

For instance, mother told her how Poland was once a great and powerful country, reaching as far as Kiev and the Black Sea. How she had many brave kings and knights who fought for centuries against Germanic and Muscovite tribes, against Turks, Tartars and Swedes. How, five hundred years ago, the German knights had been beaten at Grunwald by Polish and Lithuanian forces in a great, bitter battle. How nearly three hundred years later, Poland under King Jan Sobieski was the only country in Europe to help Vienna, which had been besieged by the Turks. King Sobieski delivered the besieged city, repulsed the Turks for good and left Europe free of the Moslem threat. How the Swedes, very aggressive toward their neighbors during that time, had occupied a great part of Poland until they invaded the monastery of Jasna Góra, which means "Mountain of Light." In it, there was an old Byzantine icon of a Madonna, blackened by age.

The Swedes were inside the monastery, swarming all over it, when one of them struck twice at the icon. Immediately their fate was sealed and their luck cut short. The whole triumphant, victorious campaign turned into disaster. In a short time, the Swedes were expelled from the monastery and eventually from the whole country.

That is why the Madonna was crowned Queen of Poland. It was not just a story, Irene knew, but the real truth, like the story about Joan of Arc is a true story in France. Every Pole went to visit Jasna Góra at least once in his lifetime to see the Madonna and to look at the two deep cuts on Madonna's face made by the sword. Many people go there once a year. Irene was taken to Jasna Góra the first time when she was two years old.

Mother told Irene that Russia and Germany grew strong and greedy, and together with Austria, which was just as greedy, they grabbed Poland and divided her among themselves. This time Madonna no longer seemed able to help, in spite of the fact that every Pole prayed and fought and prayed…

"Maybe the Madonna could not help because nobody cut her face with a sword again," Irene thought. "The Russians and Germans used bullets, not swords anymore," maman said.

In spite of the fact that the Russians and Germans were very strong and cruel, mother had said, twice within the last century the Poles staged uprisings and fought like lions to regain freedom. And before that, they hoped that the French emperor Napoleon Bonaparte would help them, so they fought on his side, too. But it all ended up in a great disaster, because not one country in the whole of Europe raised even one finger ("How can a country raise a finger?" Irene wondered) to help Poland.

Many men from Polish nobility and the gentry fought in these uprisings, including her father's and mother's relatives. One of mother's great-grandfathers had been a general who fought with Napoleon's army. His portrait was hanging in the salon, above the green couch. He looked very young.

"How can a great-grandfather of anybody look so young?" Irene wondered.

Sometimes mother would talk about more recent happenings. She had been born in the part of Poland under German domination, so she knew many stories from there. Like, for instance, the story about the children of Września.

The Germans wanted the Polish children to become German, so they not only had to speak, read and write German as soon as they went to school, but they were also ordered to say morning prayer in German. Each morning the teacher would call a different child's name and order him to say the prayer — and each morning the child would get up and say it in Polish. The teacher would punish him, beating him until he looked like a bloody pulp. But the next day, another child would get up and say the prayer in Polish again. All the children were so badly beaten and mistreated that it became a big story in the papers, and there was so much indignation that the Germans had to stop. The children had won.

"Mother moved from the German-dominated part of the country to Warsaw when she got married. Warsaw is the capital of Poland, but under Russian rule; everybody knows that," Irene thought.

Irene had a good memory for poems. In fact, she had been able to recite poems ever since she was two years old. It started when Jadwiga went to see an operetta and later, while playing the piano, sang some arias from it. Soon Irene, still baby-talking, started to imitate her. So, for fun, everybody began to teach her poems and songs because it was so amusing to listen to such a small child reciting a grownup repertoire.

At five, she knew dozens of Christmas carols and most of the poems that her brothers and sisters had memorized aloud for school, many of them in three foreign languages that she didn't even understand.

Mother also taught her the poems of Maria Konopnicka, a great poetess and symbol of hope for all Poles in regaining their independence. Like for instance:

And learn how to hate, my child,
Hate with all your soul.
Hate is the flame of human might,
Force that breaks the chains of slaves...

So, Irene learned how to hate. No Pole would call a German "German"; they were called *shvabs*, which was a synonym for roaches, vermin. Russians were called either *Moscals*, or even more despicable, *catzaps*, a synonym for cruel, primitive brutes.

Part of an unofficial national anthem, forbidden to be sung in public, ran as follows: *

The German will not spit in our face,
Nor our children will he Germanize.
Our cadres are armed with God's grace,
Spirit will take the leader's place,
We'll march when the Golden Horn resounds...
So help us God — so help us God!

---

* M. Konopnicka, *Rota* (1908)

PART I — CHAPTER TWO

For a child, growing up in this atmosphere and being taught such poems, it was as easy to hate the oppressors as it was to breathe.

That morning, after Irene finished struggling with D and W and F, and little b which carries a stomach in front, and d which has a seat behind, she wanted to look at the family picture album.

"Maman, may I look at the Album?" she asked.

"All right, but wash your hands first. They are full of ink."

For a while, Irene sat on a little stool near her mother, with a big, heavy leather-bound book in her lap. She knew all the brownish, thick, cardboard-like pictures by heart.

On the first page, there was a large wedding picture of her parents. How young they looked!

"Maybe Papa did not change much, but Maman, in her white crinoline looks beautiful! It was twenty-five years ago. Now Maman is *terribly* old. She is forty-five and is getting gray hair. Papa is fifty-five, but he has no gray hair at all yet."

Irene asked, "Please tell me how you met Papa."

"Well," began mother, "you know that I had seven brothers and seven sisters. I was the youngest of all the girls. By the time all fifteen of us had gone through boarding schools, music lessons, and the boys were getting their higher education, the girls were getting married, one after the other. Each got a lovely trousseau, some jewelry and, naturally, a dowry. So, my six sisters made very good marriages and settled in new homes. When my turn came, Father did not have any money left for a dowry."

"The news spread quickly among the neighbors that I was without a penny, so not one young man became interested in me. Here I was: an old maid of twenty years, possessor of a fine trousseau, one fur-lined coat, one ring and one broach. All my sisters had married much younger. At twenty, I was considered a hopeless case of spinsterhood."

"But some well-wishing relative found a widower with five children who was willing to marry me. I took one look at that awful man with the bushy, dark beard, and swore that I would rather die than marry him. I said to my mother: 'I can't. I simply can't marry him.' She said, 'You have no dowry. You can't be choosy.' I said, 'All right, but let me go once to see a big city during the winter season; let me attend a ball once in my life; let me go to concerts and theaters before I get married'."

"Mother agreed. I was to stay in Warsaw at my eldest sister's house. You know, Aunt Nathalie, the one who died last year."

Mother stopped talking for a while as if reliving once again her life of twenty-five years before.

"And then what happened?" asked Irene.

"I packed my clothes and left, knowing that no matter what, I was not going to come back home to marry that dreadful widower with five children. I settled at Aunt Nathalie's house and was caught up at once in a whirlwind of social activities. At the first private dance, I met your father. It was love at first sight."

Irene did not know what "love at first sight" meant, but from the way maman's voice quivered, she knew it must have been something very desirable and wonderful.

"After that," continued mother, "your father spent every free moment with me and soon asked me to marry him. I wrote a letter home saying only that I was going to get married, and would they please send my trousseau."

Irene turned a few pages of the Album.

Grandfathers, grandmothers, uncles, aunts. Men with small or long moustaches... with or without beards... ladies in wide dresses with hair covered by lace or by little bonnets... ladies with tiny waists and big bosoms, in funny hats with parasols, or without hats... with long hair undone, standing by a column, or elaborately coiffured, sitting in a chair and holding a book...

She turned another page: two babies, sitting on a fur rug.

"That's Mila and Staś," Irene said.

"Yes. They died of scarlet fever even before Jadwiga was born."

"How strange to have had a brother and sister you'd never seen, who will never be anything else but two smiling, little babies in a picture," thought Irene.

One of the last pictures in the Album was of a group of all the children — except Irene, who had not yet been born — all much younger than they were now, of course. Standing between two sisters was Tomasz, Irene's brother, who had died two years before.

In a few flash pictures, Tom appeared in her mind: a tall, blond boy, serious and unsmiling, mostly sitting at his desk reading or writing. She could remember very well the morning he died, though she had been only three years old at the time... children getting ready for school, then leaving... some argument between maman and Tom at the table about spilled milk, which was dripping from the tablecloth onto Tom's suit and onto the floor...

Afterwards, maman had left with Janka for the market (Janka wasn't in school yet) and Irene was following Ursula, their maid of two years ago, from one bedroom to another and watching her make beds.

Another picture appears vividly in Irene's mind: about an hour later, maman, still in her hat and coat, was leaning over the couch in the salon where Tomasz lay moaning and twisting in pain. Maman was crying and shouting for Ursula to bring soap, and she poured milk straight from the big can into Tomasz' mouth. The milk spilled all over the couch because maman's hands were trembling, and because Tomasz was tossing his head about in such pain... The groceries were all over the floor...

Ursula brought the soap — she was crying, too — and with maman they made Tomasz bite the soap and drink the milk. This made him vomit something awful. Now why would maman be so cruel and make him eat soap until he vomited? Maybe that's why Tomasz died?

She remembered maman shouting to Ursula:

"Run to the pharmacy and ask for an ambulance!"

The men came and took Tomasz, and that was the last time Irene ever saw him. On the day of his funeral, she had to stay with a neighbor because Ursula had gone to the funeral, too. Irene was too small to go.

She looked at the picture of Tomasz for a long time and finally said:

"Tom died, too."

"Yes, he died, too," mother replied softly.

"... How do you keep on living, knowing that you murdered your own child? How do you face the world, without being punished for it? How do you cope with the bankruptcy of all the things that you smugly evaluated as being right? You and your husband live for years, considering yourself good parents. You believe that you do your best to work, protect, support and guide your children — and one day the whole structure of self-satisfaction and self-esteem crumbles into ashes. You find it is not enough to love, but that you must show love; that it is wrong to judge things only from your point of view. That feelings and judgments of your own child, your seventeen-year-old son, might be more important than yours..."

After Tomasz' death, mother had found a diary among his school books. There was so much wretched loneliness in it, of feeling unloved, misunderstood and unappreciated... so much jealousy toward his older sister, Jadwiga.

"Did we really treat Jadwiga with so much more love and attention than Tomasz — the way he wrote... 'There is always plenty of money for Jadwiga's gowns, trips to relatives, theater tickets... but when I ask for a new school uniform or a new pair of shoes, I am told: they are good enough; it can wait'?"

"But I only wanted to help my daughter find a husband. Jadwiga had just finished school; it was only proper to send her into 'circulation' elegantly clothed. I was right, wasn't I?"

"You were wrong," said a small voice of conscience.

The woman, sitting in a chair near the balcony door sewing, was trying to smother that small voice, to push it back into the deepest, darkest place of her being. But it was growing, spreading, choking her. "You were wrong!" it was shouting loudly. "You were wrong, whatever the reason, to show more love and attention to one child at the expense of the other. You killed him!"

... The night before he killed himself, he had asked again for a new suit. His old one was too tight and shiny at the elbows. And mother had said that the tailor could let it out at the seams and steam press it. She had been very mad, because Jadwiga had told her that she was going to marry that "Moscal" engineer, who was then an officer in the Russian army.

"What a shame! She will never be able to face any of her relatives. And who, of all people? Jadwiga! Beautiful, elegant, educated... to marry a 'Moscal'! Why, she could have married God knows how well..."

Tom said: "No! The tailor can't let the seams out because it will show, and the steam will not help."

Mother had been so hurt by Jadwiga and the Moscal thing that she had to get it out of her system. She shouted:

"Stop bothering me with your silly suit! A boy in school should think about education, not about clothes! Don't you realize that Jadwiga is getting married... and Moscal or *their* family can't have a reason to criticize *our* family...? And Jadwiga must get as good a trousseau as a girl from a good family is expected to get? Don't you realize how much a trousseau is going to cost?"

PART I — CHAPTER TWO

And Tomasz had said: "Mother, is that *all* you can tell me?"

She said "yes" and slammed the door.

The next morning, he spilled a whole pitcher of milk, and mother had shouted that he had done it on purpose, but if he thought he would get a new uniform because he ruined this one, he was very much mistaken. He would wear this one even if the stains from the spilled milk didn't come out. She went out to the market and came back and... "Oh, Lord, have mercy on me..."

The last picture in the Album was that of Irene. She was standing on a tall, carved chair, holding onto its sides with her little, plump hands. Irene pulled a pin from mother's pincushion and punctured both eyes in the picture.

"Now, why did you do that, you naughty girl?!"

"I don't know," Irene replied.

CHAPTER THREE — Tom

Tomasz was sitting at the table in his room. Actually, it was not a room, but a nook in the hall between the kitchen, dining room and salon. There was just enough room for his bed, a small table and chair, and a double shelf on the wall for his books.

When the family moved into this apartment, he was given this "alcove" as the only place he could call his own. But, as it was part of a hallway, he never had any privacy or quiet for studies... or day-dreaming.

There was the constant presence of parents, children and the maid crossing the hall. Jadwiga would always choose to do her piano exercises when he had to study, or his two youngest sisters would play hide-and-seek all over the flat — including his room. Or, like today, he could overhear every word of an amicable argument between mother and Jadwiga as to what should be the size of the monogram on her trousseau.

Every afternoon he could hear Ursula doing dishes in the kitchen; stacking piles of plates and silverware, banging pots and pans, slamming cupboard drawers. It was almost impossible to concentrate with all this constant noise in the home.

He asked mother many times if he could study in the salon. It seemed silly to him that the biggest room in the house should be wasted for piano playing and entertaining guests only. But mother said no. She always said "no" to everything he would ask for.

"If only Ursula would finish those dishes! I can't stand the noise anymore," thought Tomasz.

"... I think the crown above the monogram should be one-third the size of the letters, don't you think so, Mother?" came Jadwiga's voice from the next room.

PART I — CHAPTER THREE

"She is getting married. Maybe it will be more bearable to live here without her... that selfish, self-centered 'wonder child'," thought Tomasz hopefully.

Ursula had just dropped a pile of silverware on the floor, and the sudden noise made Tomasz jump in his chair.

It was his last year in the Górski private school for boys — the best school in Warsaw. Years ago, he had been reluctantly admitted, without tuition, to the First Class. But later, he had shown such unusual talents in his studies that his parents were told that they would never have to worry about tuition; it would be a privilege for the school to have such a gifted student.

All the other students, however, were from wealthy families, many of them being "only sons." The boys wore regulation cadet-style, black uniforms, high-collared with leather belts. These had to be custom-made by a tailor out of the best English cloth, and they were expensive.

As far as he could remember, Tomasz always recalled the suit as too large for him ("to grow into," mother would say to the tailor at the fitting) or outgrown — too small, shiny at the seat and on the elbows. This fall he had been promised a new suit; then mother had suddenly changed her mind. He asked his father about it, but papa had said: "Let Mother decide."

It is not that he paid such attention to clothes, but he was shy and liked to be inconspicuous in the crowd. In Górski School one could hardly be inconspicuous by being poor or shabbily dressed, only by being wealthy and well-dressed.

Tomasz' classmates always had plenty of money. They would sneak out at night to the pool parlors (which, of course, was absolutely forbidden by the school) or even to the fashionable bordello. There was a lot of whispering about it between lessons.

Tomasz never had any pocket money; his only entertainment was skating in the winter. During the summer months life was a little easier. The family spent two months up in the country in a rented house. They could visit any of their parents' rich relatives, all of whom had big country houses and estates, but his parents had enough sense to understand that a family with eight children is not welcome even by the closest and richest of relatives. Besides, they were mostly mother's relatives, and father was proud and wanted to show that he made sufficient money to take care of his wife and children in a proper way.

"Yes, it will be better in the summer, when I can take long walks in the woods — alone — but it's only the end of November now. How am I going to endure this winter?" Tom wondered. "And after I finish school, what? Oh, I know that I will go to Warsaw University... but studying what? *You have to take law or engineering to make a decent living* was what Mother always said. But I don't want to be either an engineer or a lawyer. I would like to study philosophy, astronomy or archeology. I would like to travel much, maybe write poems or make inventions..."

Ursula crossed the hall several times with trays full of dishes. She was making the same noise now that she made when in the kitchen, putting the dishes and silverware away in the dining room sideboard.

"What homework do I have for tomorrow? German: Goethe — *Faust*. French: Alfred de Vigny. Math: calculus — that's easy. Organic chemistry: I am a few lessons ahead of what is required. What else? ... History, Latin, Greek? No, not tomorrow."

The door from the dining room opened. Jadwiga crossed the hall, going to the kitchen to get a glass of water.

Mother was standing at the door. Tomasz got up.

"Mother, I am supposed to read my essay at the Christmas party, on the stage. I can't show up in my old suit. It's too tight, and shiny on the seat and elbows. You promised me that I would get a new one at the beginning of the school year. It's November now..."

He could not study that evening, and he could not sleep all night.

The next morning he got up and dressed; his head was aching from the lack of sleep. As he was putting a coffee pot on the tray at the breakfast table, he overturned a milk pitcher. Before he had a chance to get up, the hot milk spilled on the table, on his lap and on his trousers. Mother was shouting that he had done it on purpose. He had not! So help him God, he had not!

Mother went out. "How can I go to school with all these awful stains on my suit? I can't. I have to take it off. How ridiculous. Take it off, and what? Stay here all day? Wait until Mother comes back from the market and nags and nags? And soon Jadwiga will get up, and will laugh: 'Well, re–a–lly, Tom spilled milk like a little child and could not go to school... how perfectly silly!' "

He sat at the table in that wet, messy suit, holding his head in his hands. The shelves full of books were right before his eyes: Goethe — *The Sufferings of Young Werther*. Werther committed suicide when suffering became unbearable and life lost all meaning. Weininger: a philosopher genius, who wrote a book at the age of nineteen, killed himself shortly afterward...

"Is not life just one silly but painful joke?"

He got up. "Better hurry before she comes back," he said to himself.

He went to the entrance hall where the dark wooden medicine cabinet hung from the wall. Aspirin, quinine, bandages, Vaseline, mustard plaster, ammonia, iodine...

"They won't even let me be buried in the cemetery," he thought bitterly, holding a bottle in his hands.

He was wrong. The church, by special dispensation, graciously permitted his parents to bury him in the family grave, instead of outside the cemetery walls in a place called "The Alley of Suicides."

If one of the students died, it was the custom of the school to send a few of his close friends-classmates to the funeral.

At Tom's funeral, not only his close friends were present, not only his class, but the entire school was closed for the day.

The teachers, grief stricken, served as pallbearers, and the principal — an elderly man who had spent all of his life transforming boys into well-disciplined young gentlemen, who could master emotions under any circumstances — was crying uncontrollably like a child.

CHAPTER FOUR — Madame Zariza's Dream Book

"Emily, remember to light the dining room stove," said mother while putting on her hat in front of the hall mirror.

"This time she is surely going to puncture her head," Irene thought, watching her mother insert the long, sharp hatpins.

But mother turned around, took her muff from the chair, and without appearing mortally wounded, asked:

"Did anyone see my pocketbook?"

Mother was always forgetting where she left her pocketbook. Stefa brought it from the dining room, where it had been lying on the sideboard.

"May I go with you?" asked Irene.

"Not today," replied mother as she put on her galoshes. "It's very muddy in the streets. Some other time." And with a "be good," she left.

Irene watched Emily light the stove. It was tall, up to the ceiling and made of white tile, but when you looked inside, through the little iron door, you could see that it was built of brick. The same stove went through the wall to the salon where it was also faced with white tile and likewise reached the ceiling. It had no iron door there, but this didn't matter since it was warm there on the outside anyway.

First, Emily removed all the ashes and put them in a bucket. Then she put in some kindling wood and lots of coal and lighted the whole thing with a match. She closed the heavy iron door, but left the smaller lower door open for a draft.

PART I — CHAPTER FOUR

She took the bucket to the kitchen, and naturally Irene followed her, since mother was not at home and could not scold her for staying in the kitchen.

"I — am — go — ing — to — tell — mo — ther," half shouted, half sang Janka.

Irene turned and stuck out her tongue at Janka. Not much, like some naughty children do, but just a teeny-weeny tip of the tongue to show how much she despised Janka for being a tattletale.

The kitchen was cozy and warm. The big brick, white-tiled stove in the corner, topped with iron, was giving off a steady heat. In the other corner was Emily's bed, covered with a pretty blue bedspread, a gift from Irene's mother the Christmas before. On the wall hung a few photographs and religious pictures.

Then there was a big table, scrubbed so clean that you could smell fresh wood when you put your head down on it. There was also a chair, a few stools of various sizes, a sink with a cold water faucet, and a cupboard. Warm water was always kept in big pots on top of the stove, and a copper teapot was nearly always whistling away — gentle, barely audible music.

Irene knew that Emily had come from the country to work here because she needed the money to get married. A girl could not marry until she could buy a cow, a horse, or whatever her fiancé thought they might need to make a new home. Emily was not "engaged," but "spoken to"; that's how peasants refer to it. But it was the same thing, Irene knew.

Right after Tomasz died, Irene's parents had moved to this apartment and hired Emily, since Ursula had made enough money to go back to her folks and get married. Before Ursula, there had been a maid by the name of Josephine. She had also married, but all this happened before Irene was born.

"Emily, do you like to work here?"

"Sure. Why not?"

Sure. Why not? Back home she would have to get up at dawn, work in the fields, clean up stables or chicken coops all day. She would live on bread, cabbage and potatoes, sleep three or four in one bed in wintertime, and on straw in the barn during the summer. She would not be able to get married in her village because her parents were poor, and who would marry a peasant girl without land or money?

MADAME ZARIZA'S DREAM BOOK

Here she had her own bed, plenty of food and meat six days a week. Once a month Madame would call her into her bedroom and hand her six rubles, and Emily would say "thank you Ma'am" and kiss mother's hand. When she saves two hundred rubles, she will go back home and get married.

Every second Sunday after dinner, she was allowed to go out for the evening. The time was usually spent in church, or in the kitchen of one of the maids in the neighborhood, where they would gossip about their employers or talk about the folks back home.

"What are you writing, Emily?'

"A letter home."

Emily was writing slowly. Her rough, red fingers were holding the pencil clumsily, but she was proud to be able to write. When she had first come here, she could neither read nor write. Helena taught her for almost two years, day by day.

The first book Emily bought was *of course* "Madame Zariza's Dream Book" — "... more than ten thousand dreams explained in alphabetical order." For instance, you dream of a knife, so you look under *k* — "knife, to cut bread with: you will be well provided for in your old age." Or, "to see a knife on the floor: beware of a relative who hates you." Or, if you dream of woods, you look under *w* — "woods, to see from the distance: a trip," or "to walk in the woods: be careful of a gentleman you go with."

Madame Zariza's picture was staring at you from the cover with her big eyes. She was dressed like Cleopatra (or at least the way *she thought* Cleopatra should be dressed) and was holding a glass ball in her hands. Madame Zariza apparently knew everything! Obviously she had little difficulty in writing her book. You could not please Emily more if you told her what you dreamt of the night before, and asked her to look it up in her book to see what it meant.

Helena, sitting in the kitchen and teaching Emily how to write would sometimes open "Madame Zariza" and laugh her head off — reading aloud, for instance, that dreaming of snakes meant that you "can't go out *at night* with a tall, dark man."

"Does it mean that I can go out with a *short, blond* man, or that I can go out with a dark man *in the daytime*?" she would ask Emily with a terribly serious face.

The other book which Emily had acquired was a book of poems and ballads. These were poems sung to popular, repetitious tunes, mostly about valiant knights saving maidens in distress, or about lovers meeting secretly under a weeping willow, or romantic stories about murder, punishment and the repentance of wicked wives or husbands.

Emily knew the tunes to almost all of them, and she would sing in her thin, never properly set voice, making up with a *tremolo* for what it lacked in schooling. Some of these songs were perfectly ridiculous, but many of them were very old, with the charm, simplicity and poetic beauty of classic poetry.

As to "Madame Zariza," Irene was not quite sure whether she was on Helena's side or Emily's, that is, whether she believed what was in the book or not. But as to the other book, she certainly loved it and never tired of listening to those charming tunes.

Emily finished her letter, signed it "Your loving daughter, Emily," and put it into a cheap, pink envelope, the top of which was imprinted with two kissing doves.

"Sing something, Emily, please."

"In the garden, in the full-moon light... The knight was kissing his sweetheart's lips..." started Emily.

One by one, first Janka, then Stefa and Sophie, and finally Helena — all the girls came into the kitchen, sat on stools and began to sing with Emily.

"Look who's here — the Greek chorus," said Henryk, popping his head through the half-open door. "I'm hungry: how about some toasted bread? Do you have hot coals in the stove, Emily?"

All the girls jumped from their seats.

"Yes! Let's have toasted bread!"

"Me too!"

"I'm hungry, too!"

Everyone started to look for kitchen forks. Helena brought a big loaf of bread from the dining room and started to slice it, while Emily removed the round iron covers from the top of the stove and poked the hot coals a few times with a poker until sparks burst almost in her face. Each child was now holding a fork, stuck into a piece of bread, over the stove. First they toasted one side, then the other.

Meanwhile, Emily brought a dish of butter from the balcony, where it was kept cold and firm, and started to butter the toasts.

For a while, one could hear nothing but the crunching noise of toasted sour bread as it disappeared into a half a dozen hungry mouths.

The whole procedure was soon repeated — the toasting, buttering and eating of bread.

When they finished eating, they all sat where they chose ("Not on my bedspread!" cried Emily), talking and laughing. Henryk was teasing Sophie, Janka *of course* wanted to take everybody else's seat, and they started to sing again. Henryk was imitating an opera singer while fighting a duel with the poker. This went on until they heard a key in the front door. Before mother had time to open it, they all had run out of the kitchen, resembling a flock of sparrows in flight.

"Emily! You forgot to shut the vent in the dining room, and the heat is escaping from the stove!" cried mother.

CHAPTER FIVE — A Visit from Aunt Juta

Helena was sitting in the dining room, sewing. It was the eighth of December, a religious holiday, and the school was closed.

She was planning to make a few blouses for herself, a pinafore for Irene, and a new school dress for Janka. Irene was standing next to her, watching. Helena had a natural talent for making clothes. Whenever mother brought home "remnants" from the store, Helena would put a piece of material on the table, draw a few lines with the tip of her scissors, and presto! "Hroup, hroup, hroup" went the scissors as she cut the material into something or other — without even a pattern — and whipped up a new outfit on the sewing machine.

"May I turn the handle, Helen?"

"All right. But when I say 'stop,' I want you to stop, or you will run over my fingers."

Irene started to turn the handle of the sewing machine. It was black and cold; even on the hottest summer day it seemed cold, and it made a funny *"tig, tig, tig"* noise when you used it. On the top, gold letters spelled out "SINGER".

These were the first letters Irene had learned how to read. After that came the title of the daily newspaper, names of stores, signs, and such, until she could read everything without being taught.

Stefa, Sophie and Janka had gone to school to rehearse for a Christmas pageant. Janka wanted awfully to be an angel, but they made her play the part of one of the little shepherds instead. She cried all day yesterday, but didn't cry today.

Sophie was going to play Saint Mary, because mother said that she has the face of an "Italian Madonna."

"How come the Mother of Jesus is Italian?" Irene asked herself. "I always thought that she was Jewish, because she is a relative of David, and in the little picture book that Janka has, it says that David was King of the Jews. Well, anyway, Sophie looks like Mary, Mother of Jesus, and that's that. And she is not Jewish."

After many an "all right, go ahead" and "stop," Helena took out the garment. It was finished! It had frills and tucks in the front. Helena took off her sister's old pinafore and had her try on the new one. It fitted Irene just right, but it smelled funny of new print, like all new materials do.

"May I wear it? I want to show it to Maman."

Helena, standing up, nodded her head. She already had another piece of material on the table, and the scissors went "hroup, hroup, hroup" again.

Irene went into the salon where mother was playing the piano.

Maman's fingers were a bit stiff, mainly because she had no time to practice her scales every day, and if one doesn't practice, one's fingers are not as nimble as they could be. "But she plays well," Irene thought, "although I prefer it when Sophie plays." When Jadwiga was living at home, she used to play a lot, too.

Helena, Stefa and Janka have no ear for music, maman said, so they don't play. How can one have, or not have, "an ear for music"? Everybody has ears.

Irene had ears, and an "ear for music." When mother struck a false note, it would hurt Irene somewhere inside in a way she did not know how to explain.

Sophie played the piano "with feeling." Mother just played, but Irene liked it just the same because she liked music.

Right now there was a sheet of music on the piano with the title in large print reading *Valse Triste*. Triste means sad in French; Irene knew that. The music was slow, and it did make her feel somewhat sad. Sometimes mother played *Valse* from the opera *Faust*, or Tchaikovsky's *Chant d'Automne* and *Romance*, or Chopin's "easier pieces" like preludes and mazurkas, and Paderewski's *Minuet*.

Irene, listening to mother's playing, was sitting near the table on which there rested a tall lamp. She wondered why it did not overturn, standing there on just one, thin leg.

In the next room, Helena while sewing was listening, too.

"All of Mother is in her interpretation of music," she thought. "Well taught, efficient and without feeling."

Since Tomasz' death Helena had felt estranged, if not hostile toward her mother. She had read Tom's diary, too. His accusations of a domineering, unloving mother, and of an indifferent, passive father, had left her with a certain impression. Of course, she appreciated all that her mother was doing for the family, her endless struggle to keep things going at the highest possible level, albeit within their meager means. And she knew that in her own way, mother loved her children very much. Yet, she felt also that something was missing in their relationship — a spark of tenderness, perhaps, or a sense of humor that could change their family from a group of relatives living under one roof, into a unity of people bound together with true devotion.

Within the circle of the family Helena had always felt herself to be on the same side of the fence as Tom had been. Nobody was hovering about her, beaming with pride for her achievements or talents. Nothing extraordinary was ever happening to her as it was to her sister Jadwiga. Her good marks at school were accepted by her parents as the ordinary, normal work of a child of her age, and her looks were never mentioned. So, she assumed that she must be ugly.

Indeed, when Helena looked in the mirror and saw that pale face, small nose and mouth, large gray eyes and straight "mousey" colored hair, she had to admit that there was nothing to get excited about.

"Tom lost his battle because he was too demanding, too sensitive. He was a genius; that's what his principal said in the funeral eulogy. Well, I am not a genius, and maybe that is why I have no intention of going to pieces and quitting life. No matter how drab it may look for a while, I am going to do something extraordinary and great, something that will make me want to live and others want to look up to me. I don't know yet *what* it is going to be, but I feel strong and confident that I will reach that goal."

The doorbell rang. Mother stopped playing the piano. Helena heard Emily opening the door and in a while, mother's mildly enthusiastic exclamation:

"Why, Juta! What a surprise! And Camilla! Come in, please come in!"

Aunt Josephine, called Juta (the youngest of father's three sisters) was a woman of strong character, strong opinions, and of an unending determination to make mother's life miserable. Although she was always very sweet and agreeable, there was always that drop of poison in every spoonful of honey-flavored affection. To say the least, mother reciprocated that affection in a similar way. Each visit of Aunt Juta in their house — or mother's at Aunt Juta's — was an elaborate well-performed duel, with point and counterpoint, and which culminated in a *touché*. Mother and Aunt Juta carefully counted, silently in their minds, how many points each one had to their credit.

It would start casually about their children's marks (beside Camilla, Aunt Juta had two boys) or new clothes. Or next summer's vacation, until it would end in a big battle about some political issue.

"... I don't agree. I think that *every intelligent person* has to recognize the vital importance of..."

"Oh, so I am not intelligent?" the opponent would think bitterly.

"... considering that I have six daughters..." ("She has only one, and what can she do about it?").

... or, "Well, Henry is only fourteen and his marks are excellent, too. Your Władek is fifteen, is he not... and in the same class as Henry?"

"What are they trying to prove?" Helena thought, half amused, half disgusted at this display of human weakness. But in the face of a common enemy, she always felt a great deal of solidarity with her mother.

Aunt Juta, right after taking off her coat, entered the dining room and in a matter of seconds, made Helena feel like a Cinderella.

That "why – are – you – slaving – at – the – sewing – machine – you – poor – child" look made Helena hostile right away. Mother was giving instructions to Emily about the tea, so Helena and Aunt Juta were alone.

"Do you *have* to sew, Helen?"

"I don't have to. I like it."

"Where is Henry?"

"He is out, skating."

"Why aren't *you* skating?"

"Because I would rather do my sewing. Why is Camilla not skating?"

Camilla had just entered the room, having disposed of her coat and galoshes. Nobody could call her anything else but unattractive. Her long, thin face, too long a nose, and small eyes reminded one somewhat of a camel. That is what Henryk had called her years ago, and she looked every inch of it. She was the same age as Helena, and both girls had been used by their mothers as stabbing weapons in their mortal duels.

"Some people have hidden virtues," mother would say, discussing an unimportant matter and looking intensely at poor Camilla.

"Yes," Aunt Juta would reply. "I am sure that your Helen is one of them."

In fact, Camilla did have hidden virtues. She was intelligent, studious and determined like Helena to achieve more in life than her mother had.

The girls came home from rehearsal, Henryk from skating, and mother busied herself serving tea, so for a while there was a truce. Presently father came home from the office and greeted his sister with reserved politeness so as not to annoy mother, who was jealous of any sign of affection toward his sisters.

Soon though, Aunt Juta and mother succeeded in finding a topic for a political discussion, which kept them busy for a half hour in the heat of argument.

Suddenly, Aunt Juta got up and, as if nothing had happened, started to say affectionate good-byes. Like ancient Greeks who found elevation and purification of their souls by watching tragedies in great outdoor amphitheatres, mother and Aunt Juta had their *catharsis* after a spent battle. They both felt good, as if they had achieved something creative and important.

"We have to run now, dear. Come to see me soon," said Aunt Juta, kissing mother.

"Don't worry. I will," replied mother, helping Aunt Juta with her coat in the hall.

CHAPTER SIX — Bed Time

"Come on, Irene, get dressed. I will take you with me to the store."

Mother did not have to repeat it twice. In a minute, Irene was ready and waiting, all dressed in her coat and leggings, white fur bonnet, muff and galoshes.

Every few weeks mother went to the "Colonial Store," which was a large, elegant store on Marszałkowska Street, a fashionable shopping center. There she bought coffee, tea, dried fruit and spices, all of which she required in great supply for such a big family.

It was winter: a crisp, frosty afternoon, and it was already getting dark. The night before, there had been a big snowfall, and the streets looked cozy and cheerful under so much snow. All the horse-driven coaches and *drożhki* (open carriages) had disappeared; instead there were sleighs drawn by horses that went along in a gay, easy trot. They all had bells attached to their harnesses, and the streets were filled with the sounds of these tinkling bells, each one a slightly different tone. Together they formed a simple, unique orchestra.

Irene moved at a trot, too; it was difficult to match mother's long stride. In a few minutes they would reach Marszałkowska Street, where there were more lights than on any other street. All the stores had such lovely displays that Irene's eyes simply popped each time she was there.

Before they reached the corner, she saw a beggar sitting right on the bare snow, all cuddled up, his face hidden in the collar of his worn-out jacket, trying to warm himself with his own breath. His shoes were so worn that Irene could see his bare, frostbitten feet and toes.

She pulled at her mother's arm and stopped. Without a word, mother opened her bag and gave her one kopek, which Irene put in an old hat lying on the sidewalk. Resuming her trot, she could hear from behind: "Thank you, little angel."

Right around the corner, there was first the chocolate and candy store; Irene simply *had* to stop and look in the window display at the house made of gingerbread, cookies, candies and marzipan. Hansel and Gretel were standing on both sides of the house with an expression of admiration and awe that could be matched only by Irene's enthusiasm.

Next, there was a corset shop with dolls as big as life, dressed in frilly petticoats and corsets of all colors — even red and black!

Then there was the SINGER store, and in the window was a huge doll sitting at a sewing machine... just like Helena when she was sewing.

After this store, there was the greatest magic of all: the entrance to the movie house, called the "Illusion." The lights were simply blinding at the gate, and inside Irene could see *a real Negro* in a green and gold uniform, handing out programs. He was the only Negro in the whole city, in the whole country; really black, like the sequins on maman's evening gown.

Mother once went to the "Illusion" with Irene's older sisters, and afterwards they had talked about it for at least a week. "Someday maybe I will go, too," thought Irene, watching the Negro holding a stack of pink programs.

"We will stop first at the Aunts' house for a minute," said mother.

"The Aunts" were the two older sisters of papa. Both unmarried, they ran an exclusive dress shop, which sold fancy wedding gowns and trousseaux. They catered only to a very rich clientele from the nobility. The store had no sign at all; it was just a large apartment on the main floor.

Mother and Irene walked in and were greeted by Aunt Theodosia, called "Tota" and Aunt Helena.

When one saw them, one could not tell how old they were or whether they were attractive, but one certainly could not fail to notice how distinguished they looked. Soft spoken and graceful, they were always showing a polite interest in their brother's children. Mother would never argue with Aunt Tota or Aunt Helena like she did with Aunt Juta. They were sitting at the round tea table, sipping tea and talking very politely.

"She is getting more beautiful every time I see her," said Aunt Helena.

"She has a fantastic memory. I have to keep her away from the room in which the children study, or she would memorize all the poems they are taking in school," said mother. "She will easily be ready for Preparatory Class next year."

"At six? Incredible. Eight is soon enough," said Aunt Tota.

"What are they talking about?" wondered Irene, though by now she had become interested in what was going on in the next room, the door to which was half open.

There she could see a very large, long room with many, many lamps on the walls, and crowded with young women. Some were embroidering monograms, others attaching little pieces of delicate lace to silk cloth, still others busy turning the handles of sewing machines. They were mostly quite young; some looked almost like children. The only older woman in the room was one standing near a headless manikin, adjusting a dress on it.

"Irene, close the door and behave yourself," said mother.

"Come, have some *petit-fours*," added Aunt Tota, making the scolded child feel more at ease.

Irene took one cookie and started to explore the salon. It had two mirrors reaching to the ceiling, each with a mantel on which stood figurines of Saxe porcelain. Her favorite one was of a man, elegantly dressed in a white wig and stockings. He stood near a beautiful lady sitting in a swing, who was wearing a white wig, too. She had such tiny slippered feet, like Cinderella! Irene wanted to touch her, but all-seeing mother called:

"Don't touch anything, Irene! Come, we have to go now."

Finally they reached the "Colonial Store," where the pungent smell of freshly-ground coffee, vanilla, cinnamon and tea filled the air.

Big sacks of almonds, nuts and raisins were on the floor; rings of dried figs were hanging from nails in the dark woodwork, and the shelves were full of colored tea boxes.

The salesman measured freshly-roasted coffee beans into a stiff, shiny bag. Then he made a big package of tea, coffee and all the things that mother bought for baking Christmas cakes. Then they went to the back room, which was filled with unsorted odds and ends of china.

Mother chose some dishes, which she got free as a bonus, and had them wrapped.

Out in the street, with two big packages in her hands, mother hailed a passing man with a horse and sleigh.

"Will you take us for thirty kopek?"

"Thirty-five, my lady."

They sat down, and the driver tucked a big leather apron around their legs. Then he whipped the horse, which started up in a trot. What a ride!

The sleigh was almost at the front door when Irene noticed in the semi-darkness of the street lights, a familiar looking, tall figure walking toward their house.

"Papa!" she cried, and jumped from the sleigh as soon as the horse stopped.

Father, smiling, bent low and kissed the child. Irene felt his cold nose and frosty moustache on her cheek, and kissed his hand as she always did.

"Be careful," said mother, handing him the packages. "There are some dishes inside. I got them free. Emily is so hard on china, so we can certainly use them."

It was supper time. Emily spread a tablecloth on the table, which the children had just cleared of books, pens, papers, blotters, pencil sharpeners, and such.

Supper was called "tea," and tea it was, with home-made jam, and some leftover meat and gravy.

Afterwards, Emily cleared the table and covered it again with a dark-green velvet spread on which parents and children once again put their books. They all sat around on tall leather-upholstered chairs within the ring of light, and read until bedtime.

Mother was reading an afternoon paper that father had brought home; she had glasses on, and her lips moved silently, ever so slightly. Father had a book in front of him, and so had the others, except Irene, who was looking through issues of a weekly magazine called "Family Evenings." The last page was for small children. There were special stories in big print, pictures and riddles: for instance, "what has no legs but runs, two hands and strikes, and a face without eyes?" Irene, naturally, knew right away that it was a clock!

The table was too tall for her, and after a while her hands got tired of turning pages, so she crawled on top of the chair, knelt, and read that way. She wondered how long it would take mother to notice. Mother very soon said:

"Irene, get down. You are ruining the upholstery with your knees."

Irene got down, sat in a "proper way" and felt the cold leather of the chair on her seat. Soon her eyelids became heavy, and she put her head down in the cozy nook of her arms.

"Irene, don't sleep here. Go to bed."

Every night she went through the same ritual.

"Emily, will you hold the lamp for me?"

Emily took the kitchen lamp off the hook, got a pitcher of warm water from the stove, and went with Irene to her room. There, Emily helped her to unbutton her shoes, undress and wash. Irene hated to be washed!

"Emily pulls your arms, chokes your throat, and her fingers are too big for your ears, so they hurt and turn red, especially after wiping with a towel," Irene complained silently to her invisible, sympathetic friend. "It's not that Emily is so rough because she is mean or hates you: all grownups think that a child is made out of wood and sawdust (like toys, I guess) and Emily thinks so, too."

After washing, Irene had to put on a cold nightgown and crawl into a cold bed. Emily would leave right away, taking her lamp, so Irene had to remind her every night:

"Leave the door open, would you?"

She was a little afraid to stay alone in the dark, at least until Janka got to bed, too. But usually she fell asleep right away.

Soon, one by one, everybody would undress and go to bed; by the time the grandfather clock struck ten o'clock, all the lamps in the house would be put out.

The children were soon asleep, but their parents would lie awake in their beds, staring into the darkness of the night. Since their son's death, the few feet dividing their beds seemed like an impenetrable gulf.

Each of them, lonely and sad, would turn from one side to the other, waiting for sleep to come and spread a veil of forgiveness over their minds. But he was a man and needed a woman's love, the assurance of a tender caress, the safety of her arms around his arms.

She, desperately lonesome, staring at the ceiling, would not make — rather, dare not make — the first move.

Finally, he would timidly cross those few feet and get into her bed. She would turn her head away to avoid his kiss, but would cling to his body, trying to silence a sob that was rising in her throat. He and she, who had begotten ten children in love, would make love in silence, both feeling guilty in the sharing of this moment of happiness.

Afterwards, they would lie without a word, until he, thinking that she had fallen asleep, would creep back to his bed. But in a few minutes he could hear her in the darkness, pouring water into a basin, and to the sound of splashing water, he would fall asleep.

CHAPTER SEVEN — Christmas

The last few days before Christmas were full of excitement: mother and Helena, after shopping almost every afternoon, would come home with poker faces, insisting that they had not bought anything special. Emily, more busy than usual, was hanging clean curtains all over the house and waxing the floors, so slippery that you had to be careful so as not to fall.

At night, after supper, nobody read any more: the table was full of crepe paper and shiny, multicolored paper, out of which chains and other Christmas ornaments were cut and glued together. Helena's specialty was to make ornaments out of blown-out egg shells, while Henryk was in charge of gilding walnuts, sticking toothpicks into them and attaching strings so they could be hung.

Janka liked to glue paper chains together, while Sophie and Stefa concentrated on turning out round, puffy balls of crepe paper and on making angels. Irene did not know yet how to do these things, so mostly she was used as an "office boy": her job was to look for scissors, pick up papers that fell to the floor, or hang paper chains on doorknobs to dry... and she was happy.

Father would tease them, saying that all this work was wasted, because he *definitely* would not buy a tree this year.

The day before Christmas Eve was the most exciting of all. The schools were closed; everybody was allowed to stay in the kitchen because it was baking day, and mother could use all the help that she could get. The children had to beat eggs, turn egg yolks with sugar, cut orange peel, grind spices in a mortar, and shell almonds. Emily mixed the dough in a long, wooden kneading bowl, while mother added sugar, flour and melted butter.

Later, when the dough was rising near the warm stove, nobody was allowed to walk near it, or even to breathe hard. Finally, the batter was divided into many parts; some was mixed with rum and light raisins in the form of *babas*, another batch would be filled in long, flat forms as coffee cakes with crumbs on top. Others, with fancy stuffing of fruit, nuts, almonds and poppy seeds, would go into delicious strudels and stollens.

But that was not all. The most important part was coming now. One had to move all the baking forms, filled with the dough, to the bakery. On the dark, snowy street in early evening the procession, consisting of the parents, Emily, and all the children, carefully carrying containers, looked like an ancient *bas-relief* depicting some religious ritual.

The bakery was around the corner. On the outside, it was a drab looking brick building, low and long. But once one was inside, it was the most wonderful place in the world. The air smelled of freshly baked bread and pastry. In front of the huge brick ovens, men in shirt sleeves, white aprons and little white caps stood moving loaves of bread and rolls, in and out. With wonderfully quick and nimble movements, any one of them would pick up loaf after loaf on his long, flat wooden paddle and take it out of the oven. Or push unbaked ones into the oven as if they were jumping in by themselves. The baked loaves were placed on long wooden planks, where another man dressed in white would brush them with goose feathers dipped in water. Steam rose above the hot loaves, and the smell of bread was in the air.

In another corner of the bakery, a man would shape round or oblong loaves, placing them one next to the other on wooden planks. From time to time an assistant would come, lift a plank with pale, unbaked loaves, and carry it on his head toward one of the ovens. Still another would fill large wicker baskets with baked loaves and carry them out of the bakery proper into another room. Irene watched all of this, her blue eyes wide open with the greatest of interest.

She could see some other customers in the bakery who had also brought their forms filled with dough to be baked. A man came with a piece of chalk and marked each batch of forms with different symbols: cross, circle, two crosses, and so on, so that later, when they would be taken out of the oven, he would know which belonged to whom.

"Come back in two hours," he would say to all the customers.

"You stay here, Emily, until we come back," said mother.

"Yes, Madame."

"Maman, let me stay here with Emily, please!" begged Irene.

Mother looked around. Except for flour dust, the place was clean and warm. A few other maids would wait, like Emily, until the pastry came out of the oven. Around Christmas, mother was in a generous mood.

"All right. But remember, Emily, don't let her out of your sight for even a moment."

"Yes, Madame."

Emily sat down on a long, narrow bench along the wall, talking to a few maids whom she knew. Irene sat down, too, watching what was going on for a while. In the wall crevices, a few crickets that had found refuge from the winter cold were chirping monotonously but sweetly. The warmth and the song of the crickets soon made Irene sleepy…

When she opened her eyes again, she noticed people all around her, including her family. Maman and Emily were covering the freshly baked golden pastries with linen dishtowels, and soon they all walked in the same procession back home.

At the very end ran Irene, trying to keep pace with the others, carrying a little cake which mother had made out of leftover dough, especially for her. Still warm, it smelled delicious — and it was her very own.

CHAPTER EIGHT — The New Year, 1914

In spite of father's threats about the absence of a Christmas tree, there was one, naturally, high up to the ceiling with so many candles that it took a long time to light them all. Each night everyone blew them out carefully, so as not to disarrange the decorations or cause a fire.

As the tree was in the salon, the family spent most of the time in that room during the holidays. Mother and Sophie played Christmas carols, while all the others sang as best as they could. The carols were beautiful, the lyrics being many centuries old, simple and touching in their love and adoration of the Christ Child. The music was lovely, yet void of any pretentiousness and slick "perfection" of Christmas songs composed much later in other countries of the world.

Twice a year at home, father was the center of attention. In the fall, before the start of school, he took all the children to the cobbler to buy their shoes, and at Christmastime he took them to the circus. The circus was open all year, with a monthly change of program, but the December program was considered the best of all.

Until now, Irene had been considered too young to be taken there, but this year she went with all the others. It was her first contact with the world of entertainment of any kind. She had heard so much about the opera, operettas and the "Illusion," but she could not visualize what it really was. Jadwiga used to play and sing some arias when she lived at home before her marriage, and Helena talked, for instance, about Rostand's *L'Aiglon,* which she had seen recently. "Little Eagle" was the son of Napoleon Bonaparte, who died young. He was played by such a handsome and talented actor, Helena said, that women simply fainted from adoration and emotion when watching him on stage.

Maybe the circus was not like those spectacles that her sisters were talking about, but it did have performers, costumes, makeup, glitter and pomp, and the thrill of the unusual and unexpected.

Throughout the performance, Irene sat spellbound, unable to utter a word. Ballerinas on horses, men and women on the trapeze, little white dogs performing tricks, and other animal numbers were exciting — like fairy tales. But most of all, she liked the clowns. There was a whole bunch of them, all excellent acrobats, musicians and actors.

"Well, what did you like best at the circus?" father asked Irene when they were coming home in a sleigh.

"The clowns," she replied, as if in a trance. "The clowns were wonderful."

"Because they made you laugh?"

"No, because they were so *real*."

"That's a strange thing to say about clowns," laughed father.

"You are stupid, Irene," said Janka. "How can you call clowns *real*, with noses like balloons and clothes and shoes big enough to swim in?"

Irene was too young then to understand what attracted her so much to the clowns, but subconsciously she knew: it was acting. The animals and circus people were *performers;* the clowns were *actors*.

"I want to go to the circus again," she said... and fell asleep.

The next day she was told that it was the New Year.

"Will you remember, Irene," said mother, "the year is one thousand nine hundred and fourteen. Repeat after me..."

"That's easy," said Irene. "One-thousand-nine-hun-dred-and-four-teen."

CHAPTER NINE — Father's "Name Day"

Father's "name day" was at the end of February. Little children like Irene had their birthdays remembered, with presents and good wishes; all others observed only "name days," that is, the Saint's day for which one was named. Father's name was Aleksander, so the great feast was on St. Alexander's day.

The preparations started long in advance. Helena composed appropriate little poems, which each child wrote on stiff, white paper embellished with flowers. Irene's handwriting was not yet very neat, so Helena wrote a poem in pencil and made her go over it in ink. On the top, Irene drew a picture of their house and colored it with crayons.

"Our house has a gray roof, not red," criticized Janka.

"So what?" replied Irene. "It looks prettier that way."

Mother, of course, was preoccupied mainly with food. It was a "game" month, so for weeks a huge piece of venison hung outside on the balcony to cure. Also there was a hare, with long fluffy ears and its legs tied up, hung upside down. Irene looked many times through the balcony doorway at the poor fellow, and wished that he were alive and jumping all over the place. Instead, of course, he was to be cut up, cooked and made into a pâté.

On St. Alexander's day, mother and Emily had been busy since early morning. Brandy flavored jelly doughnuts, light as a feather, and "favors" so crisp that they would break in your fingers, filled the house with a tempting aroma. The pâté and jellied meat salads, prepared a day before and kept cold, were being elaborately decorated with bits of fruits and vegetables. All sorts of hors d'oeuvres, mixed, tossed and cut up at the last minute, were put on the dining room table that was made even longer with extra leaves that Emily put in. The smell of venison roast in sour cream sauce made everybody hungry.

FATHER'S "NAME DAY"

Irene loved the excitement of the preparations, and she was looking forward to the coming of the guests. They were always asking her to recite poems, and they called her "adorable" and "beautiful," and *everybody* was in such a good mood, including maman.

From the very beginning, Irene remembered life as being incessantly pleasant and secure, and she was more often than the others a center of attention. She was neither spoiled nor conceited; she accepted it as something natural — like she considered a flower or sunny day to be beautiful. Life was good, pleasant and secure when one felt loved and appreciated. Later, as she grew older and encountered someone physically disabled, ugly or mentally inferior, she always felt humble and grateful that it was not she.

Right now the salon was humming with the voices of all who had come to dinner: papa's sisters with Aunt Juta's husband — a doctor — and their children, some other uncles and cousins, and papa's best friend, Julian, who was an engineer and a director of the City Water Works. Papa was showing everyone his greeting cards with Helena's poems. Irene was asked to recite her greeting, which she did, and everyone clapped their hands and exclaimed: "How wonderful!"

On the way to the kitchen to check with Emily to see if everything was ready, mother bumped into Janka, hiding behind the door.

"Janka, what are you doing here? Why aren't you with the others? Don't be so bashful!"

But Janka ran from the hall into her parents' bedroom and hid in the big wardrobe.

Nobody, nobody had noticed that she was not in the salon. *Nobody* asked about her, or asked her to recite her poem.

Irene, who was following mother and saw Janka, ran after her.

"For pity's sake, Janka, what are you doing in Papa's wardrobe?"

"Get out of here! You big show-off! Go dance, sing, recite poems, go on! Get out of here! I hate you! I hate you! Everybody hates you! They only let you be born because they thought you would be a boy. They called you 'little Michel,' and when they saw you were a girl, they wanted to throw you out of the window!" cried Janka between sobs.

If the roof had fallen on Irene's head, she could not have been more stunned. Red in the face, with inflamed eyes, she burst into the salon and cried:

"Is it true, Papa, that you wanted to throw me out when I was born, because I wasn't little Michel?"

"What?!"

"Janka says that Maman and you hate me because I am not a boy!"

Everybody in the room laughed.

"It's true that I thought you would be a baby boy, and I did say 'little Michel'," said mother, "but when you were born, we loved you the minute that we saw you."

"I swear," said father, "I never wanted to throw you out of the window."

Everybody laughed again, though Irene did not see anything funny about it.

"Well, let's sit down to dinner," said mother. "Helen, will you please do something with Janka. She is sulking."

Janka, in her father's wardrobe, could hear all the familiar noises coming from the dining room: voices, chairs squeaking on the floor, feet shuffling, and exclamations of how nice the table was set. She did not want to miss all this and especially miss the good food, but to appear now was impossible. She just could not face all those people.

She was sobbing bitterly, mostly because of the mess that she had put herself into: now she was not part of the feast. She was wiping her nose with the sleeve of her dress when suddenly someone put a fresh handkerchief to her face. She heard Helena's voice:

"Janka, stop crying. You are not such a small child anymore. You are almost nine years old. I know *why* you feel miserable, but you can't go through life being jealous and trying to be someone else. Accept what you are. It would not do *me* any good to be jealous about Jadwiga's looks or her popularity, just like it would not help you to try to be Irene."

"Why do I have to study a poem for a week and still get mixed up, while Irene just remembers everything right away? Why can she sing and dance and is always happy and..." Janka started to cry even more.

"Now, you stop that. Come, wash your face. You don't want to miss all the good dinner, do you?"

Helena pulled Janka's hands from her face. Looking at those small red and swollen eyes, that red pudgy nose, she felt compassion and tenderness for the first time in her life. Until now she often thought about her own feelings, but not about those of others. She washed Janka's face and combed her hair with mother's comb.

"Come on, everybody is so busy eating, I am sure they won't even notice when we come in the room."

"I don't know why I was so mean to Irene, why I said all those things. I don't hate her at all. I love her very much," said Janka while following Helena.

But Irene, seeing her coming into the room, suddenly felt miserable again, as if something had died a little within her.

"From now on I will recite poems to myself, when I am alone in the room," she decided.

CHAPTER TEN — The Jewish Quarter

It was a warm, sunny afternoon in April. Emily was clearing the table after lunch and asked mother:

"Maybe you would like me to take Janka and Irene to the park, Madame?"

"Yes, I think it's a good idea," replied mother.

Irene noticed right away that Emily hurried more than usual in doing her chores; she did the dishes in no time, and put them away with much more noise than usual.

"Hurry up, girls. Take your ball and hoops, and let's go," she said, trying to conceal her excitement.

As soon as they left and reached the corner of the street, Emily stopped.

"Listen, I have a favor to ask of you, but promise you won't tell your mother. Promise?"

It was very flattering to be so important as to be asked to keep a secret.

"We promise," said Janka.

"Irene, you too?"

"Yes, I promise, cross my heart."

"You see," began Emily, "I got a letter from home that my relative is coming today. I want to see her, to hear all the news from home. You know I haven't seen anybody from my family for two years, so, instead of going to the park, we will go to Grzybowski Square, all right?"

THE JEWISH QUARTER

"Where is Grzybowski Square?" asked Janka.

"You will see. Just hold my hand, and let's go fast. It is a long way." *

Instead of going through the residential section toward Ujazdowski Park, Emily turned immediately to the left and very soon they were in the Jewish section, crossing innumerable streets.

Everything was so different around there, that in spite of the quick pace that Emily kept, Irene, looking to the left and to the right, could not miss thousands of unusual things.

First of all, the streets she knew so far were always almost empty of people; to be seen were only some private carriages and *drozhki*, and a few persons walking. Here, the streets were so full of people that you had to push your way through. There was constant agitation and noise, shouting and arguing in Jewish jargon. Big carts were being unloaded of crates full of live poultry, rags or second-hand furniture. Others were loaded with bedding, garments, leather goods, and moved slowly toward their sundry destinations.

There were men in orthodox attire: long black coats and little black caps, bearded and with long hairlocks hanging on the sides of their faces (called *peyes*). They were arguing, gesticulating with their hands, exchanging money. Little boys, also in orthodox dress and leaving *heder* (a Jewish school for boys), were running and shouting, and looked like a nest of little black beetles you see when you lift a stone in the park.

Stores, stores, thousands of stores. No apartments in the fronts of buildings. On wider streets, where trolley cars were running, the stores were bigger: garments, horse gear and leather goods on lower floors; on upper floors, pathetically ugly manikins in dusty bridal gowns; signs with primitively painted birds advertising "goose down and feathers." On narrow crooked streets, small untidy stores with sagging thresholds. Onions tied into long rings, wooden buckets of salted herring, live poultry for kosher killing cooped up behind a dirty window pane…

Street peddlers, hundreds of them. Besides wholesale dealers and shopkeepers, there were thousands of people trying somehow to make a living. They stood on the streets all day selling anything: suspenders, handkerchiefs, spools of thread, needles, shoelaces, bagels, and sticky, fly-covered homemade sweets. If one makes a few kopeks, one can buy a loaf of bread, an onion or a herring. If ten mouths to feed are waiting

---

* about 1 km

at home, you divide one herring into ten parts and slice an onion and bread... the only meal of the day. One has to save a little money to buy a candle, to light it on Friday night for the Sabbath...

Every building in Warsaw had a wide-open gate leading to a courtyard. In the house where Irene lived, the yard was big and clean-swept, and there was a carpet beater and a large wooden garbage container. Emily came down once a week with the rugs, hung them on a frame and beat them with the wicker carpet beater.

Here, when Irene looked through the gates as she passed, she could see small, dark courtyards, slimy and wet, littered with piles of rags, broken furniture, old papers and empty crates. Pale, skinny, unkempt children were playing there, or using it as their bathroom. A woman emptied a bucket out in the yard: the foul-smelling water ran down the street, where it would join other refuse swimming slowly in an open gutter.

A very old Jewish woman (wearing a reddish-brown wig, as was the custom) sat on a store's threshold whisking a child's hair for lice. A refreshment store, painted bright aqua. Three fruit syrup glass urns: raspberry, strawberry and orange-colored. A large copper soda-water syphon with one glass for all patrons, "rinsed" in a small bowl of water after each using.

Irene wanted to adjust her hoop, which she carried on one arm, so she slipped her hand out of Emily's. Two or three passersby came between them for a moment. Emily frantically caught Irene's hand.

"Do you want to be killed for *matzohs?*" she cried. "Don't you let go of my hand again!"

Emily firmly believed that each spring before the Jewish holidays little Christian children were caught, killed and the blood drained out of them, to be baked into matzohs.

"There *must be* at least one drop of Christian blood in every matzoh they eat," she said.

How this superstition started, nobody knew, but it was not Emily alone who believed it. Probably, years ago, a child sex crime had been committed at this time of the year, and thus began that bizarre accusation.

They finally reached Grzybowski Square. Irene's feet hurt, and her left hand was all red from being squeezed so long in Emily's. If the ghetto streets were crowded and noisy, the square was even more so. It was the center of all wholesale poultry dealing. Big peasants' carts with covered tops filled most of the cobblestone square. Among the carts were people, Jews and Christians alike, some pulling down crates with squeaking, frightened fowl in them, others carrying sacks of chicken feed or baskets.

These carts, which were used by the peasants as hay wagons, had once been utilized for regular transportation by Jews and peasants. It was often too far to any railroad station from the small towns and rural settlements, so it was much easier and cheaper to travel in a covered wagon.

Emily (like all other girls from the country looking for a job) had come in such a wagon two years before, and she would leave for home someday via the same transportation. Some people came for an operation, or to buy things unavailable in rural districts, like mirrors, window glass, and such. One cart, filled with people sitting on two benches along the sides, was just leaving, while another, equally filled with people, crates of quacking geese, ducks and chickens, was pulling to a stop. In all the excitement, Emily left Irene and Janka alone, looking for her relative.

The girls stood, watching all the commotion around them. They saw Emily crying, laughing, kissing some woman, and hugging a few other persons whom she apparently also knew. Then they talked and talked until it was almost dark. Then the kissing, hugging and crying began again.

"I am tired, Emily," wailed Janka. "Let's go home."

"Me too," said Irene.

"All right, all right. We are going. Don't you worry, girls; we will take a trolley car and we will be home in no time at all. And remember, not a peep to your mother about where we have been this afternoon."

Not one of them thought for a moment that the simplest thing for Emily to have done was to ask maman for the afternoon off.

CHAPTER ELEVEN — Stepping Out at Last

As in any other city in the world, there were in Warsaw good sections and bad sections: rich and elegant homes of high class society or diplomatic corps, and houses with upper and lower middle-class dwellers. There was also the poor workers' section and the Jewish ghetto.

The most common house in this city of over a million inhabitants was a three-story building (not counting the main floor) named from the French, *parterre*. It had front apartments with a pretentiously elegant stairway made of dark oak woodwork. There was an alcove on each floor, seated in which was a scantily clad pseudo-Greek statue holding a gas lamp in one hand. Each floor had two apartments, with a door to the right and to the left. In the courtyard, the building had three more wings: on two sides and in the rear, with simple stone stairways. The whole structure of each building looked, from a bird's eye view, like a square block with a smaller square of a courtyard in the center.

Thus, on the same street, in the same building, literally under the same roof lived people of different social and financial status. The people from the second floor front apartment not only had nothing in common with the dwellers of the "backyard" apartments, but would not even greet those who lived on the floor above… and were snubbed themselves by those from the floor below. So, the city "intelligentsia" was divided and subdivided into innumerable little classes, according to the price of the apartment they occupied.

STEPPING OUT AT LAST

It was quite an achievement for Irene's father, supporting such a large family, to have a front apartment on the second floor. Father was associated with the Warsaw-Vienna Railroad. Occasionally he had to take business trips, after which he wrote long reports. That particular day, after an early dinner, he was packing his suitcases. Mother and Emily were with him, brushing this and bringing that.

Irene was in her bedroom with Janka. The day was warm; the windows were open, even though the room leading to the courtyard was not sunny. Irene was watching through the window as the children from the "back" apartments played catch and hopscotch. She wished that she could play there, but, of course, she was not allowed to put even one foot in the yard.

"Come on, Irene, why don't you play?"

Janka wanted to play with dolls. It bored and irritated Irene the way Janka was playing. She pretended "for real" that the dolls were her babies, pouring water into their mouths, changing diapers, and all that stupid stuff. Irene liked to use dolls only as actors and actresses in some story, having something terribly exciting happening to all of them: running away on a chair (which was a flying horse), fighting duels, and falling to the floor, mortally wounded. Janka wanted to cook some silly dinner in her little china dishes.

"Oh, I don't want to play."

Just then, she saw two men coming into the yard, carrying some folding partitions and a box.

The children outside stopped playing and stood in a semicircle. The men adjusted the stand into a little square room. One of them disappeared inside, while the other placed a small cardboard house on top. Suddenly, the funniest nasal voices started to come from the box: two little puppets were dashing here and there, popping from the box's windows or the top of the roof. One of them was holding a stick, and between the funny nasal exclamations one could hear the *bang, bang, bang* of his merciless strikes at the other puppet.

"I simply must see all this from the yard," cried Irene. "Let's go, Janka."

She ran to the front door, opened it, and dashed down the stairs, followed by Janka.

When they reached the courtyard, the little black puppet was still teasing and chasing the other one, hitting him with the stick. Coins, thrown from open windows, were rolling on the cement floor. The children, some holding smaller ones in their arms, were laughing and clapping their hands.

Finally, the men finished the act, picked up the money, folded their things and left.

Irene stood there, still enchanted by the performance.

"Come, Irene. If Mother sees us, she will be awfully mad."

"Wait a minute, Janka. I want to see a little bit of what is going on here."

She would not dream of playing with the "other" children, but she wanted to watch them. Poorly clad, with scuffed shoes and runny noses, they were not as nice to look at as the children in the Park, but they seemed to have just as good a time playing as did the rich. Irene walked around the courtyard and was surprised to see, through small windows at the ground level, that people lived there — in the cellars. She always thought that cellars were only storage places for coal, vegetables and fruit, but apparently not all of them were used in that way, for she could plainly see beds, coal iron stoves, chairs and tables. It was quite dark in there, but people had a need for beauty in those drab surroundings. There were flower pots on almost every window sill, mostly shade-loving plants like ferns or fuchsias, but occasionally a few pots of geraniums were kept outside in the yard in places where the sun's rays would reach them for a few hours. Right now, the patch of sunlight disappeared from the yard and started to climb higher and higher toward the top of the wall. Women came out and brought their plants back inside on the little window sills. Some of the women put water in their mouths to sprinkle the flowers with a fine mist, so they all looked fresh and shiny.

These few plants represented their "real estate"; they also symbolized man's eternal longing for beauty, from the most primitive scratches on cave walls to the most magnificent achievements of modern art.

"Come upstairs, right away," Irene heard Helena say, feeling a slight pinch on her arm. "Mother is furious."

Running upstairs two steps at a time, Irene thought that it was worth it to be scolded by her mother… to see the puppets and stay in the courtyard.

Mother, of course, gave them a strong lecture on proper behavior, after which Irene went out on the balcony to play. Suddenly, she saw her father, halfway down Miedziana Street, carrying his suitcase. "Soon he will reach the corner and will get into a *drozhki*," she thought.

"Why didn't anyone tell me that Papa is going away?" she cried.

Every time he left, she had to kiss him goodbye. Seeing him going away like that, she had the impression that she would never see him again. In a strange panic she ran downstairs and out of the house, trying to catch up with her father.

"Papa," she yelled, out of breath.

Father stopped, turned around and smiled.

"What are you doing here?" he asked.

"I forgot to tell you goodbye."

He laughed, put his suitcase on the sidewalk and kissed her. She kissed his hand, and all the panic gone, happily skipped back toward the house.

It was the first time she had been on the street alone.

CHAPTER TWELVE — Easter

Churches in Warsaw were numerous and for the most part quite beautiful, although not as old as in other parts of the country, especially the former capital of Poland, Krakow.

People did not belong to any particular church. They went to the one nearest their home, or the one that was popular for unusually good organ music, or good sermons.* One went there when there was need for communication with God. They were always open. One went there in complete anonymity, preferably in old, inconspicuous clothes. One stood or knelt on a hard, cold marble floor; the few benches were occupied by the old or weak. One did not necessarily go every Sunday — more often than not on a weekday, before work, children before school.

A dark, empty church, with a flickering light at the altar, gave strength, courage and hope when needed. Its undemanding, sober tranquility probably straightened out more lives, resolved more problems, and cured more ailing souls than could a modern psychiatrist's couch. One was not asked for donations or offerings. An old iron money box was there, and one gave an offering in the simplicity of a spontaneous need for sharing.

During Holy Week, from Thursday on, the church was not a place for meditation but the center of pilgrimage. Somehow the weather was always sunny, the air smelled of freshly-turned soil and of spring

---

* Irene's baptism was in the local parish at the Church of All Saints, Grzybowski Square.

flowers. In each church a large, life-size statue of Christ lay in the grotto of the sepulcher, among literally thousands of flowers. The whole church was fragrant with daffodils, hyacinths and tulips — a feast to the eyes of delicate, pastel hues of vegetation. Canaries singing softly, sweetly, would be flying high among the church beams.

There was no atmosphere of death or the sadism of human sacrifice; no feeling of medieval, masochistic self-flagellation for one's sins. God was asleep and will awaken. Death was rest, quiet and beauty.

The idea was to be in as many churches as possible: visiting one church after another gave a humble pilgrim serenity, a soul-cleansing *catharsis*, and gave strength to start a new, better life. Resurrection Day, after three days of pilgrimage, was the culmination of the victory of life over death.

Later, when Irene would be in college, her professor of the History of Culture would show her the similarities between Easter and the cult of Osiris, whose spirit was carried every spring in processions and culminated in his resurrection.

The custom of "visiting the tombs" — as the churches' pilgrimage was called — was, it seems, influenced by the ancient customs of the Osiris cult. Was it, therefore, pagan? Perhaps. But were not all religions under the influence of the most primitive, remote customs? Was not a biblical satan-serpent connected with a snake cult? Does not a theme of virgin conception appear time and again in myths? Did not the idea of human sacrifice for pacifying angry gods merge with the Christian idea of redemption for our sins? Are not the days of the week even today called after the sun, the moon, the planets or gods? Did not, in time, human sacrifice change into animal sacrifice, finally to be replaced by bread and wine offerings? Was it not natural, then, that one of the religions on earth believes that bread and wine symbolizes — or changes into — blood and flesh?

The important fact about religious customs is not how and when they originated, but what moral, positive and beneficial influences they have on the great masses of people.

A mother, holding a small child in her arms and watching a flowery procession of Osiris a few thousand years ago, had perhaps the same feeling of elation and purification as a mother who showed her child the statue of Christ in church lying among flowers. That feeling came from a unity with nature and God.

PART I — CHAPTER TWELVE

Irene did not go to all the churches in Warsaw, but to as many as her little feet would allow her in three days. Dressed in spring clothes and her new Easter Bonnet, she tiptoed on the cool marble floors so as not to awaken God.

All that she knew was that Jesus, who at Christmastime was a little smiling baby in a crèche, grew up to be a man, lived, suffered and died. But death was only a sleep among beautiful flowers.

CHAPTER THIRTEEN — Beggar's Soup

"Today, everything will be upside down," Irene thought. "Maman will be doing chores around the house that she usually does not do, and Emily will not do a single thing that she usually does."

It happened twice each month with the regularity of a sunrise and sunset: the grand laundry day. Mother will make beds and clean the house, even do the cooking and wipe the dishes, because Emily will be busy all day at the big wooden tub full of hot water, washing clothes on the washboard and wringing them out in the wringer. All the clothes have to be washed twice and boiled in a big kettle. By late evening they will swim in cold water, stay like that overnight, and tomorrow Emily will rinse them in blue water, and with the help of a neighbor's maid carry them to the attic in a big wicker basket. There, they will dry for a couple of days. Afterwards, Emily will bring them back down, pull and sprinkle, roll them into small bundles and iron all day. What a pile of clothes there is for eight people! And all those huge tablecloths and sheets, which two people have to pull and fold!

On laundry day mother won't even mind if Irene goes into the kitchen now and then. She knows that Emily will be much too busy to talk to the children about ghosts. Irene, sitting on a stool and dangling her feet, watched Emily.

On washday Emily was always sulky. Her arms, bare to the elbows, were red, and when she turned the wringer, Irene could see funny wrinkles on her fingers. Emily's sleeves were pinned up with two safety pins, and her apron was wet on her stomach. From time to time, she tried to push back in place a few unruly streaks of hair that were wet with perspiration. The air in the kitchen was damp from the steaming pots of hot water on the stove; it smelled of soap and bleach.

For Irene it was fun to watch: long, flattened-out clothes coming from the wringer and falling into the basket. On washday Emily had an extra "second breakfast" at about noon (bread, and coffee mixed with milk) because she got hungry from working so hard.

Suddenly Irene heard the doorbell ring and then voices of her mother and a neighbor:

"Could Irene come over after dinner and play with my little boy? I have to be away all evening, and I don't trust my new maid too much. If Irene is there, I am sure the baby won't be neglected or mistreated."

"Yes, of course she can play at your house."

Irene did not care at all *to play with a little baby boy* — in fact, she hated it — but it was always fun to go to a strange home and talk to a maid, especially on a day like this when Emily did not talk to you at all.

When Irene got there, she found Jagna, the maid, in the kitchen doing ironing. The baby was supposed to stay on a blanket, spread in the corner, but he was, of course, all over the place, and Jagna did not seem to pay attention to what he was doing. She gave Irene that "another-brat-under-foot" look and kept ironing.

"My name is Irene. What is yours?"

"Jagna. Why don't you take Kazio to his room and play there?"

"I don't want to play with him. He is too small. How can you play with someone so small? He can't even talk."

"I don't know. Why did you come then?"

"Because I wanted to meet you."

Jagna's face suddenly looked less sulky, and her voice became less hostile.

"Oh? Why?"

"Because I like to meet new people. Don't you? Here, would you like a candy?" Irene took two "honeybees" out of her pocket.

Jagna put the iron on a stand and took a candy.

"Why, I don't mind if I do."

"Do you like poems, Jagna?"

"What?"

"You know... stories in verse. Songs."

"I don't know any. I can't read."

"I know lots of poems. Do you want me to tell you one?"

"How can you know anything? You can't read either — you are too small."

"Oh yes, I can read... some. But you don't have to read to learn poems; you just listen to someone else, and you learn. You know, like prayers."

"Aha."

Irene told a long poem about a rabbit who was so afraid of everything and everybody that he couldn't eat or sleep, and he finally decided to kill himself by drowning. But he stepped on a frog who ran away from him in a panic, and that gave him new courage to live. He found out that everyone is afraid of something or someone else. It was a funny story in the style of La Fontaine, and Irene acted it out in an amusing way: trembling with fear, shedding crocodile tears, and facing suicide in the grand manner of a knight facing a mortal duel.

When she finished, Jagna laughed out loud.

"You are a funny one," she said.

She put away the ironing board and clothes, fed Kazio some cereal and milk, and put him to bed. They sat in the kitchen and had another "honeybee."

"What are you going to have for supper, Jagna?"

With one indignant sweep of her hand, Jagna emptied a small paper bag that was on the kitchen table.

"This," she said. "When they are away for the evening, this is what they give me to eat."

On the table were leftover pieces of bread, broken crusts, and pieces of hard rolls that were dry as a bone.

"I am supposed to make myself *smelka*. You know — smelka, the beggar's soup. You cut dried bread into small pieces, pour some boiling water or milk on it, and season it with salt, and a dab of butter... *if* you have it."

"But... Emily eats the same food that we do," said Irene, surprised. "Sure, we also have dry bread, stored in a bag. Mother says that it is sinful to throw bread away: bread is mentioned in the Lord's Prayer. But we do use it for bread crumbs or stuffing."

"*She* keeps everything locked."

Irene noticed that Jagna said "she." Emily always said "Madame."

"And she is not the only one," continued Jagna. "I can tell you because this is not my first place. They are *all* like that."

"Not all! My mother is not like that."

"I know. That's why Emily likes it with you, even though she has plenty of laundry and dishes — what with eight people in the house."

"All of our maids stayed until they got married, and then they got a present."

"You may be sure that I won't stay *here* long. I am already looking for a new place. But you never know what you get. You go, see a nice rich house, and you think that it will be fine. But you find that the richer the people, the more stingy they are with the servants."

"Wait a minute, Jagna. I will be right back."

Irene ran home, asked mother for a piece of bread with butter and preserves. It was nothing unusual, as the children often had a snack before supper. When she came back, Jagna was already making *smelka*.

"Here, Jagna. Have this bread for your supper."

"No, I am not going to eat your food."

"But why? You eat my bread, and I will eat a bit of your smelka. I want to taste it, all right?"

Maybe because it was something different from what Irene always ate, but the smelka tasted very good. And for the first time in Jagna's life, it tasted good to her, too. Somehow, it was not "beggar's soup" any more.

Maybe it was because she shared it with a companion.

CHAPTER FOURTEEN — Vacation in Russia!

Because Irene didn't go to school yet, and didn't have much chance to play outside, except for trips to the park, she spent most of her time observing things and people around her.

Papa, for instance, disliked arguments and avoided them with his quiet, gentle manner. Maman unconditionally made all decisions, though she always took papa's wishes under consideration. Helena was so smart and dependable that Irene had the feeling that if maman had to be away for any reason, Helena would take over without much change in the family's life. Henryk was smart, but he was "just a growing boy," as Emily said, so he liked to tease his sisters. Sophie did not like to do things that were "expected" of her; she would often get poor marks because, instead of doing her homework, she would spend all day writing stories or poems. Last summer she hid all of her "works" inside the stove in her bedroom, and last fall Emily, not knowing that anything was in there, lit the stove and burned all of them. Sophie's petticoat showed most of the time, and she had to be reminded to comb her hair. But she was beautiful anyway.

Stefa was quite different from Sophie. She was never late for school, had her homework done, and never lost anything. With so many people in the house, someone was always looking for something, but not Stefa. Janka always wished that she had things someone else had, or wanted to do things someone else did. She was constantly picking up things that she did not need at all, putting them away in her room in empty candy boxes. Whenever someone was looking for a misplaced item, sooner or later at the suggestion — "Did you look in Janka's room?" — it would be found there.

"Well, Irene, do you want to go to the Halles with me?"

Every morning mother would, more or less, ask the same question, and every morning Irene replied with more or less the same answer: "Coming!" or "I will be ready in a minute!"

During the month of May it was more fun than ever to go to the market. Everything looked so pretty: peasants' carts loaded with lettuce, radishes and baskets of strawberries were so colorful and gay-looking. Butter was golden yellow and smelled deliciously fresh when the peasant unfolded the cool, crisp, green cabbage leaf in which it was stored. This time maman did not make indignant faces when she put some in her mouth to sample, but instead nodded her approval.

"Why is the butter so yellow?" asked Irene.

"Because cows are now eating plenty of buttercups and other flowers in the meadows. Here, hold the milk can and basket, Irene. I want to buy some of these flowers."

Mother was very fond of spring flowers. Her name day, like Sophie's, was in mid-May on St. Sophia's day, and she always enjoyed buying forget-me-nots, lilies-of-the-valley or roses on that day.

They came home loaded with lilac branches. Mother could not even open the door with her key, but rang the bell for Emily to come and help her.

"There is a letter in the mailbox!" exclaimed Irene.

Letters rarely came. Occasionally one of their relatives would write if something unusual happened: a death, new birth or illness in the family.

Mother opened the mailbox with a little key. "It's from Jadwiga, but the return address is not Astrakhan anymore; it is Tula."

She hurriedly put on her glasses and began to read.

"Well," she said after she had finished, "let's look at the picture."

There was a small snapshot included with the letter. Irene saw Jadwiga and her husband, Vladimir (called Vlodek) standing next to Niania, who was holding a little boy in a white sailor suit. In the background were camels — *real* camels.

"Camels! Maman, look!"

"Yes, in Astrakhan they have camels. It is far, far in the south of Russia at the Caspian Sea, where the great Volga River flows into the sea. I will show you on the map. Where is Henry's atlas?"

They found the atlas and picked out Astrakhan on the map.

VACATION IN RUSSIA!

Mother seemed unusually excited.

"Emily! Come here, Emily!" she called. "Do you know that we have been invited by Jadwiga to come and spend the summer in Russia? Her husband got an excellent new position. They rented a big summer house and want all of us to come!"

Long ago mother had decided that Vlodek was not a *Moscal*. After all, his mother is Polish, and she *doesn't* call him "Volodya," as Russians would call Vladimir...

"Oh! Does that mean I can ride a camel?" cried Irene.

"No. Jadwiga and Vlodek are not in Astrakhan anymore. They are in Tula."

"Where is Tula?"

Mother showed Irene and Emily where Warsaw was on the map and where Tula was.

"See, a little south of Moscow. Jadwiga's husband did such a good engineering job in Astrakhan that he is now one of the chief engineers at the Imperial Armaments Plant.* You know that in Tula there are factories where they make samovars, but there are also factories where they make all sorts of guns and ammunition."

"Do you think Madame's husband will be agreeable to your going?" asked Emily.

"Why not? It will save us money. Otherwise, we would need to rent a summer house here, and the rail tickets will be free, of course, because as the family of a Warsaw-Vienna railroad employee we can travel first class all over Poland and Russia at no cost."

"That is about the nicest thing that could happen, Madame. And it would be easier for me to go... I was thinking that I have saved enough money to get married, and I would like to go back to my home as soon as the children's school year is over. If you go away, it won't be so hard for me to say goodbye to you all."

Emily's eyes began to fill with tears.

"Don't cry, Emily. It's time for you to start your own life, and I know you will be very happy, you'll see," said mother, clearing her throat. She was fond of Emily and hated the thought of her going.

---

* Тульский оружейный завод

PART I– CHAPTER FOURTEEN

"We will get you a nice wedding present," said Irene, who loved to see people get presents.

With mother's plans working out so smoothly, and all the children so enthusiastic about a possible trip to Russia, father was easily persuaded to agree with everyone's wishes. The next weeks were filled with feverish preparations: new clothes for all, and sandals for the children. A seamstress was hired for a few days, who fitted and sewed from morning till night, and slept in the salon on one of the sofas. Mother put everything in mothballs, and Emily covered the furniture with white sheets. Letters were exchanged with Jadwiga, who finally sent a last note saying that she would be waiting for them on June 29th at the station in Moscow.

Finally, the last day at home came. Emily packed her trunk, said tearful goodbyes and left in the morning. Father took a half-day off and saw the family to the station. It was agreed that in August he would come to spend the rest of the vacation with them, and then they would all come back together. A new maid would be hired after their return. Father would eat his dinners with the Aunts and send his laundry to the washerwoman.

Before the train had even left the station, Irene had explored every compartment. Some of them were first class and some second class. The difference, it seemed, was only in the color of the plush upholstery: red or brown. The third class cars were further back. Irene had never been inside them, but she knew from Janka that they only had wooden benches.

They all kissed father a hundred times, and when the train finally pulled away, they waved through the open window.

"Remember to water the flowers!" cried mother.

"Will see you all in August!" father shouted, waving his hat.

He stood there on the station platform until the train, making a sweeping turn, made him disappear from their sight.

PART TWO: RUSSIA — WAR AND REVOLUTION

Moscow, 1914

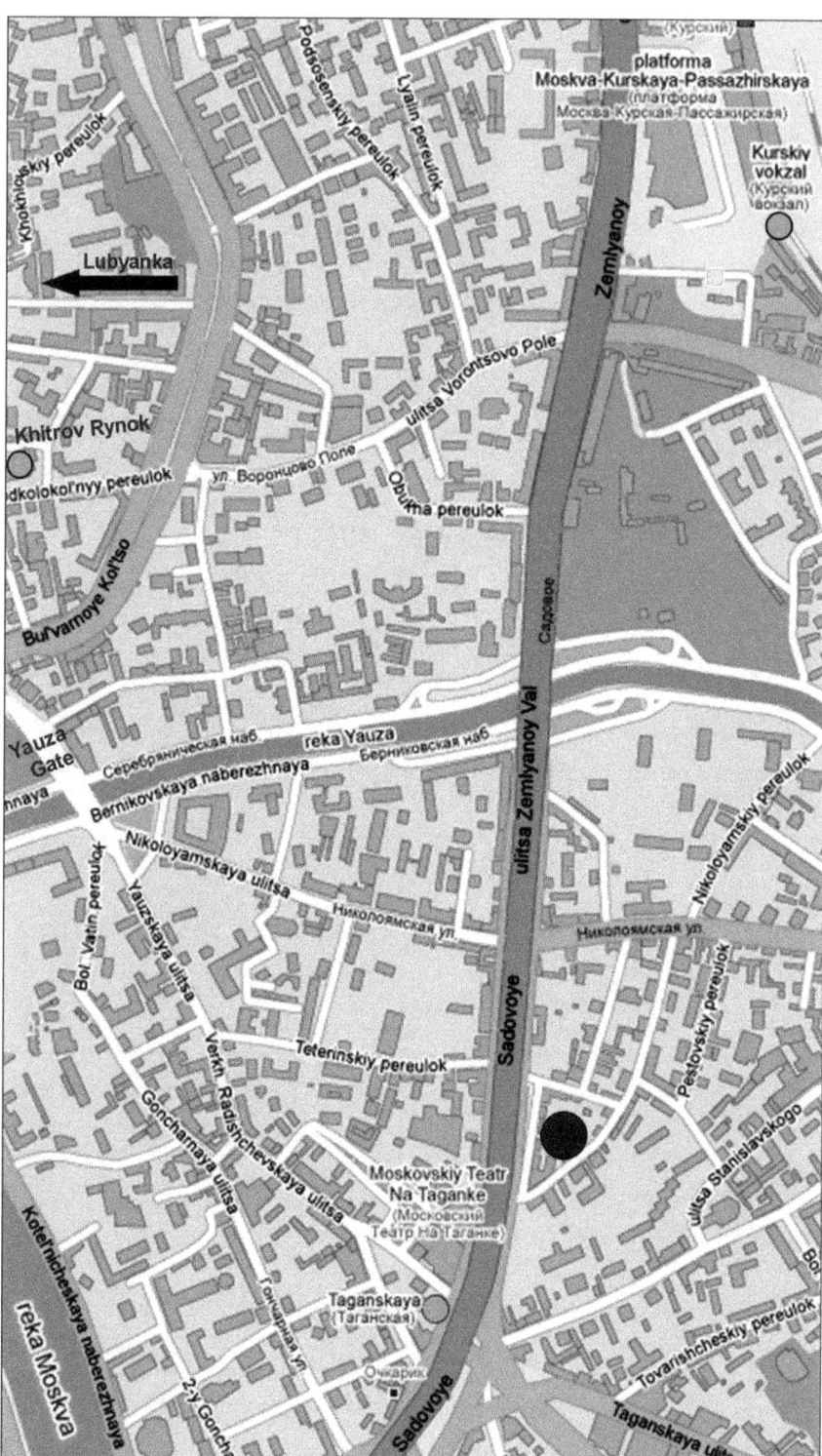

CHAPTER ONE — Jadwiga

JADWIGA was pacing back and forth on the station platform. It was still about fifteen minutes until the train's arrival, but she left the waiting room because it was stuffy there, and the smell of Russian *mahorka* tobacco made her dizzy. Besides, she was getting restless waiting.

In spite of her good figure, dazzling complexion and unusual beauty, Jadwiga looked older than her twenty-two years. Maybe it was because the clothes in fashion in 1914 made women look older, or maybe it was just her quiet reserve and dignity that set her above others of the same age.

Marriage and motherhood had brought out more personality in her young face and had given her more poise and assurance than she had in her adolescence.

How long was it since she had seen her family? Almost nineteen months. The children must have changed, particularly the little ones who must have grown up a lot. And mother... she was always good to Jadwiga. Everybody was always good to her. And now she had a husband who loved her so much, and a child, servants — everything. Friends, too. She had come to Russia afraid that she would feel lonesome and uprooted; instead she found the people of the upper middle class just as cultured and friendly as the ones she had left behind. Her two best friends, wives of engineers that she had met in Astrakhan, had since moved to Moscow, and that is where she intended to put up her arriving family for a few days. They would do some sightseeing and then go to Bykovo, where a house had been rented for the summer.

"Tula — Vyazma — Kaluga..." the stationmaster's voice, informing the public of an outgoing train, broke Jadwiga's chain of thoughts for a moment.

Yes, she had always been liked... and loved; everything had come to her so easily. She spoke four languages without the trace of an accent, and she never had to worry about her looks, health or popularity. It was easy for her to like people, too. You just returned to others what you received all the time. Yes, it was easy to be good; out of egocentric self-satisfaction it was easy to radiate "goodness," which only augmented one's popularity.

"... But were you always good, Jadwiga?" asked an inner voice. "How about your brother, in need of friendship, understanding and guidance... how about TOM? Did you ever stop to think of his emotional needs? Even after he died, all you did was to run, run away from everything that could remind you of him. You moved up your wedding date, not even waiting for your precious trousseau to be finished, and you had to give up the reception because people were still in mourning. You got married and ran away from that house, from that bed, table and shelf of books in the hall, from that medicine cabinet which was ajar when you had come out of your room, hearing Mother's cries...."

"Kursk — Briansk — Oriol..." the stationmaster was calling.

"...when you came back to have a baby, it was in a fresh apartment, with a new maid; no bed of Tom's, nothing to remind you. You were so preoccupied with your pregnancy that nothing else existed in the whole world. Brothers, sisters, parents — they were only actors in minor roles on a stage where you were a constant heroine..."

The station bells started to ring, announcing the arrival of the train from Warsaw.

"They will be here very soon. How lucky I am!" thought Jadwiga, moved almost to tears.

She ran quickly to the Restaurant Waiting Room, and at the counter bought the biggest box of chocolates that they had.

CHAPTER TWO — First Days in Russia

Irene would not remember much about the trip, except that it lasted more than two days, that she did a lot of jumping in long corridors between compartments, that every night the backs of the seats were lifted and made into two upper beds, so that in two compartments they had eight beds. Irene had to climb up and down, and it was great fun.

Sometimes the train stopped in a large station, and they had a hot meal in the station restaurant. They all looked the same: long counters of dark wood with shelves on one side, and in the middle of the room, tables and chairs with one or two dusty palm plants near the windows.

Early in the afternoon of the third day, just when Irene was getting restless and bored, mother and Helena started to pack into a suitcase all the things that had been used during the trip. Everyone washed again in the washroom, combed their hair and straightened their clothes. In the golden mist of a summer day, they could see a big city stretching out across the horizon. It was Moscow.

Never in her life did Irene see and learn so many things in such a short time as she did in those next few days. The first impression of the city was of great vastness and emptiness. Many streets were very wide, with few people in them; maybe it was because summer was here, school was out and the people were away at their *dachas* — summer homes in the country. Irene learned that Russians did not call each other by "Mr." and "Mrs." and last names like Poles did. Instead they would ask you what your father's first name was, and they would call you by your name and your father's given name, or patronymic — *otchestvo* in Russian, from *otietz*, meaning "father." Thus, Irene was Irena Aleksandrovna, Jadwiga was Yadviga Aleksandrovna, while mother was called Zofia Marcelevna because grandfather's name was Marceli.

Mother, Helena and Henryk were staying with one of Jadwiga's friends, Maria Eremeyevna, while Irene and her three other sisters were put up with the parents of another friend, Lydia Alekseyevna. Her father had died recently, and she had taken over his spacious apartment after she and her husband had returned from Astrakhan. They had two girls, Nina and Ira, both about Irene's age.

Everything was so different! The rooms were much larger than those in the Warsaw apartment, but some of them had no windows. To Irene, brought up in a house where space was precious because of a large family, this waste of rooms that served no practical purpose seemed incredible. There were rooms simply filled with an accumulation of odd furniture, a room for sewing, and one room literally filled with toys — toys on shelves, in chests, boxes, closets, and toys on the floor. Irene, who had left her only possessions behind in Warsaw (two books and a few dolls), could not believe her eyes. There were musical toys and mechanical toys. There was even a cow, a perfect copy of the real animal, with a *real* fuzzy cowskin body. It had a hidden lid, which you could lift, pour milk inside, and then milk the cow!

Nina showed her new guest an old icon of Madonna in one of the rooms. A small flickering light was kept in front of it, night and day. Nina taught Irene how to cross oneself and bow three times, Russian Orthodox style.

"Do you never make the cross just once?"

"Never. You have to cross yourself three times and bow."

"Why don't you touch your left arm when you cross?"

"I don't know. That's the way we do it. It seems strange to you, but it seems strange to me how you do it on both sides. Well, anyway *Christos* is the same, no matter how you cross yourself, is he not?"

There were three samovars in the house: a big silver one for serving tea to guests, another smaller one of brass for the family, and a third — a very old chubby little fellow — that stood on a side table and was never used. It had been in the family for generations.

In the kitchen Irene found many strange things, different from what was in their Polish kitchen back home. It was enormous, with a brick oven and stove in one corner called a *pyechka*. Pyechka was so big that Dunya, the maid, slept on top of it, keeping her straw mattress there. It must have been fun to sleep somewhere halfway up between floor and ceiling!

Dunya was doing some ironing with a strange iron. It was tall, with a lid that you could lift up and put in some hot charcoal.

"How strange!" exclaimed Irene. "Your iron has no soul."

"Soul? How can an iron have a soul?"

"Our irons have iron souls: you take them out, keep them in hot coals for a while until they are red hot, and then put them back into the iron."

"Ha, ha, ha, what a strange custom," laughed Dunya... "to have iron souls!"

"Ha, ha, ha, what a strange custom to have charcoal souls!" Irene laughed back.

At tea time she learned how to drink tea from a glass, not from a cup, and to eat preserves bit by bit from a silver teaspoon with each sip of tea. This was called *chai s varen'em*.

"You can also have *chai na prikusku* — to bite a lump of sugar with each sip. Or you can have *na prilizku* — to lick the sugar, or *na pridumku* — to *look* at the sugar and *dream* that you are using it," said Nina.

"The *na prilizku* and *na pridumku* is a joke, of course," said Nina's mother, laughing. "We are not such barbarians."

The next few days were filled with sightseeing, dinner and supper parties at both houses, and a trip to the photographer. Jadwiga was wonderful. She was never too tired or too bored to show them anything that could be of interest or fun to all of them. The weather was fine, and they did a lot of walking, but sometimes they took a horse-drawn coach or *izvoshchik*, or an open *drozhki*.

Just as in Warsaw, there were streets with funny names: here, too, they had names that had nothing to do with places. The street car conductor called out "Krasnye Vorota," which means "Red Gate," but Irene looked out the widow and there was no gate and nothing red in sight.

On "Krasnaya Ploshchad" — Red Square — there was no red pavement either, but there was on the square a huge "Tsar-Kolokol" bell and a "Tsar-Pushka" cannon. The bell and cannon are both so enormous that the Russians could never use them. The bell tore off the chains the first time that it was lifted, leaving a gap so big that when you stood inside the bell, it looked like a big gate. The cannon-balls, too, are so big that they were too heavy to be fired into the air!

PART II — CHAPTER TWO

They visited countless Orthodox churches, called *tserkvi*, as well as the Kremlin, the Kustarnyi Folk Art Museum, and finally, the Tretyakovskaya Galereya: the great art gallery.

At the Galereya two pictures impressed Irene most. One was as big as a wall and showed Tsar Ivan the Terrible, who had just killed his son, with blood streaming through his fingers where he was trying to hold his son's head. The other picture was called *Vsyudu Zhizn*, or "Life Goes on Everywhere." It shows a family of prisoners with a little child, on their way to Siberia, seated behind the barred window of a cattle wagon, feeding sparrows.

One day, passing through the Lubyanka district in a streetcar, they saw a dark, gloomy building through the window.

"This is Lubyanka Prison," said Jadwiga, "called *butyrki*." *

It was strange to see *a real prison* right in the middle of the city. Suddenly, it seemed to Irene that on that sunny, hot day in July, a cold wind had swept through the streetcar. She kept her head turned with her eyes glued to the buildings long after the car had passed them.

Maria Eremeyevna's home, where mother was staying, was very different from that of Lydia Alekseyevna. Maria was a small, dark, shapely woman with delicate bones and features, and big, black eyes. Both of her parents hailed from old families of the Caucasus region. Her home was filled with old, rare Oriental carpets and an exquisite collection of old arms: knives (called "kinjals"), short and long sabers, and pistols, some of them elaborately hand carved and inlaid with precious stones and metals. Because of so many antiques, the apartment, although large, seemed small and cozy. Her husband, Boris, a bright young engineer and a powerful, big man, seemed to move among the small Caucasian-style furniture like an elephant in a china shop. Their only son, Yura, was neither spoiled nor pampered. At ten, he was considered and treated like an adult, and his interests were those of a precocious child. He hated toys, and unlike the house where Irene was staying, there was not a toy to be seen, except for some wooden and metal pieces from which Yura was constantly building something, tearing it apart and starting something else. Like his mother, he was small, delicate and sensitive.

---

* *butyrki* is used here in the generic sense for "prison". *Butyrka* is a separate prison several km farther from the center of Moscow.

FIRST DAYS IN RUSSIA

The few days of whirlwind activities — sightseeing and parties — came to an end. Jadwiga took the family to the Bykovo dacha, where Niania and little Tadyo were waiting for them.

Vlodek came on Saturday afternoon from Tula and seemed to accept with resignation all the commotion in what up to then had been a quiet summer place. Suddenly, it was resounding with the noises of a large family settling in.

When you first met Vlodek, your immediate thought was "how could Jadwiga have fallen in love and married a man like him?" The typical "what did she see in him?" was an overpowering thought. Just as she was beautiful, he was homely. As she was refined, he seemed crude. As she was delicate and sophisticated, he gave the impression of being a primitive simpleton. He was of average height with slightly bowed legs, far from being svelte, and his round face looked like the Lord had sat on it before catapulting him into this world. In spite of being only in his early thirties, he was getting bald, making his forehead seem unusually large.

This was the first impression that Irene got of her brother-in-law, whom she hardly remembered from the times before Jadwiga's marriage. But it did not take much time, once you got to know him, to change your mind completely.

As an engineer he was brilliant; as a husband he was considerate, thoughtful and gentle; as a man he was physically powerful. His interests were diverse; his hobbies were reading and opera. He himself had a nice bass-baritone voice. Altogether, when you were with Vlodek, you had the feeling of being in the company of a bear: gentle, but capable of being powerful and intelligent. Although he loved — and adored — his wife much more than the average husband does, he was firm.

One day, early in their marriage, when she resisted stubbornly, like a spoiled child, to his reasonable advice, he simply lifted her up with one arm and carried her out like a sack of flour, all the way from the house into the garden. All this without a trace of anger or brutality. Jadwiga came to her senses and realized, for the first time in her life, that she could not get everything she wanted just because she was beautiful or loved. In fact, it was she, not he, who told others of this occurrence. She was proud of his physical strength and of his masculine, stable personality.

Besides Vlodek, who was in Bykovo only on Sundays, Irene met another Russian, but he belonged to an entirely different social class. His name was Sergei, and he was originally Vlodek's *denshchik* (orderly). After they both left the army, Vlodek kept the young man in his house. Now, Sergei was simply indispensable. He was the first to get up in the morning, and the last to go to bed. He took care of the baby when Niania was busy; he was a maid, a cook and a houseboy. He never seemed to be tired, overworked, hostile or critical. With seven extra guests in the house, there was bedding to put up each night, cleaning to do, and piles of dishes three times a day.

Sergei must have put in a nineteen-hour day, yet he was always a cheerful fellow, even though quiet and a little bashful. He was a small, slightly built blond and blue-eyed boy from the Western Ukraine. This part of the country belonged to Poland for centuries, being incorporated in turn into Russia or Poland, depending on the successes of the wars between the two countries. The great landowners — the gentry of the Western Ukraine — were Poles, while the peasants were for the most part either Polish or of mixed stock, or at least under the influence of Polish customs. Many young men of the Polish gentry were "improving" the peasants' blood by sexual relations with country girls. During the summer on hot, sultry nights, a bunch of peasant girls, including maids from manors, would go to the river for a swim. Quite often, like mythical nymphs, they would be ambushed and ravished by young men from nearby estates, who "just happened to be around." The girl usually got a substantial monetary award to dry her tears and was hurriedly married by her parents to some suitable peasant boy. And so it was not unusual to spot among the small specimens of peasant stock, a young man of unusual looks, grace, breeding and intelligence. There was one case of a "peasant boy" who knew that he was the son of a Polish Prince. His father belonged to one of the oldest families of Polish aristocracy. The son moved into the city, joined the "intelligentsia," and did not mind in the least being unofficially recognized as the son of a Prince.

Did Sergei have some of the Polish gentry blood in him? Who knows? He definitely did not look like the average Russian peasant. His bones were fine, his face delicate, and his movements and behavior naturally restrained and gentle. When he had a little time to spare at night, he would play a small harmonica and sing sad, romantic and melodious Ukrainian *dumkas* and *shumkas*.

FIRST DAYS IN RUSSIA

Irene liked Sergei very much and tried to stay with him as much as possible. He taught her how to dance Russian folk dances, including the Cossack *prisyadka* — dancing while sitting on your bended legs with your arms crossed. Irene's legs were thin and strong from much running and walking, so she could do this dance with the greatest of ease. As to Sergei, he had the perfect small and light figure of a ballet dancer, so together they had a lot of fun.

From Sergei and children living on other nearby dachas, Irene learned to speak Russian in just a few weeks. She had some knowledge of it listening to her brother read Russian poetry aloud while doing homework back home, but she never tried to speak it until now. She found it easy and was attracted to it by its melodious, uneven accentuation, and by its charm in using diminutives. Many words were used in the diminutive sense of "little," without using this unattractive word at all. You simply changed the original word into another having an ending that meant "little." In comparison with the Polish language, which is rather dry and sober in its use of words (a child is called by name, never "dear," "darling," "honey," "sweet-heart" or such), here was a language sweet like music, caressing and tender.

The following simple song used in children's games is like a string of shiny, colorful beads — like Beethoven's composition "Souvenir à Elise" — a musical piece for a child:

Ogurechik, ogurechik
Nye khodi na tot konechik
Tam detki zhivut
Tebie khvostik otorvut!

which means:

Little cucumber, *little* cucumber
Don't go down that *little* path
Little children live there
Who will tear off your *little* tail!

In English translation this song is crude, repetitive and silly, using the word "little" five times. In Russian, the same song is funny, melodious and charming — yet compact — like a few notes struck on the piano by a skillful hand.

In fact, changing a word into its diminutive form does not always mean to express "littleness" but rather something that was nice, cute or dear to you. The neighbor was not "sosyed" but "sosyedushka," a relative not "kum" but "kumushka." If you called someone a dove, it was not "golub" but "golubchik"... a darling little dove.

So, Irene, called "Irene" by her family and nothing else, was suddenly "golubchik," "dusyenka" (sweetheart), "pupsenka" (little doll) and "angielochek" (little angel).

In this strange country, so different in its customs and with its strange language, Irene did not feel awkward or out of place. On the contrary, it seemed like the friendliest place in the world. The large house, with her family always around her, her playmates, and Sergei — it was all that a six-year old child needed.

There was also Niania, who was not at all like the maids that Irene knew back home. Emily would not enter a room unless called by mother or unless she was cleaning. She stood up if mother happened to come into a room, and she kissed mother's hand every time that she would get her monthly pay. Not this niania. She did not even wear an apron, except when feeding Tadyo, and when she was not working, she sat and talked in the same room with the rest of the family.

One night something happened, after which Niania's prestige became even greater than ever before. Little Tadyo, stricken with a gastric fever, became very ill in the middle of the night. The fever was so high that the child went into convulsions. There was no doctor for miles around, and even if Sergei were to run to the station and send a telegram to Vlodek, or tried to telephone, it would be hours before the doctor could come.

Irene was awakened by shouts and commotion — the lights were on all over the house. She crept out of bed and went into the room where Niania usually kept Tadyo. She found Jadwiga there, crying hysterically, and Niania, trying to convince her that she was right in what she wanted to do. She had to shout to be heard above Jadwiga's cries. The two women seemed to be fighting over the body of the little boy, like the biblical mothers in King Solomon's court.

"You are going to kill him!" Jadwiga kept shouting.

"I have to do it! It is the only thing that can help him! Let me do it!" Niania was shouting back in despair.

In the midst of it stood mother, bewildered and upset, trying to calm Jadwiga down.

"Will you hold back your daughter, please, so that I can put Tadyo in the water!" Niania finally cried to mother impatiently.

FIRST DAYS IN RUSSIA 77

Mother grabbed the struggling Jadwiga and held her, while Niania took Tadyo, still convulsing, undressed him and put him into a small tub of water that stood nearby. The little body, burning with fever, stiffened, and trembling with convulsions calmed down in a few minutes. Niania took him out, dried and wrapped him in a light flannel blanket. He fell asleep, and his temperature went down visibly.

The next day, except for a light diet, he did not need any extra attention, and two days later was as healthy and bouncy as ever. Nothing was said about that night, as Jadwiga probably felt foolish but would never admit that she had been wrong. Niania, on the other hand, was treated more than ever like a member of the family, not like a paid servant.

The only disappointing thing to Irene in her new surroundings was Bykovo dacha itself. The house was primitively put together of rough, unpainted wood planks. It had no shrubbery, flower beds, or even a porch. The soil was sandy, covered with clumps of wild grass burned by the hot July sun into yellowish little islands in the midst of gray, parched soil. There were no large, shade trees around the house. It was quite a distance to a narrow river that flowed along the flat unattractive country. Some of the other houses where Irene went to play had a few bushes of gooseberries or currants, and a few flower beds of thin unattended plants, perpetually dying of thirst.

How different it was from the countryside that Irene was used to playing in during the summers in Poland! There, the house itself was built of solid logs, painted white or pale blue on the outside. It would have a large, sagging porch on which the family ate all their meals, and sat at night chasing away big moths attracted by the light of the kerosene lamp. And they watched dark, silent bats and owls performing their nocturnal rituals among the darkened shrubs and trees.

There was always a garden in full bloom when they came in June. There were simple flowers, grown mostly for fragrance, not for effect… nicotiana, matilija, mignonette, pinks, and sweet-and-pungent smelling nasturtiums. They were cut daily and kept in a low bowl on the porch table.

There were always old, stately trees about: chestnut trees and linden trees, some of them so old that under their branches a few hundred people could find protection from the sun or from a sudden shower. There were old country roads, shaded by stately poplars, with quiet brooks running through colorful meadows, accentuated here and there by an old wild pear tree, a weeping willow, or a graceful weeping birch.

The house which they rented for the summer in Poland was always near some rural settlement, where "near" meant a few miles away. Polish peasants seldom, if ever, built houses on the land that they possessed; instead, they had them built in a little town called a *wieś*. The houses, whitewashed or painted pale blue, with thatched roofs, had little crooked fences that encircled small gardens. There were always flowers in abundance around these simple houses: hollyhocks... wild, fragrant roses... sunflowers and daisies... a patch of vegetables... old fruit trees...

When mother came with the children for the summer, all she would bring from the city in the line of food and utilities was sugar, salt and soap. All the rest was bought from the local peasants. You often waited for the bread to be taken out of the oven; you watched vegetables being gathered from the garden, and waited for cherries or green apples to be picked from a tree by a peasant boy. You watched the cow being milked, the milk passing through a fine sieve and left to cool off in the cellar, to which one could enter only through a small trapdoor in the earthen floor...

Although you were "letniki" (summer people), you were not only friendly with the peasants, but felt somehow to be a part of their daily chores and interests. You were worried if the rain threatened the mowing of the hay or interfered with the harvest. You worried with the peasants if the summer was too dry or too wet. You went for a ride on a peasant's cart that was carrying a few sacks of grain to a mill. There you watched a huge windmill turning its powerful wings round and round, and then rode back sitting next to sacks of newly ground, fresh-smelling flour...

At other times you roamed endless forests, looking forward to gathering strawberries, blueberries and mushrooms, or you just walked among the rye and wheat fields, picking wild pinks, bachelor buttons and red poppies. You would roll down green, gentle slopes along the railroad tracks, or just lie down near the brook, your face among buttercups and forget-me-nots. Or you might turn around, face up, and look at the greatness of the pale blue summer sky...

You would watch a heart-shaped country cheese being put out to "sweat" in cheesecloth under a wooden board, weighted with a stone. You brought home ("be careful," said maman) a basket of eggs, freshly gathered by a peasant boy from under a cackling hen, some of them still warm.

And birds. Birds were like fields, forests and rural settlements — a part of the summer way of life in Poland. The haunting, monotonous cuckoo's voice, the nightingale's night symphony, the meadowlarks and singing sparrows — they were a part of nature's wholeness.

The most conspicuous, of course, were the storks, not only by their size, but as they were considered birds that bring good luck, they were encouraged to nest on the thatched roofs. The peasants would attach old, broken cartwheels to the roofs to serve as skeletons for the storks' nests. One could watch papa and mama stork for hours, walking along or standing on one leg in the green, marshy meadow, waiting for a frog, then catching it — flying to their nest where they would feed a few skinny, shaky babies, their beaks longer than their little fuzzy bodies.

On Sunday one went to the nearest country church. Since not all the settlements could afford to build a church, one could see all the country roads leading to the church crowded with carts ordinarily used for bringing in field crops. This time the whole family sat sideways, their feet dangling in rhythm with every sway of the cart on a bumpy, country road. Poorer peasants walked barefoot, holding their shoes in their hands or carrying them on a stick, and not putting them on until they reached the church square.

Mother would arrange for transportation in a carriage with a "wealthy" peasant. The whole family was always invited by the local priest to sit in the balcony where the organist played during holy mass. From there, they had a bird's eye view of the whole church.

It looked so beautiful that Irene, thoroughly absorbed by watching, had to be pushed now and then by Janka to remind her when to kneel and when to stand up, according to the rites of the Catholic Church.

Down below, the peasants were sitting: men and boys on the right side of the church, women and children on the left. Washed and scrubbed, their sunburned necks and faces shiny with cleanliness, the men's hair wet and combed neatly, they sat in their Sunday best. The women's dazzling white, handspun and starched linen blouses were hand embroidered; the colorful bead, sequin and wool-embroidered vests; the wide, wide homespun woolen skirts, with various colors predominating according to different parts of the region. From oranges, yellows and blacks, to greens and blacks, or — faded by the sun — silvery mauve and lilac blacks. The natural vegetable colors used by the peasants were always harmonious and muted, like colors found in nature: a flower's petals, a butterfly's wings or a bird's plumage. In contrast to the women's colorful splendor — accentuated further by multicolored ribbons, strings of beads and flowered kerchiefs — the men's side was like an artist's print in black and white: white shirts, and black pants held high inside black polished boots. In some part of Poland men wore colorful vests as well, or jackets, and upon leaving church they would put on black felt hats.

They were handsome people. Not good-looking or striking in any respect, but nice, medium-sized, lean and gentle. The work in the fields and the wholesome, simple food they ate made their bodies strong and straight. They could seldom afford meat, except on holy days or special family feasts, but their bread-potatoes-vegetable and dairy diet was adequate. One never saw ugly, deformed or rickety children, as in the city slums, or puffy, unhealthy and overweight adults.

If a church was named after a saint — which was often the case — once a year there was a great feast, which was a combination of the religious observance with processions and a big market day.

Primitive, wooden stalls were built, where one could buy bagels by the dozen on strings, sweets and cakes, religious pictures and rosaries, women's coral beads and ribbons, kerchiefs, dry goods, shoes, men's pants, hand-turned and painted clay pottery, pitchers and bowls, and little hand-turned whistles in bird and animal forms that the children blew incessantly, adding to the noise and commotion. All sorts of wicker baskets, sieves and kitchen utensils hung on long strings, swaying in the summer breeze above the crowds of feasting peasants. Now and then, a few men would emerge from a nearby "restaurant," visibly under the influence of vodka. They would argue and try to fight, but overcome by liquor and the summer heat, they would finish the argument in a brotherly embrace and fall asleep on a clump of grass under the shade of a nearby tree.

In contrast to all this commercial buying, feasting and bargaining, the afternoon religious procession stood out all by itself. On that usually sunny summer day there would be a priest in white and golden robes, holding the Holy Vessel high above his head: the altar boys continually ringing, tinkling little bells... the statue of the saint, carried high among the fluttering flags and ribbons... rows and rows of little girls in white dresses, walking backwards in front of the priest, tossing flower petals at his feet from their little baskets... the smell of incense, mingling with the smell of rose petals drying in the hot sun and crushed by feet... the adoration, the purification, the collective *catharsis*.

Ancient? Yes. Primitive? Yes. Superfluous? Why?

FIRST DAYS IN RUSSIA

If an average adult sees nothing foolish about his "name day" or his birthday remembered, if an average father sees nothing foolish in spending — usually more than he can afford — on his daughter's wedding reception (the most primitive, ancient tribal custom of all in the history of mankind), why then should Saint Paul's or Saint Peter's church, remembered once a year, be looked upon as superfluous or childish?

All this: Irene's country, her people and their customs were missed by her in that first summer spent in Bykovo. She was too young to realize it as clearly and vividly as would an adult, but she felt the absence of something beautiful, simple and vital with which she had grown up... and which was part of her.

But new things, images and faces were around her. It was fascinating, and it was enough to make her happy, though in a different way from what she had been accustomed to.

CHAPTER THREE — Father Makes the Decision

It was a hot evening in August. Father took off his coat and hung it on the dining room chair. He went to the kitchen, poured some water in a pitcher, opened the balcony door and started to water the flowers.

"Why am I doing it?" he thought. "The men will move the furniture out tomorrow, and my family will not be coming back here at all."

It was getting dark outside, but the sky was still pale blue with daylight, and one could hear the squeaky noise of swallows flying in circles above.

Father lighted the dining room lamp, put the inkpot and a box of stationery on the table and sat down. He sat like that for a long time, thinking of how to begin. He was never a good letter writer, but this one was particularly hard to write.

"How quiet it is in here," he thought. "Every year, when they leave for summer, I can't seem to get used to the quiet in the house. When one lives with a large family for so many years, quiet and privacy become uncommon luxuries, but finally a burden instead of a welcome change. But, let my mind not wander: I must write and send this letter right away."

He wrote:

Dear Zofie and children,

Ever since hearing yesterday's news that Russia is at war with Germany, I have been through hours of anguish and indecision. My first and main problem was whether you should all come home immediately so that we could be together in times so troubled... or whether it would be better for you to stay in Russia and not come back at all. Divided and occupied as our country has been for so long

FATHER MAKES THE DECISION

by the alien powers, what else can it become but a target and battlefield during a war?

I thought all day yesterday and all night about it — the decision I knew that I had to make. It was so much harder for me, because you are not here, Zofie, to discuss it with me? It worries me that the decision I made, and which I felt to be the best, might prove wrong as time goes on. Your woman's intuition, I am sure, would have helped you in deciding what you thought was right, but I had to act quickly, as war could turn our country into a raging battlefield any day now.

I asked Helena and Tota what their opinion was, and I saw Juta, too. They all agreed with me that it will be much safer for us to stay in Russia for the duration of the war. Juta is leaving with the children for Kiev, and she expects that Sigismund will be a surgeon with the Russian army. Tota and Helena will stay here and run their shop, even though business might be very poor during the war.

This morning I was told that I can count on getting a position in the Moscow offices. Whether it be the Warsaw-Vienna railroad or the Moscow-Petersburg, I know that I can be useful.

So you see, my Zofie, it looks as if we are going to live in Moscow. I rented a room from our neighbors today and paid a full year's rent in advance. Tomorrow the moving men will store everything in it. The piano, our good furniture and the books are the most important. Then the bedding will be piled up to the ceiling. Whatever remains of lesser value, like the kitchen or children's furniture, I will give away to the people in the backyard apartments.

Tell Vlodek that I will be in Tula in a few days; please meet me there. We will have to go together to Moscow, find an apartment, furnish it, and have it ready for the children in time for the beginning of the school year.

I hope that you agree with me, and pray, dear Zofie, that I will never be sorry for the decision that I have made.

Your

Aleksander

PART II — CHAPTER THREE

He addressed and sealed the envelope, then went out on the balcony. The wrought iron rail railings were still warm from the day's exposure to the hot summer sun, but the freshly watered plants gave off a cool fragrance. The birds were already asleep, the city quiet, the streets deserted.

Father looked up at the sky, and as the first dim stars appeared, he looked for reassurance and courage.

But the sky, like the future, seemed distant, impenetrable and enigmatic.

CHAPTER FOUR — Moscow is Home

It was Monday, and Katyusha, the laundress, was outside finishing the laundry at the large wooden tub that stood on a small table. Some of the clothes, hung earlier, were already dry, and — as clothespins were unknown — the wind blew them off the clothesline and all over the ground. Irene looked for them among the clumps of grass. They were mostly small things like handkerchiefs, socks or children's underwear. The bigger pieces managed to stay on the line despite the wind.

After father's letter had arrived from Warsaw, Irene could feel the atmosphere change around her. There was no longer the carefree, summer-vacation behavior among the adults. Mother, Jadwiga and Niania had worried, serious looks on their faces. Vlodek did not come to spend the previous Sunday at the dacha, and Sergei left "to go back to the army."

Irene heard the word "war" many times a day.

When she was very little — so little that she had to stand on tiptoe to see what was on the dining room table — she remembered Henryk playing "war" with his tin soldiers. He had a beautiful collection of all sorts of cavalrymen and footmen in colorful uniforms — some from Napoleon's army, others from Prussian, Russian, Polish and Italian armies. It seemed that war was a handsome parade:

Left flank, right flank, frontward, back to the previous position, half encircling one group, then another... until some of the soldiers were scattered on the table with a *bang!*

"Real war must be even more exciting and pretty-looking than playing with tin soldiers," thought Irene. "Galloping horses, rolling cannons, colorful uniforms..."

She thought of Sergei being part of the handsome parade, and although she missed him badly, she was somehow proud and glad that he was one of those heroes of the big game. She was told that the family was not going back to Warsaw, but would live in Moscow as long as the war went on: "probably a few months," mother had said.

Jadwiga and mother had just left the house wearing city outfits — summer suits, hats and, of course, umbrellas. Henryk carried their suitcase, while his sisters followed him.

"I'll try to find an apartment and furnish it as soon as possible, then come back here with Father for a few days' rest before school starts," said mother. "Behave yourselves and read a lot. It is one thing to take Russian in a Polish school, but it is quite another thing to be in a Russian school and take all the subjects in Russian. Try to get some school books from the Russian children, and get accustomed to the mathematics and science vocabulary. And you, Henry, please teach Irene how to read and write in Russian. She speaks well, but she won't pass an exam unless she can read and write. You will have to study with her at least two or three hours a day, as we have only a few weeks left."

Mother and Jadwiga were to go to Tula, then [*words missing*]

They started to walk toward the station, [*words missing*] their suitcase. The girls stood and watched them go. Suddenly Irene realized that it was the first time in her life that mother had gone away without her. She was used to father's trips and to being away from him during the summer, but mother was never away for more than a few hours. She watched her mother's figure on the country road getting smaller and smaller... A desperate panic clutched her heart — the cutting of the umbilical cord was harsh and sudden. She started to run after mother and Jadwiga, screaming with all the strength in her lungs: "Maman, don't leave me! Take me with you! Don't leave me! Maman! Maman!"

Henryk turned back in disgust and shouted at her: "Stop throwing tantrums! Why don't you grow up? And stop calling her 'Maman'. Why don't you call her 'Mother'?" "*Ma-man, Pa-pa,*" he squeaked, aping her childish voice.

Suddenly, Irene felt so ashamed that she wanted to crawl into the ground and die. From that day on, she called her parents in the "adult" way, but to the end of her life she could not think of her father as anything other than "Papa."

Every afternoon Irene had lessons with Henryk. Having to teach a kid sister on a hot summer afternoon did not exactly put the fifteen year-old in a gentle or understanding mood. It was easy for Irene, with her ear for music, to learn to speak Russian. After all, the language's correct pronunciation is nothing else than following certain rhythmical accents and vocal articulations. But to learn to read was something else.

The Polish alphabet is like French or Italian: a Latin alphabet. In Russian, half of the letters were entirely different from Latin, and those letters that looked like Latin were pronounced differently. The *P* was *R*, *H* was *N*, *X* was *H*, while script *m* was *t* and script *n* was *p*.

For a week Irene was frustrated, confused and discouraged. Henryk was impatient and often abusive. To top it all, there was no simple book suitable for the beginner. Henryk took the first book that he found in the house. It happened to be Lermontov's *Taman'*, and when that talented writer and poet wrote the book, he certainly didn't have in mind a struggling, six year-old child learning to read.

Three hours a day, on hot August afternoons, almost in tears and trying to remember all the letters that were different from Polish letters, Irene struggled through *Taman'*:

Taman' — *samyi skvernyi gorodishko iz vseh primorskih gorodov Rossii...* ("Taman is the most miserable little town of all the seaside towns of Russia...")

Then, one day something clicked, and Irene started to read well; not very fast, and occasionally with the wrong accent on an unknown word, but she could read! She could also write many simple words under direction. By the time her parents returned to take the children to Moscow, she was ready to take the exams at Moscow's Gymnasium for Girls.

While the children were in Bykovo spending a carefree summer, and Irene was being introduced to the bittersweet tribulations of learning Russian, their parents were trying to establish themselves in Moscow. It was a difficult situation for Poles. They had been under Russian rule, but still remained in their own country and in their native cities. It was something different again to become physically uprooted to a strange country and a strange city.

Here, Jadwiga and her two friends were of great help to them. It was not hard to find a large, suitable apartment in those days in Moscow, and Maria Eremeyevna and Lydia Alekseyevna volunteered to furnish it almost entirely with the surplus of their own furniture.

"You will do us a favor if we can get rid of all that furniture that has accumulated in the house for generations," said Maria.

Beds, chairs, tables, wardrobes and chests of drawers were arriving day after day. All mother had to buy was bedding, linen, curtains, kitchen utensils and a dining room set.

It was a large, comfortable apartment. What was nicest of all, the family decided, was the fact that they did not have to live in a typical city apartment house. The quiet side street, called a *pereulok*, only had houses called *osobyanki* (single, private dwellings), all with a large iron gate for carriages to enter and a smaller side iron gate. All had a small private garden behind a tall brick wall, and a large courtyard paved with cobblestones.

The owner occupied the first floor, and the family moved into the ground floor. There were seven rooms; three on the street side, two with windows facing the courtyard, and two others without windows in the rear. Light and ventilation to the windowless rooms was supplied by the adjoining rooms and halls; Irene's parents chose those rooms for themselves. The biggest front corner room with six windows was given to Stefa and Sophie, but actually, with its many tables and chairs, it was more or less a family room. The idea of a "salon" from Warsaw times had been abandoned. There was no piano or fancy furniture for a salon, and somehow it now seemed old-fashioned and superfluous to have such a room.

Irene also had a front room, with a view of the street, sharing it with Janka, of course, and she loved everything about the new apartment and its surroundings. The garden was simple, overgrown, unkempt but charming in its primitive simplicity: fruit trees, now heavy with fruit, a few shade trees, and tall lilac bushes. The courtyard was oblong with a big carriage house on the right, servants' quarters above it. Then there was a stable (*saray*), a storage building with a trapdoor leading to a cellar that was filled with ice, and a laundry house. On the left side of the yard, between the edge of the garden and the laundry house was an old well, covered with boards. Was it dry? Was it good only for horses or for washing carriages? Irene never found out. There were no horses or carriages any more, and water was supplied by the waterman who came twice a week, filling to the brim a big oak barrel that was in the kitchen. The rest of the water — for laundry and washing — was caught in another barrel as it drained from the roof on rainy days. It was "soft" and much nicer to use than the regular water.

The owner of the house — a middle-aged bachelor in an old-fashioned coat, who looked like an actor from a play by Gogol — appeared only once, to sign the lease with father. He lived as a recluse with his elderly mother and did not seem ever to leave the house or to have visitors.

He kept three servants: the cook (*Kuharka*), a maid (the daughter of *Kuharka*, who was married to a soldier), and *Dvornik*, a middle-aged man whose duties were to clear the snow from the sidewalks and yard during winter, and to sweep and water them on other occasions. He was a grouchy, unfriendly character who never spoke a word.

Since the owner was never around, Kuharka seemed to give all the orders and appeared to be a very clever, capable woman.

Mother hired a maid, too. Her name was Akulina, and she was a rather ugly-looking, sulky creature who never spoke unless it was necessary, and never smiled. Irene did not like her, and that made her unhappy, because she wanted to like everybody around her.

Akulina stayed with the family for two years, until one night, mother — who always wondered why she tossed and turned so much at night on the *pechka* where she slept — went into the kitchen. She found not one, but two pairs of legs on the pechka, and crying sharply with indignation, saw Dvornik, holding his pants, jump off and disappear behind the door.

Mother did not let Akulina stay even until morning; she made her pack her things and get out right away. Whether she stayed with Kuharka, her daughter, or Dvornik that night, or slept in the *sieni* (kitchen entrance) nobody knew. But from then on, she was no longer around.

But all that had happened after the family had lived in the apartment for two years. Right now, mother was trying to settle down and balance the budget. Soon she decided that although Helena should keep her rather small bedroom for herself, it was not necessary to waste a big, sunny room, one with a single convenient entrance from the inner hall and overlooking the courtyard, for Henryk's use alone.

"Henry can sleep in the dining room, behind the folding screen," she announced one day. "We could rent his room and pay Akulina's wages with it."

Mother printed in her own hand a fancy-lettered sign and put it in the front window: « *Bolshaya, svetlaya komnata, s mebelyu ili bez* » ("Large, sunny room, furnished or unfurnished").

Very soon a fish caught the hook. A widow named Marfa Grigoryevna moved in with so much furniture that one could hardly breathe, much less walk around in the room. She was a plump, extremely gay, friendly creature, apparently in great need of social intercourse, because she constantly invited someone from the family to her room.

In addition to piles of furniture, she also had a gramophone, and she played all her records every day. She also liked to sing, so she was constantly either playing records, singing, or sipping tea.

She had brought a supply of homemade preserves, which cluttered the large double window sill. They were delicious, especially her wild strawberry jam, which was a real delicacy. With all her primitive, messy ways of living, plus her overweight figure and plain face, she was full of life and so outgoing that everyone was very fond of her.

Irene was not only attracted by the *chai s varen'em* — the tea with preserves — which was so delicious, but also by the gramophone and the songs that she learned from Marfa:

« *Marietta... Mnie stranno eto... Chto nash syn pokhozh na kadeta...* »

Or, "Marietta, it seems strange to me, that our son looks like one of the cadets..."

Marfa Grigoryevna also liked romantic, sad songs, like *Ochi Chernye* ("Dark Eyes"), which she sang quite well in her low, deep voice.

Irene especially liked one song, written just before the death of a young, beautiful actress — supposedly by someone who was in love with her.[*] The music was hauntingly beautiful, and so were the lyrics; it is hard to translate the mood and sober simplicity into any other language:

Vashi pal'tzy pakhnut ladanom
A v resnitsah spit pechal'
Nichego teper' nye nado nam
Nikogo teper' nye zhal'...

Or, "Your fingers are fragrant with incense; And beneath your eyelids sorrow sleeps; We need nothing, no more; Regret no one, no more..."

The long, hard winter passed, and spring burst suddenly, melting the snow in the garden — which had been higher than Irene's head. Easter came, and Marfa Grigoryevna took everyone to the *tserkov* for the midnight service.

---

[*] By Alexander Vertinsky (*ca.* 1916).

Irene, who for that occasion, had slept all afternoon and evening so as to be able to stay up late, was overwhelmed and a little bit frightened. The crowds were so dense that she was afraid that she would suffocate, but somehow father and Henryk managed to protect her from the bodies pressing around her. Suddenly, the crowd seemed to become even more dense, as if trying to make room for one more person. But no one seemed to be moving forward from the entrance of the *tserkov* toward the altar. Yet, from the movements of the bodies, all the way from the back of the church and gradually to the front, it appeared that "something," if not someone, *was* moving forward. Through an opening between the legs of someone in the crowd pressing around her, Irene saw a man crawling on his knees along the full length of the *tserkov* toward the altar. At the same time he was beating and prostrating himself (*poklony*) and crossing himself incessantly.

Whether he was trying to repent for his sins publicly, or simply showing happiness and adoration for the Resurrection of Christ, Irene did not know. But she thought how strongly one had to believe in God and love Him to be capable of doing such a thing in public without feeling foolish.

About the time the service was nearing its end, everyone turned around and began kissing each other. *Christos voskrese, voistinu voskrese!* ("Christ has risen, indeed He has risen!")...

Marfa Grigoryevna made a delicious *pashka*, a traditional hard cheese cake in the form of a pyramid, and many other Russian holiday specialties.

Everyone was sorry when she moved away. She left because a relative in Saratov wrote to her about a possible arrangement for marriage.

After the widow, a young bachelor moved into Henryk's room. He was blond, bashful, stammered and seemed to know only two words:

"Pozhaluysta, samovarchik." ("Please, may I have a little tea.")

This meant that he wanted a hot samovar brought to his room by Akulina. He left for work in the morning after drinking a few glasses of tea from the samovarchik. He usually came home quite late, and again after several glasses of tea, went to bed. He seemed such a quiet, nice young man that one day when he asked mother if he could invite a few of his friends in to play cards, she of course said: "yes".

After *"Pozhaluysta, samovarchik"* and several hours of hearing voices — typical of young men playing cards — mother, like everyone else, went to bed. But it seemed strange to her after a while to hear women's voices, giggles and laughter. Mother knocked at the door of Ivan Ivanovich's room and entered. There were several "ladies" in the room with Ivan Ivanovich and his friends, and they were *not* playing cards! Obviously, they had not entered through either the front or kitchen door, so they had to have been let in through the courtyard and in the window — easy to do, as the window sills were only a few feet off the ground.

Ivan Ivanovich, the nice, bashful fellow who seemed only to care for *samovarchik* had to leave, mother decided.

After this experience, mother abandoned the idea of renting the room any more, and since in the meantime Akulina had also left, there was no longer the problem of her wages and the extra expenses for food to satisfy her rather voracious appetite.

The first school year, Irene spent at home. She passed her qualifying exams and was entitled to enter the Preparatory Class, called in the Russian Gymnasium, *prigotovitelnyi klass*. Jadwiga advised her mother not to send her to school yet.

"She will be two or three years younger than the average child," said Jadwiga. "Let's not make a 'wonder child' out of her. Besides, winters are very bitter here, as you will soon find out, and for her to walk half an hour twice a day would be too hard.* As to using the streetcars, a child her age would suffocate to death standing in the overcrowded cars among people in heavy winter clothes!"

Mother hesitated for a while, but when she learned that the girl's Gymnasium would be open only for late afternoon sessions, she decided to keep Irene home.

"You were right, Jadwiga," mother said. "That long walk and coming home so late, with frost and the darkness of night... she is too young."

Irene did not mind staying home.

In the morning all her sisters were home except Sophie, who went to a Polish private school and left just after breakfast, so Irene did not feel lonesome. In the afternoon, Sophie and Henryk came back (boys

---

* The distance to the school across the Yauza River is about 1½ km.

had the morning shift), and anyway there was so much to do! She could play with little rag dolls, read, or watch mother and Akulina doing household chores. Or she could play in the courtyard and garden, except during the most bitter winter days when it was just too cold to go out. Then, the whole yard was piled with several feet of snow, except for a few paths dug by Dvornik. The garden was so snowbound that the drifts were much higher than Irene. Of course, that first winter there was Marfa Grigoryevna in the house, so Irene could spend many hours in her room, learning all sorts of Russian songs, which together with the ones that Sergei had taught her, now amounted to a large repertoire.

The kitchen, like the rest of the house in Moscow, was a warm, friendly place. It was so big that the dark oak partition in the corner, behind which was the bathroom, seemed to disappear in its spaciousness. In wintertime the big *pechka* radiated a steady warmth, day and night, and there was always something tasty and aromatic cooking or baking on the stove, or in the oven.

Even the tight-lipped Akulina could not spoil the warmth and friendliness of this kitchen, where Irene used to come to watch her remove cooking pans from the oven. They were made of black iron in the strange shapes of ancient sacrificial or incense-burning vessels, with small tops and bottoms, and very wide in the middle. In these pots Akulina baked buckwheat *kasha,* and made vegetable soup with meat stock called *shchi* and beet soup called *borscht.* Also, there was *uha*, a fish soup like the French bouillabaisse, and baked blintzes called *bliny.*

The bathroom was very primitive. It consisted of an iron wash stand and a tin tub that did not have a drain: the maid had to fill it up and empty it with a pan. As the house had no plumbing, the toilet — although elegant with carved oak sides and woodwork — was similar to toilets found in trains, and the tank, hanging from above and connected with a flushing chain, had to be filled with water by hand every day.

Once a year, before the winter freeze came, men appeared in the courtyard with a big tank on a cart and pumped the cesspool all night. Despite the fact that the double windows at this time of the year were already sealed for the winter, the terrible abominable smell of human excrement permeated the whole house, and would cling to everything for a few days. But as the inconvenience was only once a year, no one minded much the lack of plumbing.

CHAPTER FIVE — Summer, 1915

Revyakino dacha was unlike any typical Russian summer place and unlike the Bykovo dacha where they had spent the summer before.* Usually dachas consisted of houses built among fir and birch trees, more or less close to each other. The house in Revyakino stood alone among endless, wild meadows — veritable *steppes* — with wild flowers as high as a man's arm. To the left, at a distance of a few miles, ran a railroad track where one could see the station and a group of houses. To the right, the meadows ended abruptly in a long, moist *ovrag*, a ravine as wild and untouched by civilization as the Garden of Paradise. Along the bottom ran a stream. Small in the summer, but fed by the melting snow, it was strong and powerful in the spring. The rich virgin soil, a proper amount of moisture, and shade from the birch trees made the flowers grow to unusual sizes, with stronger and brighter colors.

Irene learned very soon how to roam through that veritable jungle of wildflowers and bushes. The white and purple bells were taller than she, the scabiosa and daisies as big as saucers. From morning until night Irene was outdoors, coming home only when she was hungry.

For exploring and her games, she had the most suitable companion she could ever dream of. Since the house was very spacious, Jadwiga invited Maria Eremeyevna and her son Yura, and also Lydia Alekseyevna with Nina and Ira. Occasionally Irene would play with the girls, but most of the time she was with Yura. She had met him a year ago, before going to Bykovo, but in the whirlwind of the first impressions of Moscow and all the sightseeing, she hardly noticed him then.

Here, being with him all day, she not only got to know him, but very soon started to worship him. In spite of the age difference — she was only seven, he was eleven — they became fast friends and playmates. Whether it was Irene's brightness and temperament or her

---

* Revyakino is about 30 km north of Tula.

tomboyish courage, which made her do anything that he suggested, she was accepted by him as an equal. That meant more to Irene than is usual in child relations because Yura was as versatile, able and talented an individual as one could dream of: he not only knew *how* to do things, but how to do them to perfection. Whether he was ever taught these things, or just knew them by himself, Irene never learned. All that she knew was that there was nothing that Yura did not know how to do, or did not dare to do, if he put his mind to it.

He knew how to pick the proper wood for strong, powerful bows and arrows. He knew how to carve them and paint them with red and gold paint, so they looked like medieval hunting instruments from a museum. He knew what kind and how many feathers to use for arrows to give them speed and power for flight. He made the most beautiful set for Irene in just two days — all carved and painted. These two sunburned youngsters, "hunting" among virgin meadows with bows and arrows, looked like a pair of Mongols from Genghis Khan's hordes. When they were tired of hunting and shooting, they would explore the ravine, through which countless detours led them to the lake.

The lake was not very good for swimming, as it was shallow, and the bottom was slimy, but it was large and a paradise for fresh- water fish. Yura, who had brought fish hooks from Moscow, made two long, expertly balanced fish poles.

"Tomorrow morning, we are going to come here and do some fishing," he announced. As usual, he didn't seek Irene's consent. "But we'll have to be here at sunrise: That's when the fish bite the best. Also, later in the day people will come and scare them away."

They agreed that since Irene slept with Helena, Yura would not come into her room, but would wake her up by pulling a string tied to her braids. This string, lying on the floor, led all the way to the door, through the keyhole to the outside doorknob.

It was hardly daylight when she was awakened by the pull of the string. She quickly detached the string, jumped out of bed and dressed in a hurry without waking Helena. Outside, Yura, bright, composed and efficient as usual, was waiting with the fishing poles and a box full of worms that he had dug up the night before.

The meadows, heavy with dew, were enveloped in a bluish morning mist. The smell of cool water was in the air, coming from the *ovrag*... of damp earth and of the fragments of many flowers, sweet and spicy at the same time. The sky was pale, almost white, except in the east where it was all of the changing colors of the rainbow. The very edge of the red disc of the sun was pushing its way up from the meadows. Irene stood up, enchanted by the view. She had seen countless sunsets in her life, but never a sunrise, and somehow it was not the same thing.

"Wait a little while," she said. "I want to see the sun rise."

Suddenly, it was all visible to the eye — a red conqueror's shield, from which all the delicate hues of dawn escaped in flight. Irene and Yura plunged into the *ovrag* and soon were at the lake.

The fish were biting like mad. By the time they got home for breakfast, they had more than a dozen fairly large fish. Everybody congratulated them on their successful fishing expedition, but the most pleased was Niania. With the house so isolated, she had to rely on food supplies brought either from Tula by Vlodek, or by the peddlers who passed by with meat, poultry, vegetables and dairy products.

Irene liked to listen to the singing of the peddlers, their trilly voices calling: *"barànina... telyàtina... smoròdiny"* ("mutton, veal, currants...").

Niania, of course, had some chickens in the yard for a fresh supply of eggs, and from time to time some of the hens were killed for dinner. Their desperate cackling before they had their throats cut made Irene shiver. Somehow she did not mind catching fish — maybe because they were mute?

The four weeks passed quickly, like a dream. It was time for Helena and Irene to go home. They had to make room for their three sisters, who were to spend the rest of the summer in Revyakino.

On the last day, Irene went out after supper to say goodbye to all the familiar places that had become so close to her heart. She stood and listened to the insects humming in the meadows, and to the quiet trickle of the stream. She looked at the last sunset all aflame.

"Will I ever come back here? Will I ever come back to a place like this?"

To leave Revyakino and to leave Yura was the first truly heartbreaking experience in her life. That night she slept a broken sleep, full of nightmares. A few times she heard the plaintive wailing of a passing train. Usually, the locomotive's whistle was pleasant to her ears; it reminded her of travel, of going to new places, meeting new people. But that night the whistle seemed lonely and sad, as lonely as that little child in bed, knowing she had to go away. A child of Eve, thrown out of Paradise.

SUMMER, 1915

The next morning, when she was walking with Helena across the meadows to the station, she did not turn her head even once. She wanted to believe that the house, the people, Yura, and all Revyakino had disappeared, swallowed by a great cruel giant. She did not know that a giant, even more powerful and cruel than her imagination, would soon swallow not only Revyakino, but the whole country.

With Sophie, Stefa and Janka gone to Revyakino, it was now quiet in the house. Not that Irene cared so much for Janka's presence. More often than not, she irritated her with her slow, unimaginative, backward attitude toward everything — work or play. But Irene was used to a large family. Henryk was suddenly almost a grownup, staying to himself, or with school friends, and going for hikes and trips to Sokolniki or Vorobyovy Gory ("Sparrow Hills"). Helena was constantly reading or studying for the Eighth Class, which she was to enter in the fall. It had only recently been created for girls who were planning to enter the University.

As to mother, Irene was now too old to follow her with the unending interest and enthusiasm that she had shown when she was younger. And Akulina was not like the Polish maids in Warsaw who were friendly, devoted, and almost part of the family. Akulina did what she was supposed to do, no more, preferably less, without even talking or looking at you.

By the second day after her return from Revyakino, Irene began to feel restless. She knew that she could not spend one more second cooped up in the same small garden, playing alone in that same courtyard with the huge stable door that was always closed... the carriage house, laundry house and *saray* staring at her like silent enemies. Seeing Helena in the garden reading, Irene suddenly got an idea.

"Helen, come with me to the church square. I can play hopscotch and watch other children play. Please!"

Helena agreed. After all, it was only a few minutes' walk, and, like Irene, she probably felt the need for a change of scenery.

The *tserkov*, near Taganka Square, was built on a small hill with greens and shrubbery around it. It would be just the place to play! You could sit on a stone wall, iron enclosures, or on boundary stones.

When they arrived, Irene was a little disappointed. There was only one nursemaid with a baby carriage and one girl Irene's age, who was swinging on an iron chain. The maid was drowsy with the heat, but now and then she would open her eyes and say one word: "Adela!" At this, the girl would pause in her jumping and climbing and look at the maid with a sneer, then continue with whatever she wished. Adela was pulling down a tree branch and swinging on it, when the maid opened her eyes and said in perfect Polish:

"Adela, I am going to tell your mother!"

"You are Polish!" cried Irene.

"Sure. I come from Ukraine. Are you Polish?"

"We are from Warsaw."

"Adela and her parents are also from Warsaw."

Adela jumped down from the tree and came near. Now, even Helena became involved in a chat. She talked to the maid, whose name was Ania, about how and when they got to Moscow. Irene and Adela, both starved for companionship, became close friends in minutes.

Adela was a quick, restless and bright child, who seemed to enjoy annoying and quarreling with grownups. But she did it with a twinkle in her eye, with a born sense of humor. Though not very typical for her race, with green, slightly slanted eyes and brown hair, one could see at once that she was Jewish.

"I am Jewish," she announced matter-of-factly, without pride or shame. "Mother hired Ania so that I won't forget how to speak Polish, and also so I won't speak it with a Jewish accent."

Irene, to whom "Jewish" meant the Warsaw ghetto, was surprised to meet someone belonging to that race who was obviously well-to-do.

"I am driving my mother crazy, and she is sick most of the time, so she makes Ania come here so I can play."

"Why didn't you go to dacha? I just came back from my sister's place."

"Mother is too sick; she needs a doctor often, and she would not like to be away from my father."

"Is your mother sick in bed?"

"No, not all the time. But very often."

"What does your father do?"

"He has a factory. They make shirts. You have to come sometime to see it: one hundred women in one big room, all using sewing machines at the same time... what a riot! Oh, Mother is coming."

Her mother was a tall, very thin woman. Were she not so pale and emaciated, she might have been good looking. She had enormous black eyes and regular features, but her complexion was the color of putty. Her neck was so thin that when she spoke, you could see all the bones and muscles move. She had brought fresh milk for the baby, and some sandwiches for Adela and Ania. She became most friendly, learning that Helena and Irene were Polish. After a long talk, she suddenly asked:

"Miss Helen, how would you like to stay with us as Adela's teacher? She doesn't attend any school yet, and above all she needs someone to teach her Polish. I am not well. And she does not pay any attention to what I tell her anyway. She has enough energy and temperament for a dozen children, not one. Ania does the cleaning and laundry. I do the cooking. But there are many things requiring attention, which — with my health — are being neglected, like shopping for instance... Where did you get that lovely dress that your sister is wearing?"

"I did it myself," replied Helena. "I like to sew."

"Really? That is a very elegant dress, just like from a French magazine."

"I like my sisters to wear short dresses. That is a constant source of argument between me and my mother, who would like them to wear dresses below the knee."

"Miss Helen... Would you... would you please come and live with us?"

Her voice was so imploring that Helena, besides feeling pity for that hollow-chested woman, had some unexplainable awareness of a tragic, lonesome, frightened soul crying for help.

"I could stay only one month... until I go back to school," she said in a hesitating voice. "Besides, I will have to ask my mother."

"I understand. But after school starts, you could still come and teach Adela, or perhaps she could come to your house in the afternoon?"

She left her address, and they agreed that Helena would let her know the next day.

On the way home, Helena thought it over. She definitely wanted that job; the pay that Adela's mother had offered was good. She never had earned money before, or even had any, except for a small allowance. It not only meant making money, but suddenly she would be grown up and independent.

"But what is Mother's reaction going to be when she learns that I am to work in a Jewish home?"

Mother was definitely anti-Semitic. If confronted with the question: "why" — she would not be able to explain, like most prejudiced people. How much of it was the race and religion type of prejudice, and how much just follow-the-leader behavior, it was hard to tell. It was not a question of social snobbism, because Jews and Poles of the middle class never even had the opportunity to mix. But, if the Jews were not affected by social snobbism, they could be — and were — snubbed economically. Mother belonged to the group that proclaimed: "Don't buy from the Jews."

Every time she passed a Jewish store, or during a church feast, or on annual great market days, when she saw peasants buying at Jewish stalls, she would stop and say to the startled customer: "Don't buy from Jews!" Disconcerted Jews would spread their arms, smack their lips and rock their heads in a negative way:

"Ay, ay ay, lady. What do you want from us?"

Helena knew all that, so she was afraid of what mother would say about her working in Adela's house.

Strangely enough, mother did not object. Whether it was the war, which may have changed her sense of values, or the money, which would *come from* not *go to* the Jews, or whether it was Helena's age (about the same as when Tomasz had died) that made her so understanding... who knows? She let her daughter decide for herself.

Helena threw herself with all her energy and competence into the new job. She took full control of a disorganized house and maid, and divided Adela's time into study and play periods. Young and inexperienced as she was, it did not take her long to discover the source of Adela's mother's pathetic loneliness.

It was obvious that her husband was living with another woman. He didn't even pretend much at being faithful. Except for the afternoon dinner, he was never home. At night, he came in very late, or not at all, with no excuse except abrupt explanations of "business" or "trouble at the factory," and so on. On the rare moments when he was home, his wife tried to hold his attention through pity. She wailed about how ill she was, or what trouble she was having with the maid, or how difficult and unruly Adela was. He would sit at the table, listening absentmindedly, without comment, leave money or some instructions — and he was gone.

Did he drift away from his wife because of her illness, which caused such a loss of weight as to make her physically unattractive? Or was it because of her quarrelsome, constantly complaining ways? Or was it the other way around: had she become ill and complaining because of his unfaithfulness? Helena did not know, nor could she do anything about the whole situation. But she knew that her presence in the house made the poor woman less unhappy, less lonely. She told Helena many times how grateful she was for what she was doing for her and for her child.

Adela's restlessness and rebellious attitude disappeared almost completely. Now and then she would start some fireworks with Ania or her mother, just for the fun of it, but she did not have either the time or the heart to pursue it to the end. The touch of sadism that unhappy, unloved children have deep down in their souls, and which can so easily be directed toward their parents, was gone. Adela knew from Ania what was going on between their parents. She learned it from the maid in not too subtle ways. She started to observe things, to listen to her mother's reproaches and complaints, and she hated her father for that. She was unable to hurt him because he was beyond her reach — by sheer absence. But her mother was home and an easy target. She hated her mother for her weakness, for her inability to fight back, for her disabling illness, for everything.

Helena turned Adela's mind away from sadistic quarrels with her mother toward studies. The rest of the day Adela spent with her new friend, Irene. They immediately became close friends. Irene had a need to fill the emptiness in her heart after losing Yura, and Adela found a substitute for her father's love. She and Irene played all day long, either in Irene's yard and garden, or in Adela's house — one walking the other home, then back again. Except for Irene's artistic inclinations, they were very much alike. Quick, intelligent and precocious, they found the simplest games fascinating. Playing ball, hopscotch or pebbles was an absorbing contest of skill and wits. Sometimes they fought and quarreled violently, shouting:

"I will never play with you again!"

"I don't even want to see you again until I die!"

Yet, half an hour later they would meet halfway between their homes, each one already walking to the other's house, because they could not live without each other. They would hug each other and laugh, and make fun of themselves, as they both had a sense of humor.

"How about a game of *gorodki,* Adela?"

"All right, let's play gorodki."

Gorodki was a game requiring great skill. It consisted of five pins which were placed in five consecutive formations on a small platform. The first formation was in the form of a "gun"; the second, a "frog". Then there were five pins in a straight line called a "fence". Then there was a cross figure of "soldiers". And the last, and hardest to hit with one stroke, a "letter": four pins in the corners and one in the center. From a distance of about twenty feet, you had to strike out the formation with no more than three throws using a stick about the size of a baseball bat. Naturally, to throw out all five pins from the board with one hit was a great triumph, like a hole-in-one in golf.

One day, after a game of gorodki, Adela said:

"Would you like to go with me to see our factory?"

"Why not? Where is it?"

"It's off Taganka Square, not far from our house."

"All right, let's go."

It was a large brick building. The ground floor consisted of a warehouse; at the entrance, wagons were being unloaded of bales of material, others being loaded with boxes of finished merchandise. A crude stairway of unfinished wood stood at one of the corners and led to the upper floor. The girls climbed the stairs and found themselves in a huge, high-ceilinged room. The walls on one side had many built-in shelves, stocked with bales of white and colored materials. Toward the front were many long tables at which men, with pencils behind their ears and tape-measures around their necks were cutting material with big, heavy scissors. The rest of the room was occupied by countless small tables at which women were working on sewing machines. There was also one large table where "finishers," all very young girls, were sewing on buttons and making button holes. One woman walked along the tables, talking occasionally to the workers. She was Russian-Jewish, and her name was Rachela, Adela told Irene.

"Rachela is living with my father," she said with scornful flippancy, as if talking about it could bring relief to her aching little heart.

"What do you mean? Doesn't your father live with you?"

"Oh, don't you understand what 'live together' means? They are lovers."

Irene was speechless. She never had thought that anything like that could happen to people. Father was father, and mother was mother; they lived together to bring up children, until they in turn grew up and got married. Irene noticed that Adela talked louder, and was behaving in an unnatural way — "showing off" as she had the first time Irene saw her at the *tserkov* square. She appeared to be a "brat" and a "pest" once again. Irene knew that Adela was not "really" like that. She knew better than anybody in the world, because she was with her from morning until night. What made her suddenly act like that?

Rachela came and greeted them politely. After all, Adela was her boss' daughter. She walked around with them and gave Irene a box full of empty spools and some remnants of cloth "to make dolls' clothes." Her name was pronounced "Rah-haïla," which sounded like music to Irene's ear.

All the time, Adela was chattering, laughing and jumping like a little devil — and that is probably what Rachela thought she was. But she did not show the slightest bit of impatience or temper.

"Let's go and see what my father is doing," said Adela.

Her father's office was downstairs, built in a corner of the warehouse. He was a man in his late thirties, slightly bald. It seemed strange to Irene to realize how much Adela resembled her father: the same green eyes, the long, thin nose and the small, sensitive lips.

When they came in, he was sitting behind his desk, which was piled high with papers, samples of materials, pencils, packages, newspapers, and what-not. Adela put her arms around his neck and kissed him, laughing and chattering like a parrot.

Impatiently, he took her arms off his shoulders and said:

"What are you doing here? Don't you see that I am busy? Here, go and buy yourselves something sweet," he said taking some change from his pocket.

They went out. Suddenly, Adela's artificial gaiety had dis-appeared. There is a word in Polish, impossible to translate, which more or less means "the light turned off within." * That is how Adela's face now looked — as if someone had turned off a light within her. Silently, they stopped at a small store on Taganka and bought two packets of *semiachki*, or sunflower seeds.

They sat on the *tserkov* square, splitting the seeds between their two front teeth, chewing and spitting out the husks as far as they could, like true native Russians.

---

* likely *zgaszona*

PART II — CHAPTER FIVE

When at the end of their summer vacation Janka came back from Revyakino, she found a strange girl in their house playing with Irene. They both behaved as if they had known each other all their lives. There was a kind of accord, an intimacy of "tuning" between them that could not escape Janka's eye, uncomplicated as she was. She felt a strong pang of jealousy: Irene never behaved like that when she was playing with Janka! Trying to hold on, or to retrieve the lost ground with her sister, Janka attempted to play with them, but felt like an intruder. She tried, sometimes successfully, to instigate quarrels between them, and felt happy for a while, seeing their friendship suffer a blow. But it was always short-lived; Irene and Adela would "make up," walk hand in hand and plan some new games. Janka, even more than before, was sick with jealousy.

"How do you like Adela?" Irene once asked innocently.

"I can't stand her. She is an awful brat. Anyway, she is Jewish. I don't understand why Mother lets you play with her."

"It's just too bad if you don't like her because she is going to be my friend all my life!" cried Irene.

For quite a time now, Helena had been considering studying medicine. For the time being, however, she decided to enter just the Eighth Class, which gave the girls the right to enter the University. Up to this point, girls' schools and the Russian Gymnasium had courses of only seven years, not counting the Preparatory Class.

Helena knew that sooner or later she would have to tell her parents about her plans for the future. How would they accept her decision? Apart from it being quite uncommon in 1916 for women to study medicine, how would they meet the financial problem? With the war on, and no end in sight, with the financial situation less stable than before the outbreak of the war, with so many younger children to take care of, would not her parents be justified in opposing many years of study in a profession that, at the end, might not even suit their daughter? Rather, weren't they entitled to expect her to take some job and be self-supporting? How much would tuition and the expensive medical books cost?

All this was running through Helena's mind: the hesitation and uneasiness, while trying to decide when to tell her parents about it. Of one thing she was sure: she was going to study medicine because that is the only thing in the world that she wanted to do — to be a doctor.

The occasion to reveal her plans came much sooner than she expected. Aunt Juta moved from Kiev to Moscow, and through correspondence with Jadwiga, traced the family's address. She showed up one day with her three children — Camilla, Staś and Władek — fishing for news, and as usual trying to impress mother with news of her own.

Camilla had grown in height, but unfortunately not in beauty. At eighteen she already had that ageless, spinsterish look. It was strange, because her father was very good-looking, and Aunt Juta was an attractive woman, too. Whatever the Lord spared her in looks, he lavished on her two brothers, however.

"Camilla is going to attend the Eighth Class," declared Aunt Juta proudly. "She is going to study archeology."

"Of course," mother wanted to say, "*what else could she study?* She already looks like an Egyptian mummy." Instead, she said, "How nice."

"And you, Helen. What are your plans?"

"I am also attending the Eighth Class. I am going to study medicine."

There, she had said it. She was sure her parents would not jump on her in Aunt Juta's presence. So at least she was safe for the moment.

Aunt Juta's eyebrows went up -- up, but all she said was: "How nice."

After she left, Helena expected the controversial storm to break. She braced herself, trying to keep in mind all the things that she was supposed to say to convince her parents that she was right. But she did not need to say anything at all. In spite of the financial burden that would fall on the family, they accepted her right to choose a career, medicine or not.

"Thank you, Father. Thank you, Mother," she said. "Thanks so much for understanding."

"You are a grown-up woman now, my child," said father. "You have a right to decide."

Perhaps both of them, deep down, thought of their son who could have lived, but died young. Perhaps he would have chosen to be a doctor...

CHAPTER SIX — School and Friends

After returning from the Revyakino dacha, Irene began an entirely new phase of her life: school. Like her sisters, she went to the same Gymnasium in the afternoon session. The school buildings, situated on the *Pereulok* and not far from the Yauza Gate and River, were very modern and impressive for those times: six stories high, with large windows, long corridors, and elevators attended by liveried men. There were morning and afternoon sessions. The school must have attended to thousands of children of both sexes. Irene's classes were on the top floor, and the children were brought up by elevators, but after school they had to walk down six stories to the cloakrooms.

The cloakrooms were enormous, with a few uniformed attendants in charge. Each school and each class had its own racks, but nothing was ever lost, stolen or misplaced, in spite of the abundance of winter wear — scarves, leggings, boots, and so on.

Having to go down six floors every day, Irene soon learned how to shorten the trip by running every second step. At the end of each floor there was a curved stairway and banister, where she would get a good grip and jump four steps at a time. Her hands were free, as her books were carried knapsack fashion on her back. Many, many years later she would often dream of gliding effortlessly down that stairway at a tremendous speed. Perhaps in her dreams she was subconsciously trying to return to her childhood, to the carefree boldness of spirit, courage and fantastic fitness of body. Later on, just thinking about those stony, slippery steps, skipped two or three steps at a time, made her dizzy.

Irene liked everything about the school. At seven she was, of course, the smallest child in the school, and she was immediately spotted by the older girls from the Eighth Class, who made a veritable pet out of her.

SCHOOL AND FRIENDS

Nowhere in the world did grown-up ladies pay such attention to a small "kid" — however pretty she might be — as the Russian students did. During recess they carried her in their laps like a doll, practically fighting for the privilege of holding her for a while. They called her pet names like "dushenka," "golubchik," "angielochek" and so on, to the pleasant embarrassment of Irene, who did not know what to do or say. At home, to the contrary, she was treated like a grownup — nobody ever petted her or hovered about her. Thank God, after a while the older girls left her alone: apparently she grew too heavy to be carried around.

Otherwise, school was interesting. Even in the Preparatory Class she had four languages (Russian girls didn't have to take Polish, so they had three) plus all the other subjects. The classes were six days a week, with very few holidays during the school year. Irene's classes were done an hour earlier than were her sisters', but she would wait for them, as she was not allowed to go home alone after dark. It was a long walk.

Sometimes it was even fun to wait, as twice a week there were dancing classes in the big assembly room. A small bald man with a putty-colored face taught the young ladies all the secrets of Russian folk dances, and also the ballroom waltz and cotillion. Despite being pot-bellied, he was exceedingly light on his feet. Irene liked to watch that ugly old man teach the steps of the most complicated dances, jumping and moving about the floor lightly and effortlessly, as if he were weightless.

During recess, between classes, the girls spent most of the time walking by two's and three's along the corridors, or round-and-round the assembly rooms. In a smaller room there was a large icon of the Mother of God, with an "eternal light" placed in front of it. Many girls who were not too sure of their brain capacity — or homework — would, at the bell signaling the end of recess, run to the Icon, cross and bow three times and kiss the picture. How much the Mother of God was able to help the girls in distress remained a secret.

At the end of one of the corridors was a "teachers' room." The door was usually left open, so Irene could see what was going on as she walked by with her friends. During recess, the principal usually sat in a big chair at the head of the table. Behind him on the wall hung two large portraits of the Tsar and Tsarina. The principal, a small, middle-aged man, had his whiskers trimmed exactly like Tsar Nicholas — which was not only the fashion, but also a badge of prestige. He wore a long jacket with a high collar, and to augment his prestige, never smiled. The teachers, both male and female, stood or sat around the room talking. Irene always wondered what they were talking about: school, or something entirely different, like mother and Aunt Juta did.

The other places of interest during recess were the two large washrooms. About two dozen toilets, facing each other, were situated in two large rooms, long and without partitions. You had to get used to relieving yourself without privacy, indeed with other girls doing the same thing. The fun was to pull all of the chains one after the other, or to flush all the toilets at the same time, not only to make noise but to do something punishable: the wasting of water was frowned upon.

That first school year and part of the second, until the March Revolution, were very happy and carefree, not only for Irene, but for the whole family. True, the war was going on, and for Russia very badly. Immense numbers of men were being lost in battle or taken prisoner. In turn, many German prisoners were being taken and had to be transported up north to Siberia, and south to Tiflis. Battles in *Duma* (parliament) were also going on: the anti-Rasputin group, the Liberal group, the Anarchist group... each one waiting for the right time to strike a blow against the present tsarist regime. It was true that all these dangerous ferments were reaching a peak of intensity, all aggravated by a war that — from the beginning — had taken a bad turn for Russia.

However, in spite of all the internal and external political torment, life in Moscow went on at a pleasant, normal pace. Now and then, father would buy a box at the opera; it never occurred to him that you could go to the opera and take any seats other than box seats in the "loge." Irene's parents took the children in turn, as there was not enough room in the box for the whole family to go together. Janka openly hated the opera; Stefa and Helena were indifferent, preferring instead the Stanislavski Theater. Most of the time Henryk and Sophie went with their parents, and Irene also "because it didn't cost anything" to take her. She either sat on someone's lap, or for a small tip the attendant would bring an extra chair to the box. The first year, Irene would almost always miss the third act, because by then she would be sound asleep, her head resting in her arms, which would be folded on the red plush of the box's front rail.

But whatever she did see at the opera, she could remember amazingly well. There were opera series with an entirely Russian repertoire: *Demon* (Lermontov's story of a nun bewitched by the devil), *Pikovaya Dama* ("The Queen of Spades"), *Yevgeny Onegin,* and ballets like *Maskaya Noch* ("A Night in May") with its amazing Russian folk dances.

At home Irene would sing the arias and dance, dance, dance. She imagined herself to be a *prima ballerina* and for hours practiced before the mirror in her room, watching not only the movements of her body, but also the expressions on her face. Most of all, she like to be tragic.

Her interest in ballet became much greater after Christmas during her first year in school. Like any school in the world, the Gymnasium organized a Christmas pageant. In the background of the scene there was a "living picture" of many angels, and Irene, of course, was one of them (she slept with paper curlers in her hair, so that she might have long golden locks). The angels had to stand still throughout the entire program. Some students sang appropriate Christmas songs, and finally, for the main number, two children who took ballet lessons performed — solo and together.

One girl was a pretty and shapely fifteen year-old. She was well-taught and looked lovely in her pink tights and slippers. But when the second girl — in white — started to dance, the audience sat, transformed, bewitched, and barely able to breathe. She was not pretty at all: pale with an upturned nose, thin lips and a rather thin body with loose joints. Yet, when she danced, she was beautiful. Her face and body were in such harmony, the movements and expressions on her face in such accord, that she disarmed the audience with movements of pure perfection. The most magnificent, magnetic thing that attracted the viewer besides her dancing was the expression of her large, dark and serious eyes.

Irene instantly fell in love with that pale common face, that small thin body that could perform such miracles simply through certain movements that almost anybody could be taught, yet which few could copy to that degree of artistic perfection. Her name was Viera ("Faith"); Irene looked it up in the program sheet. Whenever Irene saw her during recess or between classes, her heart trembled and her legs became weak. There was nothing sexually abnormal in Irene's attitude toward Viera, but she definitely worshipped not only Viera's talent, but adored her body as well. She knew — she felt — that without that body, her talent would not have a chance to exist.

A painter, poet, writer or sculptor can be old, or ugly, or driven by alcohol, drugs and disease almost to the verge of insanity, and still produce a work of art — as indeed many famous artists have done. But in a ballerina, the body and soul are one. That is why Irene was in love with "all" of Viera. It seemed strange to her to see Viera, dressed in a regulation brown dress and black apron, walking with and talking to friends. It seemed as if a goddess had come down from Olympus to mingle with the mortals: it was not right.

She never found out what happened to Viera — whether she survived the aftermath of the Revolution, whether her family was considered *burzhui* and was doomed to be destroyed, or whether Viera had a chance to finish ballet school and become the great *prima ballerina* that she ought to have been. In time, Irene forgot even Viera's last name, but she never could forget the thrill, the excitement, the feeling of true artistic perfection that she lived through by watching Viera dance.

Strangely enough, the custom by which all Russians called each other by their first names and *otchestvo* did not extend to the classrooms. The teachers called the students by their *last names* exclusively, and accustomed to this, the students called each other by last name only. One did not care, and often did not even know the first name of a friend with whom one shared the same double desk.

One of Irene's classmates, named Kozelkova, lived near Zemlyanka Street and often walked to or from school with Irene. She was two years older than Irene, and having a few older brothers and sisters, seemed to possess quite a wide knowledge of the facts of life.

Now, it was one thing to know "how babies were born," as Irene did, but it was something else again to learn about the differences between sexes, and where it would all lead. Kozelkova, during their long walks along Sadovaya Street, gave Irene not only a thorough introduction to adult life, but she also told her about what physical changes she could expect when she reached fourteen ("Will I ever be so *old?*" thought Irene), and also about prostitutes.

This last subject was touched upon one day when they were passing Sadovaya Street near the area of Khitrov Rynok. "Rynok" means square, but unlike "ploshchad," which is a city square, it means rather a market square. What you could see of Khitrov Rynok was a short, narrow street; apparently, if there was a square, it must have been around the corner, behind the block of houses.

Kozelkova said that Khitrov Rynok was a place where all the thieves, murderers and crooks hid from the arms of the law, and where prostitutes lived, spreading out at night to other parts of the city.

There must have been some truth in what she said, because now, knowing about it, Irene noticed that men coming from the direction of

Khitrov Rynok, looked different than did the average passerby. They never wore jackets, or collars and ties. Their caps or hats, worn out and dirty, were pushed down on their heads, as if they were trying to move about without being recognized. Their hands were always thrust in pockets of baggy coats with the collars up. Some of the men had ugly scars on their faces, as if at one time or another they had wrestled with a tiger; others had parts of arms missing, or were limping. They probably were going to streetcar stations, where they would ride in the cars during rush hours. Standing in a pushing crowd, they would prey on innocent riders, emptying their pockets of wallets or pilfering from ladies' handbags.

Coming home from school, Irene often saw women standing near Khitrov Rynok, or walking slowly down Sadovaya Street toward the Yauza River. They looked so different from mother or Jadwiga! Their faces were unusually white in some places, unusually pink in others, and though dressed shabbily, there was something in their attire that attracted attention: too many cheap flowers on a hat, or pieces of worn-out, dangling fur "boas" on their necks.

And so, the outlook on life of seven-year-old "angielochek" had broadened considerably, thanks to her classmate whose name was Kozelkova.

CHAPTER SEVEN — Summer, 1916

In the summer of nineteen hundred sixteen, Jadwiga rented a house for the summer near Kozlovka. This *dacha* had many houses, built among tall fir trees. Again, like all other dachas, it had fences around most of the houses, but no flower gardens or green grass: just woodsy underbrush and clumps of wild, dry, tall grass.

Helena was spending the summer in Adela's house again; Henryk was visiting some of his school friends, so Jadwiga one day came to Moscow and brought her four sisters back to Kozlovka.

Vlodek had long ago given up any attempt to interfere with Jadwiga's plans; he became accustomed to the constant flow of relatives and friends sponging off him during summer vacations. But he did not mind much. He no doubt would have preferred to have a weekend of quiet and privacy with his wife, but he certainly did not show it. He had an easy disposition; he could afford the expense, and above all, he adored his wife too much to make a fuss about the whole thing. He could see that it made her happy to have her family around her, trying to help them in every possible way. It was as if Jadwiga was trying to make up for all her childhood and adolescent years, when she had been so selfish that nothing mattered except her own whims and interests.

"Yadunia has a family mania," he would say to her good naturedly.

After five years of marriage he was just as much in love and attracted to her as he was on their wedding night. They made love in a wild, passionate way. She found an infinite pleasure and fulfillment, being crushed and possessed by that strong, masculine body, so primitive, yet so loving and tender. He, constantly amazed at her delicate, fragile beauty — which was in contrast to her alert mind and strong will power — was agonizingly happy each time he was back with her.

Niania must not have been too enthusiastic about these summers, when there was always that coming and going of people in their house. But she kept it to herself and never in any way showed any resentment. She called Jadwiga's sisters "aunt" since they were Tadyo's aunts. In this way she avoided calling them "miss," which would have been servile,

SUMMER, 1916

or calling them by their first names alone, which would not have been proper.

So, "Aunt Irene," together with the other "aunts" roamed the countryside around Kozlovka dacha. It was a lovely part of the country. There were magnificent woods, mostly of tall, stately oak trees, and here and there a birch, pine or fir — mixed in as if by an artist for a contrast in shape and color. That spring, when the leaves were already out, a late killing frost came and dressed the oaks in a copper brown cloak. Now, in late June, the second new leaves were coming out, their fresh, pale greenness blending softly with the browns. From a distance, the woods looked like an old French Renaissance tapestry.

Nearby, there were fields: rye, potato and buckwheat. Apart from the theater and music, Irene loved flowers most of all. Deprived of the former, she concentrated on the latter. The miracle of growth was to her a constant source of amazement. The shape, color and odor of plants inspired in her a feeling akin to pagan worship. Sometimes she would sit on the ground, on the edge of a field, in the meadow, or in the woods and pick up a small wildflower. She would observe that tiny crown, which as you walked looked like nothing more than a speck. Many specks forming a color pattern, nothing more. Yet this tiny speck showed intricate design, harmony and symmetry of petals and sepals, beautiful color combinations, and the veins and curves of a tri-dimensional pattern. Even the head of a flowering moss, seen at close range, was a veritable masterpiece of construction.

They all went often to the woods, looking for wild berries and mushrooms. The oak and birch trees provided the best conditions for edible mushrooms of the highest quality, texture and flavor. There were called *poddubniki* (from *dub* — oak) and *podberezniki* (from *bereza* — birch). They were stout little fellows with short, sturdy white or reddish legs, and small brown heads, usually growing in families. Really, there was a papa, mama and ten or so little mushrooms, from the largest to the tiniest newborn baby. At least that is what Irene thought, picking them. They reminded her of her own family.

Four sisters, besides Jadwiga, were spending that summer in Kozlovka, each one living a different life of her own. While Irene took a four-dimensional approach to everything, to Janka life was two-dimensional... flat. The walk was "killing time until supper"; picking berries and mushrooms was a necessary chore if you wanted berries for dessert or to cook mushrooms. She read books for "stories," not for something to "live through" as did Irene. It did not give her the feeling of longing to travel, for adventure or the urge for doing something strange, brave or unusual, as it did to Irene. Janka was glad that Irene was away from Adela. This way she might get back some of her sister's interest in her — she hoped. Irene felt her sister's need for friendship, but she knew that it was hopeless. It was not as if Janka was three years older than Irene; it was as if Irene was twice as old as her sister — they did not speak the same language.

Stefa took over the chores that for years Helena had done during the vacations in Poland. She washed and combed her sisters' hair, supervised their baths, saw to it that their sandals were polished, and their clothes and socks clean. Stefa was only fourteen, and her childish round face, blue eyes, and curly ashen-blond hair of a Renaissance cherub were such a contrast to her serious, efficient behavior.

"Nobody is a saint," mother used to say *a propos* to some domestic squabble. Irene observed that everybody would now and then get mad at something, argue about things, or disagree. Everybody, that is, except Stefa. Her even disposition did not come from some moronic indifference to things — she was intelligent and studious. Rather, the source lay in her self-discipline and serenity, a thing that later was called "peace of mind" — and which became more and more scarce as the twentieth century grew older.

Stefa liked flowers, too. She would come from a walk in the fields with a large bouquet and put it in a water pitcher on the table. But she liked flowers because they were "nice," not because they were little miracles as they were to Irene. Stefa liked to read because she was "learning things" from books: she did not live with every character in the book until it hurt, as did Irene.

As to Sophie, she did not give a damn about her sisters' clothes or if they were clean behind the ears, just as she did not care what she herself was wearing, or how she looked. If you were to ask her five minutes after a meal what she had eaten, she could not tell you because she did not remember. She daydreamed, took solitary walks and made up poems and short stories that she would write out while sitting outside under the trees. From time to time, a summer breeze would sway the tall spruce and fir trees, whistling a plaintive tune and bringing to Sophie's nostrils a strong, pungent smell of resin melting in the sun, mingled with the odor of moist earth and pine needles. Who could think of food and clothes when there were so many things inside you and around you that needed analyzing? Sophie read books to learn how to write well enough to be able to express her thoughts and feelings.

SUMMER, 1916

Sophie was almost sixteen now, and breathtakingly beautiful. Tall and slender, with a small, shapely bosom, she had that exquisite grace of movement that made her look like a classic statue. Her slightly tilted head, her ankles, fingers, the shape of her arms and neck, were perfection itself. Her face, with regular features, though usually serious, had an inner radiance that was unexplainable but impossible to miss. The shape of her mouth, the curve of her chin, the heavy eyelids, all this gave one the impression of a perpetual smile, of that inner everlasting smile that Greek statues often have and which Leonardo da Vinci later immortalized in *La Gioconda*. Vlodek, observing Sophie, would sometimes pat her on the shoulder as she passed by, and say with a sigh:

"*Ah! Takoye dobro darom propadayet!*" ("Such a treasure going to waste!")

If Sophie was never to accomplish anything worthwhile in her life, her existence would still be justified by just having been born! God's perfect creation.

"Aunt Sophie," Niania asked one day, "how would all you girls like to go with me to *Yasna Polyana** to see Tolstoy's grave?"

"Do you know how to get there? How far is it?" asked Sophie.

"I have been there. A few days after we came to Koslovka we all went in a rented buggy. It is not far if we take a short-cut through fields."

To Niania, anything under twenty miles was "not far away." But since they were all used to long walks, the girls accepted with enthusiasm the possibility of seeing Tolstoy's grave. One of the engineers' wives from Tula, who had a little son of her own called Kolia, and who was staying with Jadwiga for a visit, promised to watch Tadyo. Niania would not dream of bothering Jadwiga with such responsibilities.

Early in the afternoon the girls left with Niania. It was a perfect summer day. They walked along golden fields, still unhar-vested, and looked for narrow paths so as not to damage the crops — tall, heavy spikes, nodding and curtseying at each step. Sometimes the hot wind would blow through the fields, suddenly changing the colors, making

---

* *Yasna Polyana* is not far from Tula, about 190 km due south of Moscow.

gentle swaying waves in the sea of grasses. Sleepy, lazy grasshoppers would break the silence with the short, harsh noises of their wings.

By mid-afternoon Niania and the girls were suddenly there. At first it seemed so disappointing: an unkempt abandoned grave at the edge of a young woods, a meadow dry from the summer heat... Irene had often seen her family reading large, thick books by Tolstoy. The early editions even had his picture on the inside first page, with the inscription: "Graf Leo Tolstoy" (later on, he dropped his title of "Graf" — count). Here she was, then, at the grave of a very famous writer, yet his grave was abandoned, so lonesome.

"Why was he not buried in the cemetery lot?" asked Stefa.

"He wanted to repose here. See these pine woods? They say that Tolstoy planted the trees with his own hands."

They went closer and stood among the young pine trees that had been planted in neat, straight rows. It seemed to them that from somewhere between the lights and shadows of the woods would appear that well-known, bearded man, dressed in simple peasant's dress: short homespun pants, long *rubashka* shirt, legs wrapped in pieces of cloth and cord up to the knees, and feet in hand-woven *lapti* sandals.

It was quiet there. The silence was ever so slightly broken by the murmur of tall grasses and by the sigh of swaying pine trees.

They all sat without saying a word. Even Janka was apparently under a spell, because she did not say anything stupid or out of place. Finally, after a long silence, Sophie said:

"Now I understand. Tolstoy was not only great because he was a great writer, but because he understood the humble simplicity of life. That's what life is to me: simple. To be born, to live and to die. His life was so simple — how could, then, he be buried in surroundings other than these?"

"Aunt Sophie, you are only sixteen. When you grow older, you will find out that life is anything but simple."

"I did not explain myself very clearly, Niania. By 'simple' I do not mean uncomplicated. Life is often tragic and twisted, and hard to endure. Yet, when it comes to the final count, life makes room for death, and from this perspective — it is simple."

"Tolstoy's life was hard. Misunderstood by his wife and the social class from which he came, unappreciated by the peasants whose lives he tried to enlighten and improve, he was in the search of God until the last hour before his death... But it is all unimportant now. Who can count how much human misery, sweat and blood went in to the building of temples or the pyramids? Yet today the same sun is scorching these edifices, the wind is shifting the same sands in the desert, the same moon is staring into the Sphinx's eyes, while nobody remembers and nobody cares about the people who built them and then died wretched deaths."

"How many millions of people does our war, called 'The Great War', now involve? Yet fifty years from now it will occupy two printed pages in the student's world history textbook. That's what I meant by life being simple. Maybe it is not even important what we do, but what we *want to do*, before we die."

She got up and put a small wreath on Tolstoy's grave. She had made it out of pink and white clover flowers. They were already wilting in the hot afternoon sun and smelled of honey.

"I hope that they will never build a marble mausoleum here, or put a summer dacha too close to his grave. Let him sleep," said Sophie.

"It would be terribly common to let him be buried in the cemetery, would it not?" asked Janka, who wanted to show how well she understood what Sophie had been saying.

"Yes," Sophie replied, patting Janka's shoulder gently.

It was just before sunset when they began walking back from Yasna Polyana to Kozlovka. The fields and meadows were enveloped in a reddish-orange haze and were silent, except for the hum of bees in buckwheat fields that were white with bloom.

One day, Niania, bothered by a toothache, left for Tula. Sophie and Stefa promised to take care of Tadyo and do the chores that Niania would usually do during the day.

It was early afternoon, and Irene did not know what to do. It looked like a dull day ahead: no trip to the woods because her sisters would be busy here, and it was too far to go alone or with Janka.

Through the open window of her upstairs room, Irene could see Jadwiga and Kolia's mother sitting outside on garden chairs, Tadyo and Kolia playing nearby, and her sisters sitting under the trees in their colorful summer dresses. The house was built on a small hill, so Irene had a bird's-eye view of what lay beyond her window. She was thinking of how much more interesting, and prettier, people and things looked from above than from ground level. The trunks of trees seemed short, but the crowns were full, round and green. They were inviting you to fly, or at least jump out of the window, and be part of that deliciously fragrant sea of green leaves and pine needles.

The girls' dresses looked like perfect, colorful circles with dark dots in the centers. Their heads, the table, chairs and the two women lying sprawled on long chairs also had geometrical scope and pattern, yet changing from time to time like a kaleidoscope — by the running children and by the quiet movements of Jadwiga's colorful parasol.

Irene was looking for a pair of scissors. She wanted Sophie to cut some paper dolls, with which she would make up some incredibly exciting stories of sinking ships, life in the jungle, or something similar. She could not find the scissors in any room, so she decided that they must be in Niania's room. She went there, and the first thing that she noticed was a suitcase under the bed. If it had a key in the lock, or if it was open, Irene would probably not have given it another thought. But it was locked.

"How exciting! What can be in this suitcase, a hidden treasure? Where can the key be? Does Niania have it with her in Tula?" All this went through Irene's mind.

She pulled out the drawer of a small table. The key was not there. Maybe in that box on the shelf? There was, indeed, a key in the box, and it did fit the lock of the suitcase. Irene opened it. Nothing special. Some letters with the ink faded and tied with a ribbon, a box full of money — naturally. In Warsaw, Emily also kept her money in her suitcase. Irene closed the box. Some official document, folded in quarters, caught her eye. Inside was Niania's picture with a seal embossed at the corner and a long column of printed and handwritten words — First name: *Maria*... Last name: *Krajewska*... Age: ...

"How strange," thought Irene. "Niania has a first name and a last name, like anybody else."

For years, Niania was to Irene *something* that always accompanied Jadwiga and Tadyo, like a slave or a piece of furniture. But to think of her as an individual with her own name was as incredible as seeing a firemen not in uniform and standing on a fire engine, but dressed like any other man.

"How stupid I am," thought Irene. "Of course Niania must have had a mother and father. Of course she must have a name. How stupid of me! ...What else is there in the suitcase?"

There was a piece of material, some brand new gloves (apparently some Christmas present not yet used) and a thick roll of white flannel. Irene unrolled it. It was double-folded, and stitched inside at even intervals so as to form small pockets. Inside each pocket was a silver spoon. What was strange about the whole thing was that each spoon was *different*, having a different monogram of different shape and size. Irene recognized one from Lydia Alek-seyevna's house with a Russian « З » for "Zakharov." There was even one with Jadwiga's monogram; she could recognize it anywhere!

Irene sat on the floor as if struck by lightning. There were at least twenty of these spoons. A few of the pockets were empty, waiting to be filled. Obviously the spoons had been stolen. Niania a thief... a common thief! But when you steal things, it is to use them or to sell them and make money. Obviously, Niania was neither using the teaspoons, nor had any need for them, and she wasn't selling them. Why, then, had she done it.

She sat there, feeling terribly ashamed, not for Niania, but for herself. She felt as if she had opened someone's heart, not a suitcase — as if she were stepping with soiled shoes over someone's soul. She had never heard of psychiatry, Freud, mental aberrations, or kleptomania, yet she could feel with her sixth sense that what Niania was doing was not a crime and not a sin. Irene carefully folded the piece of flannel, locked it in the suitcase and put the key back inside the box.

... That woman, without family, without close friends, and going through life anonymously as a "niania," saw in each silver spoon a symbol of a trousseau, of a marriage and of a home. Perhaps at night, behind the closed door, she opened the suitcase and took out the silver spoons, touched them lovingly, played with them like children play "make believe"... Maybe in touching these spoons she dreamed of being a wife and a mother, not a paid servant known only as "Niania."

CHAPTER EIGHT — Christmas in Tula

The third Christmas that they spent in Moscow, Jadwiga did not come for the holidays as she had done for the past two years. Instead she came before Christmas, brought presents, and in the last moment decided to take Irene with her to Tula.

"There are many children of the engineers' families there. I am sure you will make friends with them and have a lot of fun," said Jadwiga.

"Yes, but how is she going to come back?" asked mother worriedly.

"Don't worry. Vlodek has to be in Moscow right after the holidays, and he will bring her back."

Irene was in seventh heaven. Just to go to any place by train was always exciting, but to go to a new, strange place and meet new people was thrilling!

It was only the first time during her stay that she went to Tula, and it was to be her only time. Most of the time there she stayed and played within the limits of the *Zavod* — the armaments plants. The engineers' apartments were in long, low buildings. Enormous oblong courtyards separated these buildings from the factories. Irene played in the snow, riding sleighs or climbing roofs of sheds (*saray*) and jumping from them into incredibly high snow drifts. During all of this time she never saw any workers going to, or leaving, the factories. Apparently, the entrance was in an entirely different part of the town. She was only aware that it was a plant because Vlodek left in the morning and came home late in the day. Once he was awakened in the middle of the night: there was some emergency — an accident — and he did not come back until daylight.

Otherwise, life for Irene was perpetual play. Jadwiga's home and their way of life was so different, and so much more luxurious than at their home! There was electricity and even a *telephone* in the hall — the first telephone that Irene had ever seen. The rooms were enormous, and there were so many of them, with floors as shiny as those in museums. Twice a week a professional floor polisher came, and barefoot with two large brushes attached to his feet, he would polish the floors with the graceful movements of a figure skater or ballet dancer.*

Tadyo was almost four years old and did not need a nurse-maid anymore, so Niania was now taking charge of all the housekeeping. But she had, of course, a maid to help her with the cleaning and the laundry. Jadwiga slept late, played piano and was always planning dinner parties.

Somewhere in Western Europe bloody battles were being fought; somewhere young men in the prime of their lives were dying each day by the thousands; somewhere people were standing in bread lines; and not so far away — in Moscow — great political struggles were taking place in the *Duma*, the House of Representatives. To Jadwiga all these events were "somewhere"; it was something that you read about in the newspapers, talked of while entertaining your friends, but it was not something that you were part of. Life went on — smooth, pleasant, well-organized as it always was, and as it always would be. It had been a month since the murder of Rasputin, three months before the first *March* Revolution would take place, but Jadwiga was living in a crystal palace, without troubles or worry.

Irene was just a child. To her war meant only the flashy titles in big print on the front pages of newspapers, or the words and names overheard in political discussions. It was remote and unreal. She thought of how lucky Jadwiga was to live in Tula. It was so different from what was going on in Irene's home!

Irene made many new friends, and she was invited to children's parties. Each child got a bag of candies and a book or toy from the hostess — it was like a dream... all like a happy dream!

---

* Over fifty years later Helena would write that although Jadwiga was very secure financially, neither Helena nor her sisters could count on her help with the expenses of higher education because of "jealousy": Jadwiga herself had always dreamt of studying at the Sorbonne but had instead opted for marriage and life in Russia. Jealous, too, was Aunt Juta: Helena wrote that she was "seething with envy" (*wrzała z oburzenia*) that Helena was studying medicine.

One day Niania took Irene and Tadyo to the children's theater in the center of Tula. Unlike the *Zavod*, which was clean and orderly, the town of Tula was very primitive, shabby and ugly. At least what Irene saw on the way to the theater was like that. The streetcars were not like those in Moscow, which were electrically powered; these were small, horse-driven cars on narrow rails. The streets were irregular, either very narrow or very wide, and the houses were mostly small, two-story buildings. The theater was situated in a primitive, wooden hall, shabby, and with a small platform for a stage. But the performance was very good: mostly humorous folk scenes, dances and songs. Anyway, to Irene, *any* theater was something just short of a miracle.

Each night, after playing all day in the snow, and after parties, Irene went to bed exhausted but happy. She slept on a day-couch in Tadyo's room, near the fireplace. The fireplace was never used, but the wind in the chimney would play a plaintive, lonely tune. From the salon, where Jadwiga was entertaining her guests, came voices or the sounds of piano playing. The voices were quiet, cheerful and gay. Irene, listening to Chopin or Tchaikovsky, and to the murmur of the wind in the chimney, felt happiness — boundless happiness — and from the bliss of semi-consciousness she would fall into the bliss of deep sleep.

CHAPTER NINE — October 1917

Shortly after New Year's, Aunt Juta and her children moved into the corner front room. Henryk's room was given to the girls, and once again his bed was moved across the hall into the dining room, behind the wooden screen.

Aunt Juta gave up her apartment for financial reasons. The war was dragging on longer than anyone had expected, and her husband, a surgeon in the Russian Army, did not make as much money as he did during peacetime. Also, she might have had a premonition of the dangerous times to come, and lacking her husband, she wished to be near her brother. Mother welcomed the idea, as she could use the rent money. The food situation was growing worse; food was scarcer and becoming more and more expensive.

Naturally, as soon as Aunt Juta settled down, the verbal battles between her and mother were again in full swing. Every night, with the samovar perking on the table, and while drinking glass after glass of tea, they evaluated the world's events and Russia's internal politics. Like skilled chess players, they would move invisible pawns (names and places) on an invisible chess board.

With all this going on, it was hard for Irene to concentrate and read, so she had no choice but to listen. More and more often she heard the words "Duma"... "St. Petersburg"... "Tsar Nicolai"... and "Rasputin," dead and buried as he was. One night in the middle of March, the word she heard over and over was "abdication." Everyone seemed excited; even father, who seldom took part in the discussions, was talking a lot with great animation.

"What is abdication?" asked Irene.

"It is giving up the rights of the crown to reign over the people. Tsar Nicolai was forced to abdicate."

"Is it good or bad?" asked Irene.

She never found out, because mother and Aunt Juta started to argue immediately as to what was good and what was bad about it, and what the consequences of Tsar Nicolai's abdication might be.

A few days later, during school recess, Irene walked past the teachers' room and as usual peeked in through the half-open door. The wall above the principal's chair was bare. The only evidence that Tsar and Tsarina's portraits had ever hung there was two large hooks sticking out of the wall. The person who had taken the pictures away was in such a hurry, so as not to be suspected of having anything to do with the people the tsar represented, that he did not waste time removing the hooks.

That summer the whole family stayed in Moscow because it was the first time that Jadwiga had not rented a dacha house. It was not much fun spending a vacation in the city, but it certainly was not boring. Without Akulina, the girls now had to help mother keep house and do the laundry. Things had to be simplified; no longer was laundry a fancy two-day affair in the laundry house. It was done in one day, in the kitchen, to conserve wood and time. At night after hanging up the laundry, they all took a bath in the same wooden wash tub, which was easier to empty than the tin tub in the bathroom because it had a drain. The girls also took turns standing in lines to get food — any food. There were always queues in front of closed stores "in case something came." Sometimes the stores were open for an hour or so, and the first few hundred lucky people returned home clutching a package as precious as life itself.

Irene's age was not taken into consideration. She had to take an equal part in the family's daily chores, just as she was given the same amount of food — no more, no less. At the age of nine she was considered grown up enough to help with the laundry and to stand in lines. Playtime was a thing of the past. Even if she had some spare time, she would not know what to do with it.

The behavior of Kuharka and her daughter changed abruptly after the March Revolution. Where were the times when the maid kissed not only mother's, but Helena's, hand in gratitude for advice and for medicine for her sick baby? The time when Kuharka *first* greeted them — with a servile smile and bow? The maid now passed them without a word, staring straight ahead; she dared even to shout at Irene and Janka and to chase them from the garden. She became grouchy because Dvornik had been dismissed (or joined the Bolsheviks), and she had to sweep the sidewalk and courtyard by herself with a big broom. She was always mumbling when she passed Irene or anybody else from the family:

"Polyaki-sobaki" ("Poles, the dogs"), or *"burzhui"* ("bourgeois capitalists") or *"bezhentsy"* ("refugees").

While the word "refugee" has in English a tint of compassion (associating one's mind with refuge — a safe place after flight), the Russian word comes from *bezhat'* — to run away — and has a tint of contempt. More and more often, Muscovites were blaming the food shortage on *bezhentsy*. It was useless to argue that the percentage of Poles stranded in Moscow was infinitesimal compared to the total population. The prolonged war, poor organization of transportation and distribution of food, and political disorders were the real causes of the food shortage. The ignorance of people in hardship forced them to look for a scapegoat on which to vent the hatred, misery and disappointments of daily life.

The summer passed; Helena went back to her studies at the University, and the children returned to school. Henryk was eighteen now, so he reported to the Army and was awaiting his draft. October was quite mild that year; no snow as yet, and the days, if not sunny, were without rain — which is unusual for Moscow.

Then one day it all started, suddenly and unexpectedly: the Revolution!

In March the fighting had been mainly in St. Petersburg; the revolt and change of government did not affect the Muscovites until it was all over. This time, Moscow became the battleground of the two opposing groups for many days. Bloody, obstinate fights flared up in all parts of the city.

Strange how the news spread so quickly and easily in those days — and without telephones in the house, or any other visible source of information! One knew that it was the *real Revolution* — that either Kerensky's group would win and continue to represent Russia as a regime, or the extreme elements — the Bolsheviks — would take over.

The eight-foot garden wall and the heavy iron gates were possibly strong enough to resist bullets and intruders, but the three front rooms had windows only two feet above street level. How safe could one be with the barking of carbines and machine guns outside of the house? News was available — one way or the other — but how accurate was it? Who could know what was the real cause of the Revolution? Who fought against whom? On whose side was the Army? Why had the Kerensky regime suddenly failed?

To Irene's family, one thing was certain: it was a revolution. Revolution is bloody, unpredictable and cruel: they all had in mind the French Revolution. What would be their fate as *foreigners* in Moscow in the first place, as *burzhui* in the second place, and as *bezhentsy* in the third place?

The front rooms were immediately abandoned. Aunt Juta and all the children moved their bedding into Irene's parents' rooms. Even Helena's and the girls' bedrooms overlooking the courtyard were considered unsafe. The water supply was being exhausted: the waterman, of course did not show up. For a few days they sat and slept, and ate whatever was available, in those two windowless, barricaded rooms. But human nature gets accustomed to danger quickly. After a while, unless the shooting was unusually near or loud, the family again moved freely all over the apartment, and even took an occasional breath of fresh air outdoors. Henryk would sometimes run with two buckets to the corner of the street and get some water from the fire hydrant.

One night, tired of sleeping on the crowded floor, they all decided to spend the night in their own rooms. In the middle of the night Irene was awakened by loud gunfire. She jumped out of bed, calling for Janka. With eyes accustomed to darkness, she could see on the roof of the house across the street, two hunched figures shooting a machine gun in the direction of Taganka Square. She ran to Janka's bed: she was not there. She ran into the dining room: Henryk's bed was empty, too. She stumbled in the dark through the dining room and ran into mother's room: it was empty!

As if in a nightmare, she was all alone in the dark — terrified and cold, with the barking, shattering sound of machine gun fire outside. With a last, instinctive effort, she ran into the inner hall and opened the door to father's room: they were all there! The shooting was so loud that everybody had scrambled into father's bedroom, and with so many people in the room, nobody had noticed that Irene was missing! Tired and covered up to the tips of her ears with a comforter, Irene had been sleeping soundly and had not heard all the commotion and shooting at first!

One morning, Henryk, like a biblical dove after the deluge, went out and brought the news that it was all over. It was safe to go out, as all the fighting had stopped. They eagerly dressed and went out. The fighting had indeed stopped, but apparently they were the first ones courageous enough to venture into the streets. Taganka Square was deserted, littered with broken glass, planks of wood, chipped bricks, stones and overturned carts. Among all this debris lay sheets of paper, printed on one side only. They picked up several of them: all were alike. A lot of headlines, with exclamation marks, stuffed with words: *Da zdravstvuyet!* ("Long live!") and *Soyedinyaityes!* ("Unite!"). The Councils of Soldiers, Workers and Peasants *(Sovety rabochih, soldatskih i krestyanskih deputatov)* were hailing their victory and calling for unity.

Who would want to wish evil to the working class? The family felt relieved and happy that the fighting was over; they felt safe, almost happy.

While the parents were standing among the debris on Taganka Square, reading the leaflets, Irene asked:

"May I go to see how Adela is?"

"All right," said mother, "but don't be long. We will wait for you here."

Adela opened the door, and seeing Irene, yelled out the most hearty greeting that Irene had ever heard in her life. Yes, she was all right, but her mother was still sick with fright and would not let Ania or Adela go out. Her father was at the factory, checking on damage — if any — and figuring out what his situation was as a factory owner after the Revolution.

"I have to run now. I'm glad you are all right," Irene cried, running down the stairs.

"I am happy that nothing happened to you. I was thinking about you all the time!" she heard Adela's voice in the distance.

Reaching Zemlyanka, they found some life on the street. Here and there one could see small groups of people; a few times military trucks passed them, going toward Sadovaya Street. Irene looked at one of the passing trucks absentmindedly, until she realized with horror that the brownish cargo, piled high and swaying with movements of the truck, was a mass of human cadavers! On Sadovaya Street several more trucks passed them, filled with dead soldiers. On Yauza Bridge people stood and watched dead people lying in grotesque positions along the banks of the river, some floating in the shallow water.

"I don't know about you," mother said, "but I have no intention of further exploring the city or watching more bodies swimming in the Moskva River." She turned back.

They all went home.

"Death is ugly," said Irene, with a shudder.

She had never seen cadavers before, and to see so many bodies in one day made her sick.

Bread was distributed that day, which lifted their spirits and shifted their thoughts from death to survival.

The next morning Helena and Henryk, after a short absence, came back with exciting news.

"All the streets are full of people! There are parades and singing, and everyone is wearing a red ribbon pinned to their coats!"

"We better get ourselves red ribbons, too. It is safer these days to do whatever the others are doing," said mother.

So Helena found a piece of red cloth and made little bows, and pinned them to everyone's coat.

"Let's go, we have to see what is going on!" shouted Henryk impatiently.

There was a sea of people on Zemlyanka Street. Twelve or more abreast, in orderly rows, were moving slowly, like a gigantic dragon, without beginning and without end. Where they were coming from, nobody knew. Where were they going? Who organized the parade? Who told them how to behave? Who taught then what to sing?

Irene and her family were immediately pulled in, sucked in, like twigs in a powerful current. They found themselves walking in line, with strangers in front, behind and beside them.

Most of the time they were singing, but from time to time the singing would stop, and you could hear only the sound of thousands of feet: one, two, one, two...

Then they would start singing again:

Vstavai, podymaisya, rabochiy narod
Vstavai na bor'bu, lyud golodnyi
Razdaisya krik mesti narodnoy
Vpered, vpered, vpered, vpered, vpered!

Get up, wake up, working people
Get up and fight, you hungry people
The voice of vengeance is resounding
Forward, forward, forward, forward, forward!

The tune was simple, the words easy to follow and to remember. Afraid to act differently, Irene and her family all sang, too.

After hours of their walking, the parade became disorganized as it reached the Lubyanka district, where the streets were crooked and narrower. While the crowds were milling at the corner for a while, they slipped away, and exhausted, walked home.

The time of rejoicing was over. What life would be like the next day, nobody knew. Maybe it was better that they did not know. Maybe they would not have the courage to face it.

CHAPTER TEN — Surviving Winter

As usual at that time of the night, Moscow streets were almost deserted. The sidewalks, covered with snow and ice, reflected here and there the dimmed light from the lamp posts.

Tonight Irene did not wait for Stefa and Janka. When she was younger, she had been afraid to walk alone, but now, past her ninth birthday, instead of waiting for her sisters she would often venture home alone. Each morning she was glad that she had school in the afternoon; it was nice to stay in bed longer and to have all that free time until three o'clock. Yet each evening she wished that she went to school earlier, like Sophie, so she wouldn't have to walk home in that bitter, cold night. She crossed the bridge on the Yauza River and turned into Sadovaya Street. It seemed even darker and more desolate here because the street was so wide, and the houses, which stood behind private fences, seemed remote and abandoned. The lights in the windows accentuated, rather than removed, the feeling of somber loneliness.

"It must be about thirty degrees of frost," thought Irene as ice formed in her nostrils, producing that strange feeling of stickiness, like clotting blood. Also, the snow was singing and cracking with each step, another sign of severe frost.

Near Khitrov Rynok, Irene felt even more lonely and scared, but no one was coming around the corner.* On a night like this the thieves and prostitutes were seeking refuge in a cheap *chainaya* (tea room), keeping warm not only with tea, but mostly with vodka.

---

* Actually, she would have passed the Khitrov district before crossing the Yauza River bridge.

The warm interlined coat (*shuba*) and boots kept Irene warm, and the collar, held up with a scarf, protected her chin and ears. However, she had to rub her nose and cheeks quite often to protect them against frostbite. This she learned during her first Moscow winter. At that time Henryk had not protected his ears with a *bashlyk* (a hood with a scarf worn also by soldiers), and although at first he did not feel any pain, his ears were white and swollen when he came home. They soon turned almost black, and within a few hours were discharging fluid. It took a long time before his ears were cured.

She was already on Zemlyanka Street, turning into her *pereulok*. Just a few more houses and she will be home! The full moon was high. Around it were several circles of iridescent light, the usual sight on a cold, clear night. Irene opened the heavy iron gate, and her hand, through a torn mitten, stuck lightly to the iron. If the frost had been more severe, she would not have been able to tear it away from the metal without leaving parts of her skin on it. She was very hungry. The long walk in cold weather was enough to stir hunger in any young child. But what she felt was not the healthy feeling for food that she used to experience before the Revolution. Now it was a constant, gnawing, dull hunger — not only physical, but mental: the feeling of never satisfying hunger, of never being free from the obsessive dreaming about food.

She thought about those previous happy years: leaving with her sisters for school after a good dinner and returning home through the kitchen entrance, where they took off their boots. In the kitchen, so warm from the big *russkaya pechka*, a good supper would be waiting for them. Akulina used to set the table in the spacious dining room, where the colored tile stove, filled with wood, roared and radiated warmth from the corner into the whole room.

Irene crossed the courtyard and opened the door. It was dark and cold in the kitchen. She removed her boots and went into the inner hall, where she took off her coat. The now familiar, repulsive odor of cooking, coming from the dining room, hit her nostrils and lungs, which were still full of frosty, outdoor air.

Ever since the past November, mother had cooked the same meal each night: sour soup with potatoes. The soup was prepared with rye flour, mixed with water and kept for two days at room temperature until it turned sour from fermentation. Then it was boiled and turned into a thin, brownish soup. In the good old days it sometimes served as a first course at dinner: with smoked sausage and buttered potatoes, it tasted good. But now, eaten night after night, without anything but frozen potatoes, it turned even the most hungry of stomachs. Potatoes, affected by frost, turn green and black and have a sweetish, repulsive flavor of decay. The combination of the rotten-sweet potatoes and the sour soup tasted like vomit, smelled like vomit. No matter how hungry Irene was, each evening she had to hold her nose so as not to smell… and not to throw up while eating. She knew that if she did, she would be even more hungry, and hunger was worse at night when you went to bed and could not sleep.

She came into the dining room. Mother was cooking supper on the Primus kerosene stove, stirring the soup and slicing potatoes into it. She didn't say anything, and neither did Irene. No one said much those days, as if trying to conserve energy needed for fighting the cold, doing chores and for walking. Irene left her schoolbooks in her room, took one of her reading books and went into Helena's room, as all the others were dark.

Helena was sitting on her sofa-bed, reading one of the enormous, thick medical books that were scattered all over her bed. She did not even notice or bother to acknowledge Irene's presence. Through the open side door Irene saw her father in the semi-darkness of his room, sitting in a chair, his face partly covered by his hand. Was he asleep, or just resting, or thinking?

If he was not asleep, what was he thinking about?

About life, as it had been before? Not easy, filled with work and responsibilities, even tragedy, but secure and allowing one to have confidence in tomorrow. Or about life as it was now? The everyday struggle for survival, which changed them from members of a family into strangers — if not enemies — or half-wild animals?

Was he thinking about the daily ritual, when mother cut a small rationed loaf of dark bread into eight pieces every morning? That no matter how hard she tried to cut it into even pieces, some *seemed* bigger and were grabbed by anxious hands before she had time to finish cutting? That whoever got the smallest piece hated everyone else for the rest of the day? Was he thinking of where had gone the times of laughter, humorous stories and entertaining? Of where his wife's love and tenderness had gone? Or, was he thinking about his helplessness in having been caught by the aftermath of the Revolution?

Irene went over and kissed her father's hand. He took it off his face and touched her hair with his lips. She looked into his eyes but said nothing, and he in turn looked into hers in silence. She half stood, half sat on the arm of his chair, feeling his arm around her shoulders. Out of her anguished, half-animal soul, corrupted and twisted by hunger, he was her last and only link with human dignity and love.

He was like Oedipus Rex, caught up by the wheel of fate, innocent of sinful intent, yet guilty. Oh! No, he did not kill his father or sin in bed with his mother. But he was like Oedipus, who, running away from his foster parents, walked into the trap of Fate. He had decided to escape with his family from the dangers and cruelty of war and was caught by an evil that was worse than war — the Revolution.

No, he did not kill his father, but he let his beloved son kill himself. Maybe that is why he was doomed to suffer and watch others whom he loved suffer as well? Irene was here, standing next to him, childishly, clumsily offering her love, and like Antigone, she could not bring peace to her father's tormented soul.

Irene's thoughts again turned to food. She could hear the humming of the Primus stove from the room where Aunt Juta was cooking supper for her children.

"I wonder what they are having for supper. I bet it's not a sour soup!"

She started to read in Helena's room. They were all great readers. After all, besides concert and theater-going, there was nothing else to fill the evenings except reading. Now, with entertain-ment no longer available, books were not only the sole entertainers, they were also hunger killers. Her favorites were English books with lovely pictures, translated into Russian. *Little Lord Fauntleroy, The Prince and the Pauper, Oliver Twist, Little Women.* And fairy tales: *Tales of India, Tales of China, Grimm's, Anderson's* and *Russkiye Skazi* (Russian fairy tales with colored pictures). Her favorite Russian story was that of a Prince escaping terrifying dangers through virgin woods *(dryemuchiy lyes)*, riding on a gray wolf and holding a beautiful woman in his arms. Another favorite was *Zhar Ptitza*, "The Firebird." Irene wished that some prince would take her away from hunger and cold on the back of a big gray wolf. "…and they lived happily ever after."

She could hear Stefa and Janka come home, taking off their boots in the kitchen. At the same time, mother called:

"Supper is ready!"

"Where is Sophie?" Irene asked Helena on the way to the dining room.

"She is in bed with a cold. I gave her an aspirin."

But Sophie got out of bed and came to the table. She was feverish and had a cough, but she would not miss even that repulsive meal that they were having.

They ate quickly and in silence. Afterwards, mother did the dishes in a dishpan of lukewarm water: seven soup plates and spoons. It was too cold to do this in the kitchen. Not that it was much warmer in the dining room. The wood supply was dwindling, and father restarted each of the three stoves in the apartment only once a week. Today was the day for lighting the stove in father's room, which heated father's and Helena's rooms, and also Aunt Juta's room via the inner hall. The day after tomorrow it would be the corner tile stove in the dining room, which also warmed mother's and Irene's rooms. Finally, it would be the small stove in Sophie and Stefa's room, which connected only with the inner hall.

With February frosts of twenty to thirty degrees below freezing, it was enough to keep them from freezing to death, but not enough to keep them even reasonably warm. The coldest room was Aunt Juta's front corner room with its six windows. No wonder, then, that as soon as she heard father start a fire in the stove, she came out of her room and sat in front of it, warming her hands. Camilla and her brothers came, too, along with Helena and the girls, and even Sophie with a scarf around her neck and all bundled up in a blanket. Everyone wore jackets, scarves, stoles, blankets — anything to keep warm — and sat on the floor listening to the crackling of the wood. The flames played light and shadow on their faces, and sparkled in their eyes. They sat like their ancestors did a half-million years before in a cave; the fire now, as then, gave them not only warmth but the reassurance of safety, of life itself.

Mother came into the room with a lamp, which she put on father's night table. She was cross because Aunt Juta was sitting on his bed, talking to him in confidential whispers. That always made mother jealous. The light of the lamp, and the noise with which mother put it on the table broke the spell of cozy serenity. She saw the children make faces and squint their eyes, and felt, or imagined, an atmosphere of hostility because of her intrusion. Mother, in turn, felt hostile toward just about everybody, but especially toward Aunt Juta. Noisily she pulled over a chair and sat on it, adjusting a wool knit stole around her shoulders. Feeling uncomfortable, Helena got up and went back to her room; so did Aunt Juta's children.

Watching the fire and absorbed by her thoughts, Irene did not pay any attention to anyone else in the room. Only when the voices started rising to a crescendo did she realize that mother and Aunt Juta were having one of their arguments. Now, however, they did not waste time on polite, formal sweetness as they had in the old days. Now they had political discussions exclusively, in which all the disappointments, frustrations, torment and anguish of their private lives were subconsciously disguised in the wraps of politics.

Irene could hear "Bolsheviks" and "Mensheviks"... "Keren-sky" and "President *Veel-son*" and "Kaiser *Veel-helm.*" Quite often they did not let each other finish a sentence, as if it were a matter of life and death to prevent the other from having the last word. Mother's cheeks were flushed, while Aunt Juta's seemed to be even more pale than usual. In the middle of the battlefield sat poor father, trying to put in a word of reconciliation here and there, but without any success. It was amazing how mother and Aunt Juta summoned up all that energy and stamina at that time, as all day long they hardly spoke.

Finally, father got up, looked inside the stove, and seeing that the wood had turned to charcoal, screwed the door and vent tightly. Mother got up, too, and with a last loud and pointed sentence, left the room with the air of a conqueror — though she actually felt more frustrated and lonely than before. She went to her room, took off her shoes, and without undressing, threw herself on her bed and began to sob.

The girls left father's room, undressed and went to bed. They could hear mother's sobs until they all fell asleep and could not hear her any more. Father could hear her cry, too; he wanted to go and console her, but he was afraid that she would cry even more. Tired and sad he, too, finally fell asleep.

The clock in the dining room struck three times.

Mother got up, lit a lamp and turned the light to a small flicker to conserve kerosene. She felt her aching head, and her eyes were swollen from crying. She washed at a small iron washstand with water that was ice cold, but somehow, today, she did not care. She was almost fifty now, and the time had come for a change in her body. After a few months of irregularity, she was now hemorrhaging. She knew that it was not unusual at her age, but her back and stomach hurt just the same, no matter what the reason. She wished that she could stay in bed longer, but as usual she had to get up to stand in line as early as possible to get a quart of milk. Milk was not rationed, but it was very scarce, and the line began to form at two o'clock in the morning; some latecomers went home with empty milk cans every morning.

She tidied herself and dressed, put on her heavy coat and pinned a little felt hat onto the top of her head. No matter how many scarves she bundled on her head for warmth, she always wore a hat. Invisible under the scarves, the hat was nevertheless a symbol of breeding and social standing to her, something to which she clung desperately during the misery of war. She sat down and started to wrap her feet in old newspapers — for insulation against the cold — before she put on her boots.

Irene, too, heard the clock strike the hour; half asleep, she automatically counted one, two, three... Covered up to her ears with blankets and comforters, she was warm, but she could feel the cold air on her forehead as it came in frosty waves from the windows. And she could smell it in her nostrils.

What awakened her was the itching of frostbitten toes. Whether it was the poor diet or the cold in the house, or so many winters now spent in the Moscow climate, this year she had suffered badly. The frostbite was not bad enough to cause sores, but the swelling and itching persisted, especially when her feet were warm. The worst part of it was that you could not scratch, because it hurt, and anyway, the more you scratched, the more it itched.

She opened her eyes and saw through the open door a faint beam of light in the dining room. It was coming from mother's room. She heard her stirring and walking. Every morning, before anyone was out of bed, mother was back from the store with a quart of milk, which they would have with tea. Irene took it for granted that it would be there on the table, scalding hot, mixed half-and-half with tea, making that miserable breakfast of a small crust of bread more tasty and nourishing. For the first time, in the middle of the dark cold night, snug under her blankets, she suddenly realized what it must have been for mother to get up night after night, and stand there until dawn in the bitter cold to get that milk.

"So that is what Mother means," she thought, "that a mother is not just a person saying nice things to you, or elegantly dressed and perfumed, entertaining guests. It is to have her near you when you are ill and thirsty because of high fever, holding a glass of water to your lips. It is standing in line for hours on a cold night to bring you some food."

An unexplainable emotion rose up in her throat. She got up from her bed, crossed the dining room and stood in front of mother. Mother had just finished putting on her boots and was taking a scotch plaid from her bed to throw over her shoulders.

"What is it that you want, Irene?"

There was so much, so much that she wanted to say! Instead she stood there, shivering with cold and emotion. All she could do was to spread her arms around mother's clumsy figure in the thick *shuba,* and stammer: "Mother…"

She began to cry.

"Now, now, little one, go to bed. It's very cold in here."

She went with Irene to her room and covered her with snuggly blankets. The bed was still warm, and Irene soon fell asleep.

Closing the heavy iron gate behind her, mother turned to the right toward Taganka Square. The moon was low in the sky, behind the trees; the street was dark and lonely. With her head heavy from lack of sleep, and her body tired and worn out, she walked like a robot. In her heavy clothes, with steam coming from every breath, she looked like a robot, too — wound and directed by an invisible hand.

… How long ago was it when she was Irene's age? Only forty years. Yet it seemed like her life had never happened; or perhaps it had, on another planet, or not in this life but in a previous reincarnation… A girl in long, lacy pantaloons that showed from beneath an elaborately pleated petticoat and dress… sitting at the piano, playing scales. A girl who grew up in a beautiful, spacious house full of servants, filled with antique furniture, rare books and family portraits… where, during holidays, with family and neighbors dropping by, there were never less than thirty people sitting at a meal. Where, besides cooks, kitchen maids, nursemaids and other attendants, there were three laundresses just to take care of the laundry, mending and ironing…

How strange that her childhood should appear so remote and unreal, as if it had never happened, yet at the same time seem so close and alive that she remembered every sound, every shape, every fragrance of those bygone days. The smell of freshly starched clothes, of familiar food, the shape and glossiness of the stairway banister, the squeaking of certain planks of wood in the parquet floor. The smell of a snuffed candle in her bedroom, mingled with the smell of lavender sachets coming from a chest of drawers. The voices of her parents, brothers and sisters… the sound of the old piano and familiar songs.

PART II — CHAPTER TEN

Maybe the real is not what "is" today, but what we remember of the past? How often do we live through happenings, unappreciated and seemingly unimportant at the time, but which acquire different values later? Is it not also true of historical facts — not only lives of individuals but of whole nations? Do we not value most, things that are gone forever?

A few hours later, on her way back home with the quart of milk, Irene's mother saw the city still dark and asleep under the cover of snow, like a naked woman covered with a transparent, blue veil. But dawn was already pulling up an opal curtain of light in the east.

CHAPTER ELEVEN — Henryk

Henryk was walking briskly past Kurskiy Voksal, the Kursky railroad station on the other side of the Yauza River. He had left the soldiers' barracks early that morning and had a long walk through half the city already behind him. As it was not snowing, he did not wear his *bashlyk* hood monk style, but folded it in half and wrapped it around his ears and chin to protect them from the frost. Now and then, he hoisted up a small bag and two packages that he held in his arms, which were constantly sliding over his stiff soldier's uniform.

He had gotten a day's pass to see his family, and he had to hurry if he was to spend a few hours home and still manage the long trek back to the barracks in time. A lot had changed in Henryk's life during these past few months. Right after the Revolution, he was inducted into the army. Poland was entirely occupied by the Germans now, and Imperial Russia had ceased to exist. But Poles were still considered by the new Bolshevist regime as citizens of "Mother Russia" and obliged to serve her. Henryk did not mind being in the army in the least. He was given brief training and combat instruction, and he was now assigned with other soldiers to clean up the mess in the city left after the Revolution. He was also busy guarding supply trains, warehouses, railroad stations, and such. He was given a carbine and given orders to shoot any "enemy of the soldiers', workers' and peasants' regime." This made him feel grownup, but he also knew that he could easily be shot on the spot if he did something that did not please his superiors. This gave him a great sense of responsibility. With all this knowledge, Henryk had nevertheless risked his life three times within the past twenty-four hours. Being one of the guards of the unloading post of a supply center, he watched crates of food being handled and stored all day. He knew that he was going to leave the next day, and he could not stand the idea of going home to his half-starved family with empty hands.

First, he casually knocked a package of lard from the pile near the warehouse entrance. His heart was pounding, as any of the other soldiers or workers could easily have seen him and denounced him. Besides, he had never stolen anything in his life, and crossing the moral bridge between honesty and crime was even harder to cope with than was the feeling of imminent danger. But the bridge was crossed; what was started had to be finished. He slowly pushed the package with his foot until he had buried it in the snow near the wall.

A few hours later, after the midday meal, he did the same thing with a bag. It was hard to the touch and made a dry, crunchy noise.

"Maybe it is buckwheat kasha?" he thought hopefully, pushing it backwards with his feet toward the snowdrift.

This morning he stole a loaf of bread. Every soldier got his loaf of bread for the day. Henryk, looking slightly nonchalant and looking into the eyes of a soldier guarding the bread baskets, took two loaves instead of one. Again his heart was pounding, his face flushed to the very roots of his hair. He wrapped the bread in a spare shirt and went to dig the other things out of the snow.

"What am I going to tell the guard at the gate?" he wondered, unable to find an answer.

He calmly placed everything on the ground and took out his leave pass. The guard nodded his head without looking around. He had made it!

When Henryk was almost thirteen years old, he had read Victor Hugo's *Les Miserables*. Of all the tragic events that the book contained, the one about the man running with a stolen loaf of bread haunted his memory the most. Now, like Jean Valjean, he was running home with stolen food. Was he wrong in doing it? Would he ever be sorry for it? He did not know. Now, after it was over, he did not even care. Life in the army had not only toughened his body and built up his muscles, but it also had affected his mind and his soul. The feeling of shame was gone, and only the sense of daring, devil-may-care courage remained.

The gray daylight of the early winter morning was creeping through the windows and into the dining room. Mother put a few more pieces of charcoal inside the tube of the samovar, and leaning over, started to blow on the coals. They must have caught fire right away from those below, because her face became orange with the glow. She stood up straight to escape the sparks, which jumped with sharp, dry noises. She took a pot from the Primus stove and started to pour hot milk into seven glasses. Milk had to be boiled to kill any possible tuberculosis bacteria. Anyway, to use hot milk with tea or coffee was the custom of Eastern Europe. The light tremor and the steam escaping from the samovar signaled that the water was boiling. Mother poured some water into a teapot and put it on the samovar to brew.

Irene was sitting at the table, wrapped in a blanket and holding a lump of sugar while watching with hungry eyes the seven glasses half-filled with milk. She was neither dressed nor combed, as right after breakfast she would creep back to bed. Helena came in, put her big heavy books on the side table and sat, waiting for the tea. She was all dressed up, as her classes started early, and it was a long walk to Moscow University. Sophie was dressed also, as her school was still on the morning shift, but Stefa and Janka came in looking more or less as messy as Irene. Finally, father came, he too holding a lump of sugar in his hand.

On the first of each month the sugar rations were distributed: thirty lumps per person. You could eat them all in one day, or one each day, or half a lump twice a day — or use them in any possible other way. Each member of the family kept his ration hidden some-where: in a drawer, locked safely away from temptation or theft. Just when mother filled the last glass of tea, there was a knock on the kitchen door. It was Kuharka, who brought their daily ration of bread: one loaf for the family, one half for Aunt Juta. Kuharka had their ration coupons and got the bread for all the people living in the house.

Just then Władek came to take the bread and samovar to Aunt Juta's room. As he had poor eyesight, he was not in the army, but instead was studying mathematics at the University.

"I will bring the samovar back as soon as we make our tea," he said.

It was a small, dark, round loaf of bread.

Mother took a kitchen knife, made a small cross above the loaf (because bread is mentioned in the Lord's Prayer) and started to cut carefully, with mathematical precision. She felt all eyes on her hands, and they trembled slightly. There was silence and tension in the room, as if something extraordinarily important was about to happen. Today Helena and Janka grabbed the two pieces which seemed the biggest (how much bigger — a few crumbs?). The rest of them managed to take the second best pieces and started to eat it in a silence heavy with hostility.

Two pieces of bread were left on the table. One was mother's, who never reached first, and one extra — actually Henryk's ration — which, despite his being in the Army, was not taken away. They were very small, miserable crusts of bread. Mother wrapped one of them in a cloth napkin for father's extra meal. He was coming home from the office much later than dinner time these days. As frugal as the dinners were, it filled their stomachs at least temporarily. Father needed something to munch in the office, to kill the gnawing afternoon hunger.

Now mother started to eat, cutting her bread into small bites with a knife, as if she wanted them to last longer.

When they got up, there was not the smallest crumb to be found on the table.

Stefa combed her long blond hair and started to braid it in the back, holding her arms high and watching in the mirror to see that it was straight. She was dressed and had already made her bed, as well as Sophie's. It was her turn today to stand in line in front of the butcher's store, "in case" some meat was distributed that day. Her two younger sisters were still in bed, trying to forget in their sleep their unsated hunger. Mother was napping, too, catching up on her sleep and trying to rid herself of the exhaustion caused by a night's vigil in front of the milk store. Half asleep, she could hear someone open the entry door to the kitchen, then the tramping of feet on the floor, as if someone was shaking off the snow from his boots.

Stefa could hear the noise, too. She entered the inner hall, passed mother's room, opened the door to the kitchen and stood face to face with Henryk, who had just been ready to open it from the other side.

"It's Henry!" she yelled, with the full strength of her young lungs.

Mother sat up on her bed, trying to put aside her blanket and comforter, and started looking for her shoes.

"Are you ill, Mother?"

"No, no. I was resting a bit after standing in line, that's all. See, I'm all dressed."

She stood up and kissed him.

"You look fine. Do they feed you?"

"Yes, don't worry. We get enough bread and tea with sugar, and we get two hot meals a day: *shchi* (cabbage soup) with meat, and *kasha*, and such."

"It's very bad here, my son. We don't even have those rotten potatoes any more, or rye flour to make soup. For the past few weeks all we could get was sauerkraut or salted herring, but you can't eat much of that without bread and potatoes. All it gives you is a bad taste in the mouth, and it makes you wretchedly thirsty."

"I brought you something, Mother. It's not much, but it will help a little."

Henryk went back to the kitchen, where he had left the packages, and brought them to the dining room where mother was again blowing at the charcoal in the samovar.

"You need a hot glass of tea, that's what you need after such a long walk. What is that?" She was pointing to the bag he held.

"I don't even know, Mother. Something I could get for you, and two loaves of bread… and this is lard."

He spread everything on the table.

"Let's open the bag and see what is there," he added.

It was chicken feed. Unthreshed grain. Just what one could expect from the efficient government of the People's Revolution. A supply of bags full of chicken feed for the citizens of Moscow… who did not own a single chicken.

"All of this dragging of a heavy bag for nothing," said Henryk, almost ashamed.

"For nothing? My son, it is grain — it is food! We will take off the husk tomorrow, and we will eat it, every single bit of it. Here have some tea."

She brought out her next day's lump of sugar.

"No, thank you, Mother. I have my sugar with me."

He took several lumps out of his pocket and put them on the table. Big and strong, his face still red from the cold, he stood up and kissed Irene and Janka, who had come in all dressed and combed, with their hair still wet near the ears from a hurried washing.

"I have to go now to stand in line," said Stefa with hesitation and regret in her voice.

"Wait," said Henryk. "We will have some tea and bread. I have not eaten yet."

He gave them sugar, and he cut bread into generous slices. The loaf was tall, oblong and squared, shaped especially for soldiers to carry under their arms.

"You'd better go now, Stefa," mother said after they had eaten. "What they'll give you is mostly skin and bones, not much meat, but it makes the sauerkraut taste better." "I have been worrying about you," she continued after Stefa had left. "I thought maybe they would send you away from here."

"They might. The fighting is not over. In a country as big as Russia there might be months — even years — of fighting between the anti-Bolsheviks and the revolutionary forces. Moscow and St. Petersburg are not the whole of Russia."

"But you are not a Bolshevik — you are not even a Russian. How can they expect you to fight against those who oppose a new regime? Are you going to shoot and kill innocent people?"

"It is to kill or to be killed. Do you want me to be killed?"

He was her only son. How could he ask such a question? She did not reply, and for a few seconds a heavy silence filled the room.

"I will worry when the time comes to make that decision," Henryk continued, laughing to chase away the gloom. Right now, so long as I am in Moscow, I will try to bring you more food as often as possible."

Mother and his sisters sat and watched with admiration this handsome, cheerful and strong young man. He was so different from what they had become. It was like watching a god!

He was like a *deus ex machina* in a Greek tragedy: a god who comes in at the last moment to straighten out the tragic plot of the helpless human race.

CHAPTER TWELVE — A Sack of Flour

On the third of March in the year of our Lord nineteen hundred and eighteen, Russia signed a War Treaty with Germany in Brest-Litovsk. It was a humiliating treaty, but torn by civil war and threatened with intervention from the West, Russia had no choice.

The war was still raging in Western Europe, but for Polish refugees stranded in Moscow it was not an issue of primary importance; the problems of *when* and *how* to return to Poland were much more important.

A special committee had to be formed to arrange for the departure of refugees in "echelons" — long freight trains. The names of those wishing to leave had to be put in order, and the possible dates of leaving, drawn. It required months of preparation in the midst of chaos caused by the civil war and a new government that lacked responsible organization. Peace with Germany did not improve the food situation in Moscow; the city suffered from the miseries of famine, and with it, did Irene and her family.

Each morning mother would soak some of the unthreshed grain that Henryk had brought. Then she would sit on the window sill (to see better) for hours, taking each grain between her fingers and removing the hard husk. Irene helped her as much as she could, for her small fingers were more nimble than her mother's. Stefa and Janka cleaned the house, stood in queues, or did homework, but mother and youngest daughter would sit hour after hour, day after day, separating hundreds of grains. After many hours of over-whelming labor, there was enough to make a thin, watery soup for all. In their native language, they called it the "soup of the hand-threshed kasha."

Sitting that way for hours on a window sill gave Irene time to think — more than she could bear. She missed the opera, going to the theater, and she missed a piano in the house. She missed Adela, too; Adela had school in the morning, so they could see each other only on Sundays. There was nothing to do in the world, it seemed, but daily chores, the struggle to get food... and removing husks from grains. At night, before she went to sleep, Irene could still see in front of her tired eyes, millions of grains and millions of husks to be removed by millions of fingers, until she thought that she would scream. But she would finally drop off to sleep.

Sometimes in the middle of a chore, Irene would slip down from the window sill and go to her room, shutting the door. She would stand in front of the mirror and start acting, reciting a poem, or singing an aria from an opera, while making all sorts of tragic expressions with her face. Finally, she would start to dance.

The little face, with eyes enlarged by hunger... the thin little arms, softly, gracefully moving in a dance of the flying swan, until the body crumpled of its own inertia...

The war and hunger took almost everything from her, but not the longing for beauty, for harmony. Feeling cleansed and fortified, she would return quietly to the room where her mother was still sitting hunched at the window, clumsily splitting stubborn husks between her stiff, cold fingers.

One spring morning there came a telegram: "YADVIGA ILL. MOTHER PLEASE COME. VLODEK" it said.

Mother decided, "I am not going. Jadwiga has Vlodek and Niania to look after her. I am more needed here. After all, you girls can do only so much before you leave for school."

But by late afternoon another telegram came: "YADVIGA DANGEROUSLY ILL. MOTHER PLEASE COME AT ONCE."

She left that night by a late, crowded train, taking nothing except her pocketbook.

"Take care of yourselves," she said when leaving. "I will write you as soon as I can."

None of them mentioned Jadwiga's name, as if they were afraid that it would bring her to the attention of evil spirits.

On the third day, mother's letter came: Jadwiga had an infection of the abdomen after a miscarriage, and there was no known medicine. She was dying.

A SACK OF FLOUR

The girls managed as best as they could with the cooking and all the other chores, but nobody would get up early and wait in line for milk, so this nourishment had been removed from their diet.

Why is it that we are more hungry on some days than on others? With Irene, hunger was a constant companion, but that particular day she was so ravenously hungry that she wanted to tear apart everything around her. The morning tea and bread seemed only to stir her perpetual hunger even more. She started to look in every drawer, on every shelf in the kitchen cupboard, in the dining room breakfront. She knew that there was nothing there, nothing *could* be there, yet she looked, obsessed with the idea that she had to put something in her stomach right *then*, not six hours from then at the next meal that they would have before leaving for school (some left-over cabbage, locked up by Stefa in one of the kitchen cupboards). The last place that Irene inspected was a built-in wall closet in mother's room. It had not been used for a long time, but Irene looked just the same. She found an empty flour sack, discarded long ago, yet when she touched the corners, there was a little flour left. She shook the sack carefully into a bowl. There was about one tablespoon of flour in which silver bugs were swimming around. She fished them out, mixed the flour with a bit of water, flattened the batter, and toasted it on the frying pan over the Primus stove. She could not wait until it had cooled off, so she burned her tongue. It tasted delicious, but it was not enough.

Still hungry, in desperation she went out into the garden, trying to forget about food. It was springtime. The fruit trees had just ceased blooming, but the ground was still covered with a carpet of soft white petals. Irene looked gloomily at the tiny green beads on the trees and thought that it would be months before they grew into edible fruit. The lilac bushes were not in bloom yet, but flower stalks were already appearing between the fresh green leaves.

Irene sat under the big linden tree. "In July," she thought, "it will be covered with thousands of tiny golden flowers, fragrant with honey." Now, only the first, pale leaves had appeared. She picked some of them and put them in her mouth; they were crisp and sweet, like leaves of spring lettuce, so she picked and ate some more. Then she started to scrape around the tree, where among the last year's decaying leaves were hidden hundreds of little brown balls, no larger than the head of a hatpin. These were seeds of the linden tree. Irene removed a soft, brown shell and put a little in her mouth. It tasted good, just like a hazelnut — sweet and oily.

"What are you eating out there?" asked Janka suspiciously as she came out to shake some rugs.

"I am eating linden nuts! They are delicious!"

Janka came, tried some, and found them tasty, too. They sat under the tree, digging up the nuts and peeling them like animals. The instinct of nature, of survival, spoke to them, and they accepted its voice, for it was as strong as life itself.

Just before they were to leave for school, a telegram came. Stefa opened it with trembling hands; they were all sure that it meant that Jadwiga had died. Instead, it was announcing the Jadwiga was safe and that mother was coming back soon.

"It is a miracle," said Stefa, "but after all, Jadwiga is always lucky."

"You will never guess what I brought you, Mamochka," said Vlodek, coming home from the factory.

He called Jadwiga's mother *mamochka,* which means in Russian "mommy." After days of anxiety and despair about Jadwiga's life, he was now bursting with happiness. He kissed his wife, who was still in bed. She looked pale, but beautiful as ever. "Mamochka" was sitting nearby. She was going to leave that night for Moscow, and she wanted to stay beside her daughter every possible moment.

"What is it you brought me?" she asked.

"Twenty pounds of flour, a bag of kasha, sugar and sunflower seed oil! Don't ask me where or how I got it, but I did!"

Mother could not find any words. Tears came to her eyes and after a while she managed to say: "You don't know what it means to us!" After days and sleepless nights of vigil at her daughter's side, she was shaky and could not control herself as well as she usually could.

"Thank you so much, Vlodek. I am sorry I have to leave you all, but you understand how hard it must be on the girls to run the house and go to school at the same time. We are not as strong as we used to be, especially since the famine started."

Niania came in, bringing Jadwiga's meal on a tray.

"Dinner is on the table," said Niania, turning to mother. "You had better eat now and leave for the station. Heaven knows when the train will leave and how crowded it will be."

"You are right, Niania," said Vlodek. "Come, Mamochka."

A SACK OF FLOUR

"You did not even kiss me when you came home!" cried Tadyo. "You never play with me anymore!" He was sulking as Vlodek came into the dining room and lifted up his son.

"My son," thought Vlodek, "how could you understand that you almost lost your mother...?" He tried to kiss him, but Tadyo freed himself of his father's embrace, ran to the hall, climbed the chair and unhooked the wall telephone.

"Is this *Dryemuchiy Lyes* ("Virgin Forest")?" he asked into the telephone. "Wolf? Wolf, come quickly to eat up my father, because he is very bad!"

He put the receiver back on the hook, and relieved of all his hostility, sat down quietly to dinner. Vlodek and mother had a hard time keeping straight faces, and what the telephone operator thought, nobody ever found out.

They left right after dinner, Vlodek carrying a bag, and mother the large package of food wrapped in brown paper and heavy string.

"How are you going to carry all this home from the station? Do you think that you can find an *izvoshchik* at Kurskiy Voksal?" *

"Don't worry. I will manage," replied mother in a happy voice. "Oh, I can't wait until I see their faces when I arrive home with all this food!"

When they got to Tula station, the train for Moscow was already waiting and filled, literally, like a can of sardines. Not only were all the compartments and corridors filled with standing people, but even the platforms and the narrow metal strips connecting the cars.

"What shall I do? I simply have to leave?" cried mother, looking in dismay at the people pushing their way to the crowded platforms.

"I would not let you ride all night on the platform. It's dangerous. There is only one way."

He put the food packages on the ground, lifted mother high and pushed her, feet first, through the open window. She landed sideways, on many heads and shoulders, but somehow, after a while, slid down until she felt the floor. She stood up, leaned over to the window, and pulled in the packages that Vlodek handed her.

"Are you all right, Mamochka?"

---

* The distance to home from the Kursky station is over 2 km.

"I am… fine. Thank you again for what you have done…" she cried as the train started to pull away from the station.

The trip was a nightmare. After a while, there seemed to be more room. This was because some courageous people had climbed to the narrow racks usually used for luggage and settled there for the night — posing a threat to those sitting below, as they might fall down in their sleep. Mother, standing in the corridor and holding a package on her shoulders for lack of space, felt faint from exhaustion. She would not fall even if she lost consciousness. "That was impossible," she thought. "Even a cadaver would remain upright all night, with no one finding out about it until we reached Moscow…"

Later on, some people got off at one of the stations, and mother found enough room to sit on the floor. As tired and sleepy as she was, she was afraid to shut her eyes even for a moment, lest someone steal her food. She spent all night holding the sack of flour under her arm and a package in her lap.

It was just before sunrise when she got off at the Kursky station. There was not an *izvoshchik* in sight, so she faced the long walk home with a heavy burden. She was worn out, not only from the sleepless night spent in an awkward position on a hard floor, but the terror of her daughter's near-fatal illness was just now catching up to her. Yet there was nothing else that she could do but walk and carry the food home. She found that second, almost superhuman strength, which supposedly all human beings possess — a strength that badly wounded soldiers find when running away from danger and carrying men more badly injured than themselves… a strength that mothers of newborn infants possess when the need arises…

She was halfway home, stopping now and then to place the food packages on the sidewalk and catch her breath, when she heard a young, pleasant voice behind her:

"*V am tyazhelo, ya vam pomogu.*" ("It's heavy, I'll help you.") Mother turned around and saw a young woman, about Helena's age. She even looked like one of the students Helena used to invite into their home.

"Oh, thank you very much," said mother. "I am quite exhausted."

The girl picked up the sack of flour and started to walk briskly.

"Where do you live?"

"Bolshoi Drovyanoi." *

"That's not far. You take it easy. I will get there in no time at all."

She continued to walk fast. First the distance between them was only a few feet. Then the gap became larger and larger. Mother's legs were trembling, her heart pounding. She had to stop to catch her breath.

"Podozhdite, baryshnya! Podozhdite!" ("Wait, Miss! Wait!") Her cries were faint.

But the girl did not seem to hear her at all. She had reached the corner of a *pereulok* that was a shortcut toward Zemlyanka Street and had disappeared from mother's sight. With a final effort mother reached the *pereulok* and looked all the way down the street. There was no trace of either the girl or the sack that she was carrying. She had disappeared into thin air.

"It can't be! She must be here; she could not have reached Zemlyanka already… I just saw her a minute ago." Panic was clutching at her throat. "Oh, God, no, no… Don't let this happen! God, no!"

She stood in the middle of the empty street.

Which way to go? Where to turn? Which house… behind which gate? Even if she tried all the houses of this *pereulok*, how could she find the right apartment? Would people be willing to open their doors to a stranger — to a foreigner — and let her look for a girl? She is hiding now, anyway, and even if she did find her, how could she prove that the girl had taken anything from her? The police? Maybe there were police to arrest people and drag them to *butyrki,* but there were never any visible ones on the streets of Moscow to help a citizen in distress.

All these thoughts were flashing through mother's mind.

With every passing second she realized more and more clearly that she had been robbed, cold-bloodedly robbed of a most precious possession — food for her half-starved family. She was still praying, still hoping that the girl would suddenly appear from one of the houses and give back her sack.

Finally, she put her package on the sidewalk, sat down at the edge of the gutter, covered her face with trembling hands, and like a simple peasant woman, began to weep.

---

* Большой Дровяной переулок

CHAPTER THIRTEEN — Summer, 1918

Early in the summer, long trains started to take Polish refugees west, back home. These refugees were mainly from the intelligentsia class of Polish gentry, who had run from their towns and estates in Eastern Poland to escape the ravages of war. Aunt Juta was fortunate enough to get a place in one of these first echelons. Someone left mother, as a present, a pillowcase filled with dried bread. It was a generous gift and very much appreciated. Irene remembered how before the war the neighbor's maid in Warsaw had felt indignant about eating *smelka* — the beggar's soup. Now the family ate smelka every day at suppertime... and considered it a happy change from salted herring.

The date for leaving on the next refugee train was fixed. Now the time came to reverse the process of four years ago: the furniture had to be returned to Jadwiga's friends, the dining room set sold, and things had to be packed, sorted and disposed of. The lack of food was still the most predominant factor in their lives, but it was easier to bear while looking forward to the trip back home. Besides, summer was not as demanding on the body's energy as were the cold winter months.

Saying goodbye a hundred times to each other, Irene and Adela promised that the first thing that they would do when they arrived in Warsaw was to plan to meet again. Neither asked for any relative's address through which they might contact each other; silly, naïve children. However, just the fact that they were friends seemed enough to assure that they would meet... in a city of over one million people.

When at the end of July news had spread of the murder of Tsar Nikolai and his whole family, Irene's parents not only became worried but afraid for the safety of their family.

"If they could kill the Tsar, Tsarina and their *children*, who for over a year were harmless creatures, what might they do to us? Instead of bothering to send trains to Poland, they might shoot us like animals!" cried mother.

SUMMER, 1918

The last two weeks dragged on endlessly in the house stripped of furniture. They slept on the floor, and packed and threw out things that had accumulated over the past four years. Kuharka was more and more gloomy and hostile, and it seemed as though at any moment she might appear at the door of their apartment with a big kitchen knife, ready to cut their innocent throats.

The day came when everything was packed, and it was time to leave. Even Kuharka and her daughter were somehow less hostile that day; maybe they, too, were happy that the *bezhentsy* were leaving. They even gave the family their own bread rations of the last day... because they knew that it would be possible for them to collect until the end of the month the rations of those who had already left. Neither the owner nor his mother was anywhere to be seen.

"I would not be surprised if Kuharka, with the help of Dvornik, had murdered them long ago and buried them somewhere in the depths of the *saray*," Henryk remarked cheerfully.

It was true that in all these years the owners had not only never been seen, but no one had ever heard their steps or the moving of chairs — all the usual noises that people hear when they live in a flat below their neighbors. Kuharka came to collect the rent, and that was the end of any connection between the owner and the family.

All the trunks, suitcases and duffel bags were loaded on an *izvoshchik*. Henryk sat in front next to the driver because there was not much room inside, and they drove off to the station. The rest of the family was to follow on foot.

Father stood at the heavy, iron gate and held it open until all of them were out, except mother. She looked around the courtyard, at the house and at the garden. She took a deep breath and sighed: it was the sigh of someone who had been in pain for a long time and the pain had finally ceased... it was a sigh of relief.

CHAPTER FOURTEEN — Goodbye to Moscow

The long train consisted exclusively of cattle wagons. The car in which Irene's family was given room for the trip was clean enough. They found it by looking for a number marked in chalk on the outside of the wagon. It had to correspond with the number printed on a piece of paper that father held in one hand while carrying a suitcase in the other.

Mother and the girls stood on the platform, watchful of all their possessions: suitcases, trunks, food baskets and bedding. Irene could see Henryk following father: he was carrying some luggage under both arms, jumping from one rail to another and trying not to lose sight of father in the pushing, hurrying and shouting crowd. Then she saw both of them stop in front of one of the cars. Father turned and waved toward them.

"Go," said mother. "Take whatever you can carry, and I will stay here with the rest of our things."

Soon all of their belongings were inside the rail car. They took possession of one-half of the car, the other half being occupied by a family with small children. In spite of being tired, thirsty and sweaty from moving all their belongings, they were all happy and excited about the coming trip.

How different it was from the voyage of four years before! Then, they had been in the happy, excited mood of tourists, looking forward to a luxurious two-day trip to a new, strange country. Now, they faced a trip in cramped, primitive quarters, sitting and sleeping in uncomfortable positions, their meager food cooked on a Primus stove, a can of water and a bucket their only toilet facilities.

Yet all of them, even Irene who had left Warsaw as just a child, were overpowered by the feeling of tenderness, of sudden longing and love for their mother country, even though it was still occupied by the Germans. During the past four years they had not realized how much they missed it. Yes, life was going on in Moscow — new homes, new lives — but now their ties with that city were cut off... all was left behind, and no one felt sorry. Everyone's thoughts and plans concentrated on the future, on the trip back to Warsaw.

What they did not know was that the trip would last one whole month.

Mother tried somehow to make a home out of the small space in the cattle car. With father's help she hung a few blankets from the ceiling, which gave them some privacy from the strangers on the other side, and she made a partition for a bathroom in one corner. Once a day she cooked some soup, flour thrown on boiling water, which formed dumplings of a sort. Besides that, there was only stale bread, sausage and tea. Two small windows high up near the ceiling gave little light: the upper part of the door was kept open during the day, and this gave enough air and light.

Sometimes a whole day passed and the train did not stop at all. Sometimes it stopped in the middle of the night, or during the day, quite a distance from a station. It was just as well, because as soon as the train stopped, everyone ran out to the bushes to seek the privacy of outdoor facilities, to empty buckets, to stretch legs.

No matter what time of day or night it was, peasants would appear out of nowhere, bringing some food for sale: mostly bread, cheese or potatoes. At each station there was a big metal tank of boiling water with a faucet, and a sign on top, *kipyatok*. A Russian, traveling with a teaspoon, mug and lump of sugar, needed only *kipyatok* to make a cup of tea. Father and Henryk would go to the station and bring back some boiling water. It meant saving the kerosene stove, as some of the water was used for tea, the rest for washing. But since no one ever knew how long the train would stay before pulling out again, those trips to fetch *kipyatok* were filled with unbearable tension:

"Will Father and Henry get back before the train leaves?"

"What if they don't and get left behind?"

Of course, they were not the only ones who ventured to the station. Irene could see many nervous, tense men jumping across the rails and heading for the station with all sorts of utensils, turning their heads often toward the train for fear that it would leave without them.

CHAPTER FIFTEEN — The Train

Irene began to get restless. Sitting all day on a trunk piled high with bedding, she could do nothing but read or nap, or just look through the wide-open part of the car "door." If only there was some room to jump, to play ball... anything! From time to time she had to pull herself up, as the motion of the train made her slide gradually down the slippery comforters and pillows.

The flat, gray Russian countryside, bare after the harvest, stretched endlessly outside. Here and there, a potato or cabbage field dotted the picture with a bit of green, or a tall haystack broke the monotony of deserted fields. Irene closed her eyes and began daydreaming. She thought about Adela, about their plays, games and silly quarrels. She thought about school, trips to museums and the opera... A waltz tune from the opera *Yevgeny Onegin* came suddenly to mind:

Zachem Lenski nye tantsuyesh
Olginy ruchki nye tzeluyesh...?

Lenski, Lenski, why don't you dance
And kiss Olga's little hands...?

The train moved slowly; the cars sighed and groaned. It seemed that the one from behind was trying to push the one in front. As it started, it reminded Irene of the onomatopoeic interpretation of a train in motion that she had been taught long ago:

S"yest' khotim, S"yest' khotim, Pit' pit' ... ... Pit' pit',
Yeshche skoreye, yeshche skoreye,
Cherez most, cherez most, Pit' pit' ... Pit' pit' ... Pit' pit' ...

We are hungry, we are hungry, Drink-drink ... ... Drink-drink,
Even faster, even faster,
Through the bridge, through the bridge,
Drink-drink ... Drink-drink ... Drink-drink ...

THE TRAIN

She laughed, contented and insouciant. The motion stopped. One could hear the cars bumping into each other, one after another, one after another, from the first to the last. Finally, the sudden pull... Irene opened her eyes. She could see her mother bent over a small basin, washing some socks and stockings. Her feet apart, she was trying to catch her balance after the last pull of the train.

"There is a town nearby!" shouted Henryk, leaning out.

Everybody was trying to get a look, crowding at the door.

A man, walking along the train, was shouting, repeating over and over:

"All right, you can open the door now and get out! The train will stop here for three hours!"

Three hours! Never before were they given so much time, and told in advance how long it would be.

Parents decided quickly.

"Come children, let's not waste time. We will go to the woods!"

The woods were quite near, next to some potato fields. The children quickly jumped over the railroad tracks and ran toward the trees. How good it was to run again! How sweet and mild was the air on that sunny, autumn afternoon! How caressing the wind on one's face, singing and whispering among the dying leaves! How refreshing to the eye the green moss under the trees! How lovely seemed the timid voice of a half-asleep cricket, the song of the sparrow perched on the telegraph pole!

They gathered some dry wood and built a fire at the edge of the woods. While mother and the girls looked for mushrooms, father and Henryk dug up some potatoes. Later, they all sat around the fire, eating potatoes and mushrooms roasted on sticks, *shashlik* style. Sand and ashes were on their hands, lips and tongues. They did not have any salt, yet that simple food, prepared and eaten primitively, not only tasted good, but it gave them the feeling of belonging together, of sharing things together. They were one — a family again. A primitive instinct was stronger and more precious than centuries of civilization, culture, breeding and education.

But the time was going by fast. Father looked at his watch many times and finally said:

"We have to go. We can't be late."

His words were heavy and sad. He did not want to look into anybody's eyes. It was as if he personally felt responsible and guilty for all the tragedy and sorrow in the world... as if he were guilty for their hard, abnormal life — without a tomorrow — and for the dirt, hunger... and struggle.

He helped mother to get up. "Come children," he said softly.

After two week's of traveling at the pace of a turtle, stopping for short periods of time here and there, the train stopped one day at an ugly-looking, dirty and dismal station. They were told to get off with their belongings. It was Baranowicze. The empty train pulled back toward Russia. About eight hundred people stood on the platform, clutching their baggage, shifting uneasily from one foot to the other. For two long weeks, having traveled like cattle until they felt like caged animals, their only wish was to get out of this train. Now, free at last (or so they thought), they did not know what to do with their freedom.

But it did not take them long to realize that nobody had to make any decision. Baranowicze was the town on the line of demarcation between Russian and German dominated land. A German officer appeared, accompanied by soldiers. In correct Polish, heavy with a German accent, he told the people what to do and where to go. The people were instructed to follow soldiers to the barracks where they would get sleeping accommodations and food. The next day, all would stand in line to get necessary cholera and typhus vaccinations. They were expected to wash outdoors near the pumps and to use outhouse facilities. Then came the final, distinct words:

"This is quarantine. You will stay here for two weeks. No one is permitted to leave the camp. Any attempt to cross the barbed-wire line will be punishable."

Not a word was spoken. What was one to say? The people were tired, bewildered and frightened to the point of apathy. They followed the soldiers; a certain number of people were counted out and led to each barrack. Mother held Irene's and Janka's hands and kept repeating: "Stay together children. Helen, watch out for Stefa and Sophie." Mother had dark circles under her eyes. Her face looked haggard; her fluffy hair was in disorder. Irene held her mother's hand and felt like crying.

"Even Father," she thought, "who is most handsome, does not look nice today. His eyes are cold, and his face looks hard."

They were counted out like sheep, and then they entered the building....

That night Irene's parents found out that the trip in the cattle wagon was heaven, so far as privacy and comfort went, compared with life in the barracks.

The huge, long room was filled with primitive double bunk beds. About two hundred people, including many children, tried to settle down for the night. Tired, hungry and frightened, the children cried easily, and the adults became uncooperative and quarrelsome.

A few German soldiers brought and distributed some dark, soggy bread and black ersatz coffee. After that, all lights but one were put out.

Irene and her sisters were put on upper bunks, while their parents, Helena and Henryk slept on the lowers. Exhausted, they fell asleep quickly, but their sleep was delirious and often broken by noises and scratching. Sophie seemed to have a chest cold and coughed all night. This time, there was nothing mother could do to help her, not like in the old days when she would apply a mustard plaster to her throat and chest.

All were asleep except mother. She spent all night catching big, fat and bloody bedbugs that crawled out of bunk crevices by the hundreds and attacked the sleepers. They were evil-smelling, even though she carefully scooped them into a can of water, trying not to squeeze any. Irene woke up a few times when mother was picking the bugs from her body, but she was too tired to realize what was happening. But even in the deep sleep of an exhausted child, she could smell the abominable odor, one which she would remember to the end of her life.

In the dreary semi-darkness of the room, with endless rows of tall bunk beds towering around her, the small, leaning figure of mother drowning bedbugs in a can of water looked like a shadow from Dante's *Inferno*.

CHAPTER SIXTEEN — Quarantine

It was a cloudy, cold day. The end of September in this part of Eastern Europe is already the time of late autumn.

People stood in a long line in front of the building where the vaccinations were administered. They had to wash outside, in the cold early morning, with freezing water. Now they stood sleepy and shivering, their empty stomachs craving for warm food.

Irene's family stood in line as others did, trying to keep warm by leaning on each other's backs. They watched with envy those already vaccinated, coming out of the building and heading for another line forming in front of a big kettle from which a German soldier was scooping a thin soup into small metal containers. Later, when their turn came, they found out that it was a thin, barley soup with a few pieces of horsemeat floating in it. From then on, for the next two weeks, it was always the same soup, distributed twice a day.

Henryk, practical as ever, suggested that if they lined up later, maybe the soup from the bottom of the kettle would be thicker. It was. So from then on, they would always stay near the end of the line.

On the first day of the quarantine, right after their meal, mother decided to do something about their living conditions. It was after they returned from the cold fresh air to the barracks — in which so many people slept, where children's unwashed diapers hung, where huge bedbugs crawled — that the offensive odor of the unventilated building made them almost lose their meal.

As usual, mother would not just sit there and suffer.

"I am not going to see my children rot in these barracks and be eaten alive by bedbugs," she said emphatically. "Look at Sophie. She is shivering and sweating, in turn, and her cough is getting worse. I bet she has a fever. The big problem is not the physical torture of staying here, but what it is going to do to us mentally. You can't even compare us with animals; at least they have freedom of movement and enjoy fresh air!"

"But there is nothing we can do about it," father said. "You see that everybody lives here under the same conditions: doctors, lawyers, engineers' families — everybody. And the Germans don't take bribes, even if I were to offer one. And where would that take us from here?"

"I don't care where, and certainly I don't intend to pay any money for it. I do know that we are not going to stay here one more hour!"

Mother took a fresh, white blouse from her suitcase, put it on, brushed her skirt and shoes, smoothed her hair, and taking Irene by the hand, said: "I am going to see the Kommandant of the camp."

Why did mother take Irene with her? Was it because she was the youngest, or the prettiest, or both? Did she want to use her as a psychological softener on the Kommandant? Or was it simply because she was scared to death of what she was about to do, but could not back out after all she had said to her husband and children.

Mother did not have time to analyze her feelings, or maybe she did not care or want to. It was probably all those reasons put together that made her drag Irene with her. Maybe that thin, cold hand given to mother in full trust was all that she needed to give her courage, the same insane courage that birds show in protecting a nest against an attacker, or animals show fighting to the last breath to protect their young.

She stormed into the Kommandant's office, brushed aside a few officers and soldiers, told them that the Kommandant was expecting her, and to her amazement was informed that she could come in right away.

Here, in this office, Irene for the first time in her life saw diplomacy at work. She knew that mother hated Germans (did not everybody?), yet for a half an hour she talked with Herr Kommandant in her fluent, impeccable German, smiling and friendly. Whatever she said must have been pleasant and flattering to Herr Kommandant, because he seemed not only interested at first, but later, engrossed and amused by mother's talking, from time to time smoothed his moustache, which was trimmed à la Kaiser Wilhelm II.

He finally got up to shake hands with mother and give some instructions to the officer who appeared at the door. Irene knew from the relaxed expression on her mother's face that everything was going to be fine.

The two rooms given them by Herr Kommandant were in a building adjacent to the Germans' quarters. One room had the same crude, wooden bunk beds as in the main barracks, while the other, smaller room had a table and a few chairs. A German soldier helped them with their belongings and later brought a can of jam and two loaves of bread. He said that from then on they would get bread every morning. He also brought a pass card that authorized the family to leave the barbed wire campus each day for walks in the country.

"We are all alone! We have our own apartment! How simply marvelous! We can take sponge baths and do some laundry… and brew our tea on the Primus stove! We will have our breakfast here, and we can sleep as long as we wish!" All this from the mouths of the children as they explored every nook and corner of their new quarters.

How quickly human nature adapts itself to a new way of life. What a few months ago would have seemed to them an incredible, degrading kind of living, was now enthusiastically greeted as the utmost in luxury.

Father was a happy man, as happy as the children, about mother's successful visit to the Kommandant. Yet, in a hidden corner of his being — which all of us possess and where we store unhealed sores that we dare not touch — in that little corner was a feeling of shame. Shame that it was not he, the head of the family, who had eased their lives, but rather his wife. He felt that, if not negative, his attitude toward life was passive. He knew how to work and suffer; she knew how to work and fight. But he buried these feelings… like he had many times before.

"How did you do it, Zofie?" he asked his wife. "What did you say to him?"

"Oh, I kept talking about the 'famous' German efficiency and planning, and how I always loved to study German poetry — throwing at him Heine, Goethe and Nietzsche, and whatnot — until he melted like a snowman in the sun. But mentioning how closely he resembled the Kaiser did it, I think. I hope that there aren't any bedbugs here," she added, looking around.

She was wrong. There were, and in abundance.

After a cold spell, the weather was sunny and mild again. Sophie was feeling better. That afternoon she was trimming Helena's hair, the only one of the girls who wore short hair. Holding a mirror and clutching a towel around her neck, Helena was giving her instructions on how much she was supposed to trim off.

"I wish Mother would let me have my hair cut," said Sophie. "I am tired of my tresses. As soon as we arrive in Warsaw, I am going to cut it."

"Hurry up," said mother. "If we are to go for a walk, we had better leave now; you know how early the sun sets these days."

Mother folded the letter that she had just finished writing. It was to her cousin Pauline in Warsaw.

"I hope Pauline won't mind too much having us for a few days until we rent an apartment," she said. "I gave her an approx-imate date of our arrival. I will mail this letter right away. Hurry up, children."

Henryk and Stefa put away books they had been reading and went out. Sophie shook out the towel through the window and put on her coat.

"Thanks," said Helena, looking at herself critically in the hand mirror. "Not bad."

They left and joined Irene and Janka, who were playing outside.

"Where are the others?" asked mother.

"They are waiting at the gate," Janka replied.

"Will you wait a minute for me? I have to go to the bathroom!" cried Irene. "Janka, come with me. I'm afraid to go there alone."

The "bathroom" — or rather the outhouse — consisted of two wooden, primitive shacks: one for men and one for women. Inside, there was nothing but a long plank of wood, with many holes made a few feet apart. Another plank of wood covered the front part of the seats, and gave some support to the altogether shaky structure. Through the holes one could see a deep trench, which served as a cesspool. There were no partitions of any kind to give privacy from other people who happened to be using the outhouse at the same time.

The trench, visible through the seat openings, scared Irene: she was afraid that she would fall into that awful pit. Actually it was impossible, as the holes were not large. The odor of human excrement, in spite of the smell of a strong disinfectant, was overpowering.

Janka held Irene's legs while she sat, just to reassure her that she would not fall in. Irene stood up, and adjusting her panties, looked into the pit. The rays of the afternoon sun were coming through the crevices of the outhouse, falling into the pit.

Suddenly Janka saw her sister's horrified face and felt her arms around her neck.

"Look, Janka, down there... Look! Ugh!"

Janka followed with her eyes to the place where Irene's finger was pointing. She saw it, too.

The pit, filled with excrement, was in constant movement, as if alive. Hundreds and hundreds of round, long and sleek worms were dancing, wiggling and pulsating like a huge disgusting monster; on the top, the embryo of an unborn child was swimming.

Irene suddenly remembered how Emily, the maid, had told her that when you die, the worms crawl out of your body through the mouth and eat you in the coffin.

They both started to gag and retch.

"Let's run!" cried Janka, pushing her sister out of the building. Irene shivered for a long time. The sight was imprinted on her mind so vividly that she knew that she would never forget it, not ever.

Outside it was sunny, and the air seemed so fresh! The girls ran toward the gate where the rest of the family was waiting for them impatiently.

"What took you so long, for God's sake?" cried Henryk.

"Oh, nothing. I was a little sick to my stomach," replied Irene.

"You are not catching dysentery, are you?" mother asked anxiously.

"No, nothing like that."

Every day that it did not rain, the family used the pass that permitted them to leave the camp. It was good to get away from the drab surroundings, to forget about war, quarantine and bedbugs. They looked for hazelnuts and mushrooms in the forest, talked and laughed, pretending they were on summer vacation like in the good old days.

That day, maybe because it was warmer, everything seemed lovelier: the golden hue of the fields in the autumn mist, the purplish-black lace of branches in the trees on the pale, washed-out sky.

"Harmony, tranquility of nature, of world order. What man had brought to it — with all his superiority of brains, his talents, even genius — was for the most part ugly, cruel, selfish and degrading. What good was it for artists to create paintings, poetry and music, when it could not make man any better? Art by the few, for a few. The dark, primitive, ugly human soul is just as primitive and ugly as it was the day that Cain killed Abel," thought father aloud.

With his hands behind his back, he was walking slowly beside mother through the lonely, abandoned fields.

"Did you ever think what the world would look like without those few?" she replied. "Nature is wasteful — look at the thousands of seeds shed by the trees — only a few will grow into beautiful and useful trees. So it is with the human race; many are useless or harmful, but some reach perfection. The war brought us starvation and poverty, which affects our bodies and to a certain degree our minds. But it must not corrupt our souls. It could give us the vermin, but it could not take away from us the pride in our family traditions, in our country's noble past, in our remembrance of the beautiful things we saw, of poetry we learned and books we read. We have fine, bright children, and they are good. Nothing can take away from their breeding, their brains and their sense of good and evil."

They walked for a while in silence. Then mother continued:

"I don't know how the world is going to shape up in the near future, what kind of life our children will have to face, but I know — I am sure — that they will have the moral qualities that will let them, if not to belong to the 'chosen few,' at least to appreciate them."

Walking a few feet in front of her parents, Irene could hear what they were saying. For the first time she started thinking as a child looking at the world not from the point of view of *events*, but of the *evaluation of events*. That overheard conversation of her parents — and maybe also the image of the pit wriggling with worms — had started a chain reaction in her mind.

Suddenly, Irene was no longer a child. She was only ten years old, but the problems of life and death had become different from the ones she had known until now. It is true that fairy tales were not always fancy and beautiful, but were often packed with cruelty, dangers from demons... witches and evil people. But life was not like that. In fairy tales, good was good, bad was bad. Everything was final. In life, the same events could look different to different people — she thought — and they could affect people and impress them in different ways.

Yes, that ten-year old undernourished girl with the thin, long legs and the lovely face had grown up. She was so deep in her thoughts that she did not pay any attention to the usual chatter of others around her. She did not notice that big clouds were racing above their heads and that the sun had disappeared. It began to rain. A sudden gust of wind lifted dust and weeds from the fields and started a melancholy dance, round and round. It grew dark and cold.

Janka and Irene were the only ones who did not have their coats. Somehow mother had not noticed this when they went out earlier in the day to play. Now they were hugging each other, trying to keep the rain and penetrating wind from their bodies while following the others to the camp. Suddenly, they felt a warm coat wrapped around their shoulders: it was Sophie. Spontaneously, without even the need to think, she had taken off her coat to protect her little sisters. Sophie was like that. Now they were all running toward the camp, as the wind and rain lashed at them. Then, it was father who took off his coat and wrapped it around Sophie's slender body.

"You will catch a death of a cold, my dear," he said.

They all stopped for a minute to catch their breaths. Irene looked at her father's face. She did not know whether it was a drop of rain or a tear in the corner of his eye.

At the end of two weeks, the people in the barracks were told to pack their things and board another train. This time the trip was short. On the second day, about midnight, the train stopped outside the eastern station at Praga — on the outskirts of Warsaw across the Vistula River.

Nobody had slept. They got out of the train and watched, enchanted and moved to tears at the glow in the sky from the lights of the city. Nobody spoke. They stood and watched until early dawn made the glow disappear.

They were home.

PART THREE: BACK HOME

Warsaw, 1918

CHAPTER ONE — Pauline

COUSIN Pauline was not mother's blood relative: she was married to Aunt Nathalie's only son, Bronislaw. The circumstances under which she became his wife were quite unusual — to say the least — so poor Pauline was never quite accepted by the family.

One late afternoon in the fall of 1910, Bronislaw, a handsome young student in his last year of law school, was to meet his mother at a fashionable dressmaking establishment, after which they were supposed to attend some engagement party together.

Aunt Nathalie, mother's eldest sister, was the only one who had not married a country squire. Her husband, of Austrian origin and the owner of a fine luggage factory, kept his business on the highest level of Viennese tradition. A refined and elegant woman, Aunt Nathalie preferred the gay social life of Warsaw to the quiet, somewhat dull country life of the Polish gentry. It was at her home that Irene's parents met, and under her influence, mother chose the city life, too.

Strange, how the most insignificant decision can alter someone's destiny. Like for instance that afternoon when Bronislaw was waiting in the carriage in front of the dressmaker's for his mother. He looked at his watch and seeing that he was too early, he decided to sit in the salon instead of waiting outside.

"Are you ready, Mother?" he asked, settling down on a plush red sofa.

PART III — CHAPTER ONE

His mother, in front of a large mirror, was being attended by two fitters. "I will be ready in a moment, Bronek," she replied. "Could you take it in a little at the waist?" she asked, turning to the attendant. "My waist is smaller than that."

"We will *try*, Madame. Pauline, make two pinch pleats."

The young woman, called Pauline, was sitting on the floor with her back turned to Bronislaw, pinning up his mother's dress. His hands crossed on his walking stick, Bronek looked with a bored expression at the fitting scene. But soon his eyes concentrated on Pauline. She was kneeling down, and he could see her small waist, young firm arms, and her neck between the collar of her dress and the blond fuzz of her hair.

"How about the hem? Is it straight?" asked Aunt Nathalie.

"We will check it once more, Madame," said the attendant. "Go ahead, Pauline."

Pauline, pushing a small pillow with her knees, started to move around Aunt Nathalie. From time to time she would stop, take a few pins from the hem and put them in a different place. She was now halfway around, and Bronek could see her pretty profile and her young, firm breasts. Suddenly he felt numb with desire for that girl who was leaning over humbly at his mother's feet.

The girl disappeared for a moment behind his mother's figure, then suddenly reappeared on the other side, facing the young man who was staring at her so intently. She blushed to the tips of her hair, lowered her eyes, and taking a few pins from between pink, tight lips, continued to work.

Never in his life had Bronek felt such a desire for a woman as at this moment. Like all wealthy bachelors, he had a small apartment in which he often entertained women visitors, but they were more or less "professional" *demi-monde* type girls whom you would have one day and forget about the next.

Aunt Nathalie disappeared behind a screen in the corner of the room and changed dresses with the help of an attendant. Pauline picked up loose pins from the floor and inserted them into a pincushion. She had time to throw a few glances at the young man who was still staring at her. How handsome and elegant he was! As a dressmaker she was constantly in contact with high class, well-dressed ladies, but she had never been so close to a "true gentleman." Picking up the pillow, she stood and looked at him for the last time. This time her face was not timid or blushing. Then she left the room.

"How long is the dressmaker's open?" Bronek asked his mother on the way to the party.

"Until six. Why?"

"Oh, nothing. I was just wondering how many hours these girls have to work."

"From eight until six… the usual ten hours; they get a tea break at noon."

Taking advantage of the large, crowded reception, Bronek made his appearance and promptly snuck out.

When Pauline left for home that night, he was waiting some distance away. He followed, and finally caught up with her.

"Do you know who I am?" he asked.

"Yes, I could hardly miss you this afternoon."

"Would you have dinner with me?"

She hesitated a moment, for she thought that is what a "high class" girl would do, then said:

"I guess it is all right."

In the restaurant they spoke of trifles, hardly aware of what each other said… he burning with sexual impatience, she concen-trating on proper table manners (Which fork to take? Do I hold the spoon right?). She wanted to make a good impression on him. He was so handsome, well-bred and desirable that she would do anything to get hold of him forever!

When they left the restaurant, reached his apartment, and crossed the threshold, she was fully aware of the point of no return for her. That by losing her virginity she would never be able to get a husband from the lower middle class to which she belonged, yet she could never dream of becoming a wife to this man… that Cinderella stories happened only in fairy tales. But she did not care.

Standing immobile in the middle of the room while Bronek was hastily removing her garments, she was burning with the same passionate desire to belong to him as he felt in wanting to possess her.

Pauline was not only to love Bronek, but to worship him. Whatever happened to her that first night, she never regretted. She managed to hide her pregnancy, squeezing her swelling body into a corset, and kept on working until the last day. Delivered by her mother of a baby boy on a Sunday, she went back to her job the next day, fainting a few times from the loss of blood and from exhaustion.

PART III — CHAPTER ONE

In the meantime, Bronek passed his last exams and started his law apprenticeship. He still lived with his parents, and still kept the bachelor's apartment where he met Pauline twice a week. Mother-hood had not spoiled her figure; she was only twenty and just as fresh and desirable as when he first met her. When Pauline became preg-nant for a second time, Bronek decided to tell it all to his parents.

"I want to marry Pauline. She is going to have another child."

"Over my dead body!" cried Aunt Nathalie. "Do you realize how this kind of woman can ruin your life?"

"What do you mean by 'this kind of woman'? She is a hard-working girl who has never known another man but me. Her only fault is to love me. She never asked me to marry her, or even to support the baby!"

"What I meant is that she has no education, no breeding. She will not be an asset, but a social handicap to your career."

"I agree entirely with your mother," said his father. "Give her enough money to support the children comfortably, but don't get involved in marriage."

And so, the second child, a girl, was born to Pauline, and it seemed that her life with two illegitimate children — the life of an outcast — was set for good.

About that time, though, Aunt Nathalie began to suffer from severe headaches that soon became unbearable. Unable to sleep for weeks, banging her head at the wall near her bed, she knew that there was nothing doctors could do for a tumor of the brain, operations of this type being unknown before the Great War.

On her deathbed, she told Bronislaw:

"I was wrong about Pauline. Marry her and give the children your name."

And so, "over my dead body," Bronek married Pauline. She moved into Aunt Nathalie's elegant apartment right away and took charge of the house and of her father-in-law, now an elderly gentleman retired and living on a handsome income provided by the sale of the luggage factory. But what seemed for Pauline the begin-ning of a happy married life was, in fact, the end.

"Mother was right," thought Bronek. "Pauline is impossible!"

She irritated him from the first day with her clumsy lack of proper manners, her lack of tact and authority with the servants, and her cheap suddenly-acquired snobbism — which is so typical for social climbers

— that well-bred people have no need for. Even her love, devotion and hero-worship, which used to flatter and amuse him during their love affair, were now constant sources of irritation and disgust. How can a man love or treat his wife as equal when at night she takes off his shoes and kisses his feet? Had he loved her, he would have tried to educate her and change her strong, primitive emotions into proper channels; but he did not care to. Without any violent scenes or arguments, he simply moved out, returning only occasionally to see his father or the children.

If Pauline suffered much after losing Bronek, she did not show it, just as she had not shown any mental pressure before their marriage. She seemed happy and took care of the children and her father-in-law. Whether becoming the wife of a lawyer and assuring the children of proper fatherhood was more important to her than Bronek's love, it was hard to tell. Maybe social status was all she cared about in her life. But, on the other hand, having been brought up in poverty and struggle, maybe she had simply learned how to control her emotions and not to expect too much from life. She seemed not to be hurt by the lack of invitations from relatives (including Aunt Juta and her sisters) and was very gracious and hospitable to anyone who cared to come to her home.

Mother, who often called Pauline an uneducated social climber and laughed at her snobbism behind her back, nevertheless treated her with kindness and consideration, visited her quite often (mostly to see her widowed brother-in-law) and always invited Pauline to all holiday receptions and dinner parties.

"After all, she is not to blame for the way she is, and she is a good and devoted mother," she used to say.

Pauline had remembered mother's kindness well, and she kept that in mind that October morning in 1918 as she walked from room to room in her apartment, trying to figure out how she was going to find enough beds and mattresses to put up a family of eight. Strangely enough, she did not consider it an unpleasant chore or bother. Actually, she was excited at once again seeing relatives who had spent four years in Russia, and her ego was uplifted as she realized that for the first time *she* was doing *them* a favor, and not vice versa.

"I will give my bedroom to Zofia and Aleksander," she thought, standing at the door to the room and looking at the twin beds. (Bronek's bed was still there and untouched after all these years.)

"Two children can sleep on the salon couches, plus two on folding beds... that makes six. Two more can be put in the bachelor's room — that's eight." (The "bachelor's room" used to be Bronek's before his mother's death, and later, after Pauline had moved there, her father-in-law's room.)

"Strange," Pauline thought, "how silly names cling to one's mind. 'Bachelor's room' — that's how the servants used to call it when I moved here."

Though Pauline had dismissed all the servants during the war, she was all ready and waiting that morning, when her children, playing on the front balcony, called out:

"They came! They came! They are here!"

Three *drozhki* were standing at the front gate, filled with suitcases, trunks and duffel bags, which the drivers had started to unload onto the sidewalk. Irene stood on the street with the rest of the family, feeling uneasy and embarrassed. The feeling of being uprooted and dispossessed had hit them more strongly at this moment than ever before.

Pauline ran down two flights of stairs and met them on the street. At other times mother probably would have thought that her greetings were too loud and her behavior lacking distinction, but at this moment her warm, outgoing and somewhat crude behavior was a blessing. It chased away that feeling of humiliation and embar-rassment and made easier the first few awkward hours of bringing things upstairs, unpacking and settling down.

"It is good of you to have us, Pauline," said mother. "We are an awfully big crowd."

"Nonsense. There is plenty of room. Father-in-law died last year, and I am all alone with the children now. I have no help, though. Bronek doesn't give me any extra money, and everything is more expensive now. So, except for a laundress who helps me clean a bit, I have no one."

"Don't worry, we will do everything ourselves. We did not have a maid for the past two years in Moscow either. You haven't changed a bit, Pauline," said mother.

It was true. She was maybe a bit more plump than before, but still young and attractive.

"But how your children have changed! Why, they are almost all grown up!" exclaimed Pauline.

"How ghastly they look! How thin they all are! How Zofia and Aleksander had aged!" Pauline thought. "You are all a little underweight," she said aloud. "Was the food situation bad?"

"Just about enough so as not to die from starvation," said father. "And how is it here under the Germans? Is everything rationed?"

"No, not everything. Bread is not rationed."

"You mean you can go to the store and buy *all the bread* you want?" exclaimed Irene.

"Yes, of course," Pauline replied. "Now wash your hands, and let's sit down and have a bite. You must be hungry." She continued, "How was the trip? How long did it last?"

"A whole month, my dear. Two weeks in a cattle wagon, two weeks quarantine, then a few more days in a cattle wagon until we pulled in last night at Praga Station," mother replied. "You are very, very good, Pauline, to let us stay here for a few days until we get an apartment. But you are the only one with such a big place. Helen and Tota could take us, too, of course, but it would be very awkward. A great part of their home is taken up — as you know — by their dressmaking business, and the salon is used as a waiting room for the clients."

"Yes," said father. "It is very kind of you. But I will rent an apartment right away, and as soon as we move the furniture from storage, we will stop imposing on you."

"You are not imposing on me, but don't be so sure that you can find an apartment quickly. Times have changed. Nothing new has been built in the past few years, though the population of Warsaw has been growing steadily, especially in these past few months since the Russian-German peace treaty. People whose ancestors have lived for centuries in the Ukraine, the gentry who lost their estates to the Bolsheviks, business and property owners, town officials — they have all come to Warsaw… and are still coming. There is a black market on many things. Profiteers and the newly rich are all trying to benefit from this situation. There is even a black market on apartments."

"What do you mean, Pauline?" exclaimed father. "How can there be a black market on renting an apartment in the city?"

"You can't just walk in and rent it, like in the good old days. You have to pay the equivalent of about two years' rent for the right to rent, and then you have to pay the monthly rent anyway."

"You... you mean, like buying it?"

"Yes, except that you don't own it, in spite of paying for it."

"But I simply can't!" cried father. "I have to pay the three years' expense for furniture storage, then I have to cover the expense of moving it all to a new place. Where will I find money for *buying* an apartment?"

"Try to look, maybe you will be lucky and get something without going to the black market — maybe away from the center of the city."

"I have to! I have to! I simply have to find something!"

For the next few days the parents were out hunting for a place to live, coming home each night exhausted and discouraged. How many flights of stairs had they climbed, how many streets had they walked?

"You were right, Pauline," said father. "Any decent apartment in the center of the city is beyond our reach. They all want a 'pay off', for which I have no money."

"Did you try the 'build-ups'?" asked Pauline.

"Build-ups" were new apartments added under raised roofs, in place of attics where the tenants' maids usually hung the laundry.

"Yes, we did look at some of them," said mother. "But they all have the same faults: they are too small for us, they are in old buildings without elevators — and after all, Alex is over sixty, and I am not young either. And, above all, you have to pay a year's rent in advance."

The children did not seem to take any part in their parents' worries. They enjoyed nice, comfortable and clean beds, and plenty of bread; nothing else seemed to be important. It was fun to walk the streets of the city and see that "nothing had changed," to walk into old familiar churches and feel as if the last four years had never taken place. The same old cobblestoned, pigeon-infested Old Square, with the narrow, Gothic and Renaissance style houses in the "Old City" quarter... The only new and different thing about the city was the cruel imprint of war: one of the beautiful bridges on the Vistula River had been destroyed, dynamited by the Germans — or was it the Russians?

While Helena went one day to enroll at Warsaw University, Irene asked her sisters to go with her to the park where she used to play before the war. They all agreed, mostly because it was in the fashionable

Aleje Ujazdowskie section, where all the so-called "little palaces" were built by Polish aristocrats. Many of them still would remain in private possession for years to come, but some of them would be converted to embassies of foreign nations.

How small the park seemed to Irene that day! As a child, she used to think of it as an endless jungle. She was sure that if Emily and Janka would suddenly disappear, she would never find her way to the gate! Now, the park was just a garden, more so now because the trees were barren of foliage, and one could see the large wrought iron gate from any part of it.

"How can that be?" Irene asked herself.

"Does everything during our lives change around us, as we change? Is nothing *really* big or small, important or not, pretty or ugly, desirable or repulsive — except how we feel or think about it? If everything depends on how I feel and what I think, how can I know what is *real?* How can I know what is *right?*"

She worried.

CHAPTER TWO — A New Home

"What are your plans for the future?" Pauline asked the children, as they sat at the dining room table after a simple dinner of potato soup and "piroshki" — meat-stuffed ravioli.

"I have two years of medical school behind me, and I hope that I will be able to get through with my studies in three or four years," said Helena.

"And you, Henry?"

"I want to study engineering, particularly the building of bridges and dams. But first I have to go through with the army, I suppose. I hope they will count my service in the Russian Army and make me an officer soon."

"I have one more year of school," said Stefa. "After that I want to go to the College for Librarians. I like quiet, orderly, systematic work, without pressure or hurry."

"I just want to be through with school," said Janka. "I don't know what I want to be."

"You are very young. You have plenty of time to think about it," said Pauline. "And so is Irene... or do you have any idea what you would like to do?"

Irene blushed. "Maybe I know what I would like to be, but I don't think that I could be any good at it."

"Well, well, there's plenty of time to make up your mind. Nobody knows at ten what she can do, or how good she can be. And you, Sophie, don't you know what you would like to do?"

"I would like to study medicine, like Helen, but I know my parents could not afford to put so many children through years and years of studies. I decided to go through nursing training. This will keep me in touch with doctors and patients, at least. Anyway, I don't have much time left. Whatever I do, I have to do right now…"

Sophie left the room and started to play with Pauline's children on the balcony.

"Sometimes Sophie makes me shiver," said Helena. "She talks as if she has only a short time to live."

On the fourth day the parents came back to Pauline's house early, and very happy, indeed. They had found an apartment! It was a "build-up," but in a modern building with an elevator, and the landlord wanted only six months' rent in advance.

"Aren't we lucky!" exclaimed mother. "Father already arranged for moving our furniture from storage tomorrow, so we can settle down right away without bothering you any more, Pauline."

How "lucky" they were, they found out within the next few days. The "modern" apartment had been hurriedly built, obviously only for profit, not for the tenant's comfort. All the rooms faced north, and the bathroom and maid's room had no windows at all. It was a cold-water flat, without any plumbing in the bathroom, which consisted of a drainless tin tub like they had in Russia. There were two tile stoves to heat the apartment, and no electricity… though the rest of the building was wired and, of course, the elevators were power operated.

Besides the eternal gloom of northern exposure, the view was dismal: the black, tin roofs of "back apartments," the small windows of laundry attics gaping at them, from which stray cats, dirty with soot, would now and then dash in and out… When you leaned out from the window, all you could see was the dark square of a courtyard. Well, at least the family had one comfort — modern plumbing in the toilet room! But this proved to be haphazard. The big city, accustomed to serving three and four-story buildings, was suddenly faced with additional water usage on fifth and sixth floors, and could not provide enough pressure to reach these higher apartments. At least not at all hours of the day. Often the family would have to catch water late at night in order to have an adequate supply for the next day. Mondays were hopeless, as it was laundry day, and water usage all over the city was unusually high.

If these hardships and inconveniences were not enough, there was one that proved to be the greatest nuisance, affecting everyone's morale. Apparently the chimney was not tall enough to provide an adequate draught of air. The kitchen stove, used morning till night, constantly backfired smoke. The smell of smoke with carbon monoxide, and the bluish mist in which all the things in the apartment seemed to swim, was a constant nightmare. Everything smelled of it: curtains, bed linen, clothes, even one's hair. On cold, rainy and windy days the smoky kitchen in which mother, with the window open, had to stay for hours with reddened eyes — and the rest of the apartment smelling bad as well — was depressing to all.

As Helena asked one day: "What kind of incompetent builder did this job? I would like to know. It is obvious that they could have built an apartment with southern exposure and an attractive view of this part of the city and suburbs. Instead they built this gloomy trap... while the corridor connecting the laundry attics has a lovely southern exposure with many windows!"

"It is not incompetence, my dear," said father. "It is cunning planning. A front apartment would impose bigger taxes on the landlord, which he obviously wanted to avoid. That's why we are connected with the front stairway only by the elevator shaft, and the kitchen entrance is the same as the one to the attic and backyard apartments. We are sort of... in hiding."

"Could we not at least have electricity? It is quite silly to still live in the kerosene lamp age," observed Helena, who felt particularly hostile that day to all the inconveniences of the house.

The landlord would not hear of extra expenses, so father scraped together the necessary money and had electricity installed. It was a crude job, with wires running outside the walls, with one lamp in each room, but it seemed quite a luxury to them.

Besides three bedrooms, there was only one other large room, which became not only their dining room but also partly absorbed the former "salon" furniture and the piano. In spite of this, it did not seem too crowded, and mother even put a bed between the breakfront and the window, behind a screen: it became her bedroom.

If for a while it seemed a bit crowded in the house, soon the situation eased. Henryk went back to army duty, and Sophie left for hospital training, coming home occasionally to visit. But life was far from easy: they were not allowed to use the elevator for any kitchen

A NEW HOME

needs. The garbage had to be carried six floors down the stairs, and the coal from the cellar, seven floors up.

Irene hated these chores, in which she, of course, had to participate like everyone else. To pack dusty, cold chunks of coal into buckets and carry them up each day was a hopeless, degrading chore. The lack of sunshine in the rooms was also depressing. Now, Irene could understand why people living in dark cellars had plants on their window sills, and kept them outside in a patch of sun for a few hours every day to let them grow... All of a sudden, she became obsessed with the desire to grow something, anything, in this gloomy house. She planted a lemon seed, which soon started to grow into a nice plant, and then a date pit from dates that Helena had received as a present. To her contentment, it started to grow into a small date palm. She also got cuttings of myrtle and geranium. From early spring, on sunny days, she would carry all the flower pots and place them outside in the attic corridor on the small, high window sills where they would bask in the sun. Sometimes she would bring a chair and look through one of the small windows at the city roofs below, or she would close her eyes just to feel the warmth of the sunshine on her face. The sun was so strong that she could "see" through her eyelids the pale orangey mass of their flesh and swimming specks of light.

As soon as mother had settled down after unpacking things from the four-year absence, and had found enough space for everything (the bookcase had to stand in the hall for lack of room), she faced the problem of finding a school for the girls. They had already missed nearly two months, as it was the end of October, and all the schools were in full swing. It was not as easy as that. First, the children needed new shoes and clothes, particularly new winter coats, as they had outgrown the ones from the previous year. Anyway, in spite of the severe winters in Warsaw, nobody wore heavy, interlined and padded Russian-style outer coats here: Warsaw belonged to Western Civilization.

Now things like coats were not bought at a store. One had to buy cloth, lining, interlining, buttons, and have it made to order — something that required not only plenty of money, but also time and planning. Somehow, father found the money for all these things, and one day early in November mother went to the private school for girls that Jadwiga had attended. The woman principal remembered Jadwiga well, and listening to mother's story about all the family's trials and hardships, agreed wholeheartedly to accept all three girls without a tuition fee.

"The only thing that they have to buy is books. That will be quite a lot of books, especially for your oldest daughter. If you think that would be too much of a burden on your budget *at the present time*," she said tactfully, "you can go to the Charity Organization, which provides second-hand school books, and other things, too." She gave mother an address.

Charity Organization! The words struck mother like a whip. They could have been hungry in Moscow, they could have been living under awful conditions during the trip back home... that was something out of their control. But to turn to a charity organization now seemed more degrading than anything she had lived through.

"Be reasonable. Be practical," an inner voice said. "Which is worse — a false pride, or money set aside for food to be needlessly spent on books? Do you have a right, after years of semi-starvation, to skimp on food because you are too proud to get second-hand books from some organization? How far can you strain your budget? What do you expect from your husband — miracles? Moving expenses, six months' rent, an electrical bill, winter attire, shoes for the whole family... it is good that he got his job back, in spite of his age..."

The next afternoon mother told the girls to come with her "to get your books." She did not specify where; they took it for granted that it was to be a bookstore. Each girl had a list of books, as given by their teachers.

Instead of a bookstore, however, they came to an apartment on the main floor of a building: two poorly-lit rooms, one full of clothes, the other full of books. A nice woman greeted them and helped them find most of their books, which shortly all three girls were holding under their chins in a jumble of criss-crossed arms.

"Is there anything else you need?" the woman asked. "How about clothing or shoes?"

Mother hesitated... "Perhaps some galoshes; the melting snow and mud will ruin their shoes so fast..."

They found some galoshes in good condition that fitted nicely, and thanking the woman, they left.

Outside in the hall, the half-nude, pseudo-Greek figure holding a lamp was staring indifferently at them from her niche. Abruptly, mother turned toward the niche, put her elbows on the pedestal and started to sob.

The girls stood around, at first indifferent, then embarrassed. Janka sat down on the steps leading to the first floor and showed her impatience by stamping her rubbered feet on the wooden step. Stefa just stood there, without any expression on her face.

Irene pulled mother's sleeve.

"Let's go home, Mother," she said softly. "These books are very nice."

CHAPTER THREE — Sweets

When in November of that year the Armistice was proclaimed and German troops disappeared from the streets of Warsaw overnight, nothing spectacular took place. For the first time in one and a half centuries Polish soil was without oppressors: German, Russian, Austrian... or anybody else. But the fate of the country, strangely and always unjustly dependent on European conference tables, was still unknown. Although there was no starvation, the food situation was not good. There were shortages, black market activities, abuses. For someone with plenty of money, it was all right. For Irene's family, it meant many restrictions and limitations. The dinners were simple but adequate. Breakfasts were tea and plain bread (no butter or jam), and supper was always the same: barley soup. It was cheap and healthy, and barley, like bread or rice, has a plain taste that you don't mind including in your daily diet.

At noon recess in school, the girls were always munching their "second breakfast" — some sort of sandwich — and as no drink was provided, you had to eat it "dry" and then get a drink of water in the washroom later. Irene could bring only two slices of dark, plain bread. It was too dry to swallow, so she got used to pouring a few teaspoons of water between the slices and putting in a few pinches of sugar; in this way it was edible.

One of Irene's friends, Hala, always had a crisp, white roll with butter and ham inside. Irene could hardly remember the taste of a white roll from prewar days, but still her mouth watered at the sight of the roll and the pink, fat ham that overlapped it on all sides.

"I love dark bread!" Hala cried one day. "What do you have inside?"

"Butter and honey," lied Irene, her heart pounding.

"Oh, I love honey! Please swap with me!" She was pushing the roll with ham toward Irene.

"I don't want it! I don't want to swap!" cried Irene. She could not give the plain bread, soggy with water, to Hala. She could not let anyone know what she had been eating all this time.

"Oh, come on! Be a good sport!" Hala laughed, still pushing the roll in front of Irene's mouth.

"I told you, I don't want it! I hate rolls! I hate ham! I hate it! I hate it!"

She was all red in the face and ready to cry. All the girls, especially Hala, looked at her in surprise: it was not like Irene. She was very easy to get along with, had a good sense of humor, and was a real "good sport."

"All right, all right, excuse me," said Hala in a hurt voice.

"I'm sorry, but I really couldn't eat your roll… I have some allergy of some sort… I would be sick," Irene lied again.

Irene felt mortified, doubly mortified: first, that she was not a "good sport," and second, she wanted so much to eat that roll!

Now Janka did not have to be jealous of Irene. What could make her jealous? Irene did not sing or dance or recite poems any more, and as for looks, she was now just about as ugly as Janka. The new teeth seemed too large for that skinny face; the once big blue eyes with long eyelashes seemed small now, sunk deep into the skull. The blond, curly hair was darker and kept in one long tress, accentuating the thinness of her face. Sometimes in a daydream, Viera would appear in her white ballerina dress and look at her with dark, serious eyes… Or an aria from some opera would run through her mind persistently for hours and hours. But it was all like a long-forgotten dream, and you could not remember how it began and how it ended…

Her growing body, disturbed by the arrival of the last molars, was craving for extra food, for sweets. True, she was not starving, as in Moscow, but three simple meals a day, plus bread munched at school, was not enough for that fast-growing body. She especially craved sweets, which were never on the menu at home. The temptation arose each afternoon after school, when coming home she would pass a woman peddler with a tray of candies. But Irene had no money. There were all sorts of candies on that tray, but most of all the square milk-chocolate dairy candies attracted her. One morning, as Irene was cutting her bread for school and mother had gone out of the kitchen, Irene quickly opened mother's bag, took out a small coin, and hid it in her pocket. It was enough to buy two candies the first day, two the next, and one on the third day.

They tasted awfully good, but the feeling of being a thief did not leave her for a moment. The children were taught two things above all else by their parents: not to steal, and always to tell the truth, no matter what the consequences. Now, her conscience was bothering her for the first time in her life, bothering her far more that she would expect! Lying to Hala about what was in her bread... taking that small coin from mother's purse... She knew that if mother could, she would buy Irene as many candies as she could eat — or give her money, if only she could afford it.

"I just have to put that coin back in Mother's purse," Irene decided. "But where to get the money?"

One day after school she walked with a few friends along Nowy Świat (New World) Street, and parting with them at the corner of Saint Cross Street, started to walk home.

Saint Cross Street, whose name was taken from the nearby church around the corner, was lined with antique shops exclusively. Silver, china and miniatures were displayed in every window. There were also books — rare books, collector's items, second-hand books, and medical, legal and school books. You could buy nearly anything, and also sell nearly anything when you needed money. Anything that had to do with antiques, jewelry or books, that is.

Later at home, taking her coat off in the hall, Irene's eyes fell on the bookcase. It was a beautiful piece of furniture in the Empire style, made of fruitwood and filled with all the old and rare books that father had brought to the city years ago after the death of his parents. All were leather bound, mostly first editions of German, French and Polish writers and poets, and some translations of English poets like Lord Byron and Shakespeare.

Irene took out one book, spread out the others to conceal the empty space, and hid it among her school books. The next day after school she walked into one of the shops on Saint Cross Street. The man looked over the book carefully and gave her the price. It was probably a fraction of its value, but to Irene it seemed an astronomical number: it was enough to buy candies for six weeks and still give mother back what she had taken from her purse!

She was quite happy, walking all the way home and feeling all that money jingling in her pocket. But when she came into the house, the books in the hallway seemed to stare at her in silent condemnation.

CHAPTER FOUR — Danse Macabre

In spite of the gloomy, smoky apartment and the many chores that had to be done because there was no maid, mother, after the day's struggle, would often sit down in the evening at the piano and play her modest repertoire. All the music sheets had survived the storage: Tchaikovsky's "Romance" and *Chant d'Automne*... Chopin's "Easy Pieces"... Paderewski's "Minuet" and the waltz from the opera *Faust*.

There was one waltz* — "Danse Macabre" — with the Polish subtitle: "Dance of the Skeletons." Every time Irene listened to mother play it, she could see the same picture, or rather scene, taking place in front of her closed eyes. The first part was slow, sad, melancholy music. She could see an enormous, dark hall in a castle, with many doors both in the background and on left side of the hall, and a grand, sweeping staircase. Moonlight is coming in through long, narrow windows on the right side of the hall. In rhythm with the melancholy waltz, ghosts start to gather in the hall — some glide from upstairs down the staircase, others appear through the closed doors...

Now mother is playing the second part, which sounds louder, lower in key, and more rhythmical than the first: One-TWO-three, one-two-three, one-TWO-three, one-two-three, one-TWO-three, one-two-three, one-TWO-three, one...

Ghostly skeletons form a circle and start dancing, shifting their loose joints, grinning and grinning; they divide, forming pairs and keep dancing, keep dancing...

Mother plays the third part now, which is the same, sad melancholy tune as the first. The ghosts, leaving each other's embraces, start gliding toward the places from which they came and disappear. One last pair is still dancing in the middle of the floor... slower and slower, until they become part of the moonlight beam...

---

* by Saint-Saëns

DANSE MACABRE

Mother had not touched the piano for the past five years, and the cold Russian winters had made her fingers quite stiff. It had a bad effect on her piano-playing, but it seemed to Irene that the stiffness in playing "Danse Macabre" was not an impediment: it brought out more than ever the stiff, eerie, rhythmic qualities of the music.

One-TWO-three, one-two-three, one-TWO-three, one-two-three, one-TWO-three, one-two-three, one...

Besides book reading and visits to the museums, there was not much the family could afford in those days in the way of intellectual entertainment. Sometimes they went to the Sunday matinee concerts at the Philharmonic Hall. After a while, the concerts became a weekly must for Irene, but they did have one bad effect on her cultural development in the world of music. The programs were — though perfectly performed — too "popular." Over and over it would be Tchaikovsky's *Nutcracker Suite*, Grieg's *Peer Gynt* and such, with a few loud numbers by Mendelssohn, Liszt or Wagner thrown in. It took Irene quite a few years of attending evening concerts to free herself from this type of music and to discover the immortal qualities of Bach, Haydn, Mozart, Handel, Schubert...

Opera was out of the question. The box was too expensive, and somehow it did not occur to anybody that there were four tiers of balconies in the opera house where one could get reasonably priced tickets. It was "the loge" or nothing. Apparently, some "cultural" customs could not be uprooted even by war and its aftermath.

The only other source of entertainment was the cinema. All the girls, even Helena, became deeply obsessed with it. Almost all the time the question was whether to buy a new pair of badly-needed stockings, bathroom soap... or go to the movies. It was always the latter that won. On Sundays, half the day was spent mending stockings: "We are lucky the fashion is for high-laced shoes, not Marie-Antoinette style slippers," Helena once observed. And the soap in the bathroom would be a cake of ordinary laundry soap. But the longing for movies after six days of school — the need to get out and forget for a few hours their surroundings and hardships — was stronger than reason.

The girls could not afford the brightly lit, softly upholstered movie houses on Marszałkowsa Street. But there were a few cheap movie houses where the programs were good: plain, unadorned long halls with small, stiff wooden chairs and clickety-clack pianos.

It was the era of movie "serials," and one would simply rather die than to miss the second part of *Count of Monte Cristo* or some story about an Arab sheik in love with a British girl. Someone would be playing "appropriate" music on the piano. Apparently there were only a few sheets of music available, as they were used over and over again for each consecutive movie. It was always the same "piece," played fast and violently when the elements were against the heroes — be it storm, wind, sea tempest or erupting volcano. Another piece was used in love scenes — something à la Tchaikovsky. Finally, a third — something from Liszt — was used every time there was an escape and hot pursuit of the innocents by the villains, or vice versa.

Sitting on hard chairs and listening to music played by unskilled hands, the girls became absolutely absorbed in the handsome, courageous hero's exploits. There was no smoky kitchen, no carrying coals seven flights up, no mending of stockings. All that existed was a wonderful world of make-believe. No amount of inherited culture or acquired knowledge could, at that moment, replace the need for an escape from reality. The movies were a sort of mass therapy in those days; they were not a source of entertainment alone, but a fountain of rejuvenated spirit.

These were crude, naively directed and performed movies, the ones that a generation later would watch as "classics" in convulsive laughter. Yet the later mid-century sophisticated public would not realize how much they were missing: their later slick, super-colossal and expensive movies could never let them forget that they were watching a movie. The actor would be charming, the actress sexy, the *mis-en-scène* costly, but the audience would always be aware of "film making." In Irene's time — as one of the factors of post-war psychology — people had to believe in things unreal… and make them real, like children often do.

CHAPTER FIVE — Summer, 1919

How much the children took for granted the things that their parents were doing for them! That first summer after the war, father would not think of making mother and the younger girls stay in a sunless apartment in the city. In spite of his six-day-a-week job, the heavy burden on the budget caused by Helena's medical school fees and her costly books, he did not hesitate to find and rent a suitable apartment in the country. It was not a whole house, as it used to be before the war, but there was no need since Helena had a summer job, Henryk was in the army, and Sophie was in nursing training at the hospital.

The summer place was not far from where they had rented before, but there were no rural settlements, no thatched roofs, no small fields or pastures in sight. The enormous, privately owned forests and fields, apparently belonging to some local estate, spread endlessly in all directions. It was good to roam again through the forests and pick berries, to walk through the fields along narrow, high-grounded paths and pick wild poppies, or just brush by or caress the full, nodding spikes of wheat or rye with one's hands.

Combing her hair in the morning, in front of a small country-style mirror, Irene liked what she saw: the delicate, oblong, suntanned face, the shiny eyes and the red lips. There was no trace of that haggard, ghost-like expression on her face that she had worn for the past few years. They were eating simple but healthy food, the freshest dairy products, and things that grow, picked mainly in their presence. That is why all of them regained so quickly fresh complexions and felt so well.

One Sunday, Father, Henryk and Sophie all came together to the house for a visit. Irene had never seen her father in such good spirits: he was so proud of his children! Henryk had just been named first lieutenant; how handsome he looked... so big, strong and sunburned in his neat officer's uniform! Sophie through her training was now officially called a "Sister of the Red Cross." She wore a uniform and a band on her arm with a red cross on it. The same kind of insignia was attached to her coat sleeve.

That was one of the rare days when they again felt like one family, without thinking about hardships — past, present or future.

"Well," said Henryk, holding Sophie's arm, "as you can see, we are all set. All we need is a new war to put us to work."

Everybody laughed. It was the year 1919, a year of the Treaty of Versailles. The thought of another war seemed something incredible. It will not happen in a hundred years!

Henryk brought a book for Irene as a present. It was *The Origin of the Universe and Man*. Together with science books that she had been reading for the past few years, it completed, for the time being, the first stage of her education beyond school books. She was immensely grateful that Henryk considered her grown up enough to buy her an adult science book.

He brought a box of chocolates for Janka.

CHAPTER SIX — Goodbye to Father

Father was getting hard of hearing, and Janka invented a cruel sport in which she found consolation and escape for her hidden hostilities. When father would ask her something, she would mumble unintelligibly so that he had to ask:

"What did you say?"

At that, Janka would shout right into his face in that ugly querulous tone of voice, which made father's face twitch with pain.

One day father was looking for something, and seeing Irene in the room, asked her for it. Irene was in an ugly mood that morning, and something made her act like Janka. She mumbled an answer under her nose, and father said, "What did you say?" With that she turned around and shouted the reply right in his face.

He gave that sorrowful, quiet look and left the room. What Irene did not know was that Sophie had seen the whole scene through the open door. Irene had never seen Sophie angry in all her life, but now she came and stood in front of Irene, her eyes flashing with anger.

"How dare you behave like that!" she said, almost in a whisper. "How will you be able to live with deeds like that on your conscience after he dies? You will wish that they never happened, but nothing will help you undo them."

Suddenly, she changed her voice completely.

"Be good to Father," she said gently, "because he is going to die soon."

Ashamed and sorry for what she had done, but not ready to admit it either to Sophie or to herself, Irene was glad to change the subject.

"How do you know that he is going to die soon?"

"I just know."

"Nonsense! Father never had a cold or even a headache in his whole life."

"Irene, I beg of you, be kind to him. Don't be like Janka."

"You are right, Sophie. Do you know... I feel terrible."

"If it hurts *you* more than it hurts him, then I am sure that you will not do it again. I am leaving tomorrow to start my nursing job, and I have a feeling that I will never see Father again. So be kind to him for both of us, will you? He is a lonely man."

He was a lonely man. All his life he had been a quiet, simple hardworking man. He lost both his parents early and moved into the city with his three sisters. He was "head" of a family at sixteen — Aunt Juta was only eight years old then. They lived the first few years on the remnants of a modest inheritance, getting the best possible education, helping each other. Marriage, which brought ten children into the world, meant work, hardships and tragedies. Three children were buried, seven had to be brought up and educated. The war and its aftermath were more cruel than anybody had expected.

Now he was sixty-two and tired, very tired. There were days when, coming home from the office he felt so exhausted, he could hardly speak. Yet at home only hostile indifference awaited him. An irritable, tired wife, struggling with the hardships of a limited income and discomforts of the apartment... and children, each one living his or her own life... hating life for all it failed to give them.

"Why did we drift apart? We are not starving any more like we did in Russia... when we were also strangers under one roof. For a while, after our return from Moscow, it seemed that we became one family again, but it is gone now. All is gone. My life is gone..."

Of all the children, Sophie was the only one who showed a spark of feeling, but Sophie was now away. Irene, who used to be close to her father, had changed suddenly into a restless, defiant and growing child.

Besides that feeling of exhaustion — which at his age was perhaps a normal symptom of aging — his dental plate was bothering him, or his teeth, or his throat. It was hard to tell exactly where it hurt, but lately it hurt so much that he could not sleep. He would have to see the dentist tomorrow, he decided.

"No," said the dentist. "Your plate can't cause you any trouble, and your teeth are all right. I would suggest that you see a surgeon."

He was told by a leading surgeon that he had a growth in his neck and throat, and that it should be removed at once.

Irene was told about her father's coming operation, but it seemed such a trifle. Everybody knew that kidney or abdominal operations, or amputations, were serious, but a throat operation was something as minor as tonsils or adenoids!

When she came home from school the next afternoon and was told that father had gone to the hospital to be operated on the following day, she cried, "Why didn't someone tell me before? I did not kiss Father goodbye!"

She had not kissed his hand, as she had done all these years when parting. Suddenly she felt panicky, like years ago when she had watched her father walk down Miedziana Street with a suitcase. He was gone! He was gone, and she had not kissed him goodbye!

The next day mother came home from the hospital: the operation had been successful, but father was very weak and could not swallow. On the third day, Irene went outside after dinner. It was February* and still very cold, so she stopped at a friend's house, and, feeling restless, she persuaded her friend to go out with her. They bought some cream puffs at the pastry shop and devoured them on the spot. After that, gay as larks, they ran to the top floor of their building and started ringing the doorbells all the way down to the main floor. They hid under the stairwell, giggled and listened to all the doors opening, and to the surprised voices of people asking each other who might have rung the bell.

Irene came home in a happy, boisterous mood. Knowing that she was a little late for supper, she undressed hurriedly and went into the dining room. But she noticed that the table, set for supper, was undisturbed. The soup tureen was covered, and the plates were clean. She saw her mother, sitting on the piano chair, her face hidden in her hands. All the girls were huddled together on mother's bed.

"Father died tonight, Irene," said Helena in a quiet, solemn voice.

Irene felt numb; she could not say a word or show any emotion. She sat down on the nearest chair at the table, automatically lifted the tureen's cover, poured soup in her plate and started to eat.

---

* The year is 1920.

PART III — CHAPTER SIX

There is a belief that a man dying a violent death, as from drowning or hanging, sees his whole life flash before him in the last few seconds of consciousness. Irene, facing death so suddenly — though not her own — was now experiencing something very similar.

All those times in her life that were connected with the presence of her father were now flashing through her mind: from earliest childhood when he gave her a "ride" on his knee, through holidays, name-day dinner parties, his coming and going to work, his face when he was reading a book at night, his way of walking with his head tilted to one side...

She was lifting the soup spoon in rhythmic, methodical movements, unaware that she was swallowing food. She could distinctly hear father playing the piano and singing Schubert's song. Now she could see his face the day she shouted at him because he could not hear... She finished her soup and got up.

"You are a heartless, cruel, selfish child," she heard Helena say, trembling with indignation. "By all means, have another serving!"

Irene left the room. She threw herself on the bed, but could not cry.

If Irene's mother was the vessel in which her life had been created, then her father was that spark of God that had given her life. She now felt like a plant whose roots had been cut off... still healthy and living, yet devoid of the source of life. The plant may grow new roots and survive, but for a time the shock of the amputation will be shattering.

When she saw her Father in the open coffin before the funeral service, he seemed so different. They had shaved his moustache for the operation, and it had changed his profile. She came and for the last time kissed his cold, folded hands.

"I loved you very much," she thought. "I am sorry I did not tell you that many, many times. I loved you very much."

CHAPTER SEVEN — Scarlet Fever

It was a winter with an unusually heavy snowfall. The sidewalks were more or less clear, with the snow piled up high on both sides, making them look like tunnels. The roads, however, were simply left as they were... mashed and remashed, cut and recut with sleigh runners, trampled on by horses' hooves and by the feet of pedestrians, who in crossing streets jumped foolishly trying to find smoother, steadier places for their feet.

It was also a winter when the number of scarlet fever cases reached epidemic proportions. Many girls in Irene's school were sick, and a few of them died.

All the private schools for girls were now state owned, tuition-free institutions called "State Schools." All except one: the Countess Plater School, which had survived and was still catering to high-class students.

The schools not only did not lose, but actually gained by being nationalized. They had excellent curricula and professors, many with doctorate degrees in physics, science or mathematics. They prepared the girls broadly and efficiently, so that at graduation they were ready to study at the University those particular subjects of their choice and interest, without wasting time on general subjects. Even such subjects as psychology and logic were taught during the last year of school to complete a general education.

But Irene was only thirteen, and there was a long way to go (it seemed to her) to finish school. That particular day she did not feel well at all: a sore throat, headache and nausea had been pestering her since morning. By the time noon recess came, she could not stand the sight of girls eating their sandwiches. She ran to the washroom and became ill. In spite of that, and feeling drowsy and weak, she managed to stay until the end of her classes. Then she had to walk for half an hour through the cold, brown slush in the streets to reach home. Her feet, it seemed, were not walking on snow, but on melted butter... her legs felt rubbery... sinking, sinking...

"I don't feel well, Mother. I don't feel well at all..." she said upon arriving home, and then she collapsed.

Mother must have been at her bedside constantly, because every time Irene half regained consciousness, she could see her mother's face swimming somewhere near the ceiling. Mother was terrified: she had lost two babies to scarlet fever. To her it was a symbol of death.

When on the second day the scarlet blotches appeared on Irene's body, there was no longer any doubt. It was against the law to keep at home a child with scarlet fever, so Helena notified Children's Hospital. Two men came, wrapped Irene in a blanket, and carried her to the elevator. That was all that she remembered.

When she awakened a few days later, she was in a large room; some green plants were on two sunny sills, and on her right and left stood two beds in which girls were sleeping under neat hospital blankets. The girls later proved to be very nice. One of them had been there for many weeks, sick with rheumatic fever as a result of scarlet fever, and the other, like Irene, had to face a six-week quarantine.

At those times, doctors believed that this disease was "catching" through peeling of the skin, and that this process, especially slow on the feet, lasted six weeks. Also, it was believed that in order to best prevent complications like deafness, rheumatic fever and kidney trouble, the patient had to be kept on a strict diet. No meat. Milk was permissible, but ironically, in the Children's Hospital no milk was available at all, at least not to children of Irene's age.

For six weeks all that she was fed was oatmeal, mashed potatoes and mashed turnips. Day after day, oatmeal in the morning, potatoes at noon, turnips at night. The girls, long since completely well, were not allowed to move from bed and were kept on that rigorous diet. At the beginning they had a lot of fun together, playing "word" games, composing silly poems, and such. Halfway through the quarantine they were so hungry and obsessed by the thought of food that they could talk of nothing else, and all the games and poems became exclusively about... food.

When after six weeks Irene came home, she was a few centimeters taller, but she looked again like a living skeleton. By the time mother's food had put a little flesh on her, and she had returned to school, she realized that she would never be able to catch up with her class. Latin, mathematics and history particularly would require intensive study, and for that Irene not only lacked the physical strength, but also simply did not care. It was agreed between mother and the school principal that Irene would attend class to the end of the year, but that she would be required to make up for her lost time by repeating her class the following year.

"There is no tragedy in staying back; you are much younger than the average student. You can still finish school ahead of other children your age," said mother.

CHAPTER EIGHT — Bolshevik Invasion

All spring, mother was concerned about what to do with Irene during the summer months ahead. Watching her daughter move her flower pots out on the attic window sills, seeing her sitting in an open window, dangling her feet outside to the dismay of horrified onlookers in the backyard apartments, mother decided one day to enroll Irene in one of the free summer camps provided by the city. Janka was too old to apply, so she had to stay with mother.

It was a very primitive camp, and the children slept on straw bags on the floor. The food was simple, but plentiful. There were no camp counselors, except the head of the camp and a few women in charge of cooking, serving food, and so on. But instinctively from the first day, the older girls took care of the younger, shy and homesick ones. There is no better substitute for a mother than a warm, under-standing older child. The camp ran smoothly, and all the children were healthy and happy.

The most popular game resembled "cops and robbers," except that the children were divided into "Poles and Bolsheviks." The fights were so violent that Irene, tied to a tree with ropes one day, almost strangled herself before she managed to escape.

While the children at the camp were playing "make believe" war, another real, bloody war was going on at full swing in their country.

General Piłsudski, who was the head of a Polish Legion during the past war, realized that — as most Poles did — that the Treaty of Versailles, which assured Poland of independence, did not mean much unless the Poles built up their military strength and fortified their frontiers. No matter what the moustached and bearded gentle-men around the conference table decided, Poland was still a nut caught in a nutcracker, with the two arms being Germany and Russia pressing in on each side. Germany — at least temporarily — seemed the lesser threat, but the vast, flat frontier with Russia was a constant menace.

General Piłsudski wanted the land of the Western Ukraine to belong to the Poles... the land which for centuries had been Polish and which was soaked with Polish blood from countless battles; the land where cities, towns, churches, estates and all the cultural aspects of Western Civilization had been built by Poles. Century after century, Polish kings had led armies in defense of this land against the Tartars, the "Moscals" and the Cossack hordes.

But once again, this time it was the Bolshevik hordes, spilling over the frontier like hungry locusts, pushing west, west, west. And hungry they were, literally: the famine in Russia, especially in certain areas, had reached its peak, leading to cannibalism in some instances. The Bolshevik soldiers were told: "Go kill, destroy, rape and fill up your stomach in the *burzhui* land." By the time Irene returned from camp, which had been hastily closed in mid-summer, the growling of long-range cannon fire could be heard in Warsaw all day: the Bolsheviks were moving in to take the capital.*

Sewing rooms were started at their school, where girls made soldiers' shirts and underwear. Irene followed Janka the first day after coming home from camp and volunteered to do some sewing.

"Aren't you a little too young to do that?" asked the teacher. "Do you know how to operate a sewing machine?"

"Yes, I do," said Irene, though actually she had never been closer to a machine than she was when watching Helena. The machines there were not hand operated like the one at home: they were pumped by leg. But Irene did a good job. Part of the day you spent on sewing; then you had to make button holes, sew on the buttons, or make a "charpie." For a "charpie" you had to bring old, soft and pure linen sheets, cut them into small pieces and pull out all the material, thread by thread, to make a fluffy pile. This was the best dressing for wounds: it let the sore breathe, and it did not clog and stick as much as cotton did. It was easier to cut it off from the dried, bloody wound while changing dressings. Anyway, even if it was not better than cotton, it would have to be used because cotton was too expensive. Everybody could spare an old linen

---

* August 12th 1920

sheet and turn it into a bag of "charpie." In this way, tons and tons of charpie were collected all over the country.

In the afternoon the girls cut countless loaves of bread and carried them in big laundry baskets to the soldiers' "refreshment center."

It was a pretty town square in the suburbs. Large kettles filled with sweetened tea stood in a row, and the baskets of bread were placed on both sides. Here, each afternoon Irene poured countless jugs of hot tea, spilling a lot on her fingers, which became painfully red and swollen from abuse.

The soldiers that she was serving were not the colorful, brave heroes she imagined them to be years ago. Their drab, dirty, torn uniforms were often incomplete, and the haggard, unshaven faces were expressionless. They did not speak at all, just took a few slices of bread, a jug of tea, and as soon as they were through eating, they dropped to the bare sidewalks or to the round patch of green lawn in the center of the square. Completely exhausted, they went to sleep.

"Is Henry like that, too?" Irene wondered. He was fighting, but they had not had any news of him. They did not know exactly where he was.

She remembered that day, a year ago, when he brought her the book during vacation and had said, jokingly, while standing next to Sophie: "All we need is a new war to put us to work…"

Well, Sophie was put to work, too.

All the nations of Europe were watching with indifference the valiant struggle of Poland against the Bolshevik hordes. All, that is, except France. France did not send any troops, it is true; she had bled her youth to half-extinction during the Great War and could not afford to bleed more. But she sent a staff of capable generals, who together with Polish officers and chiefs-of-staff, drew plans for an offensive. From then on, the Bolsheviks, instead of rolling forward with the capital of the invaded country in sight, started to retreat. Once on the defensive, they were forced to withdraw toward their frontier with high casualties. The Polish Army, with ten centuries of tradition — intrepid, tough and brave soldiers, agile cavalrymen — had shown once more what determination, audacity and high ideals can achieve in the face of overpowering numbers. It was the same desperate determination they had shown in crushing the Teutons at the battle of Grunwald in 1410, in fighting and destroying the Turks at the siege of Vienna in 1683, and in the countless battles with the Cossacks, Tartars and Swedes, before, in between and afterwards.

Even after the partition of Poland, the Poles twice staged bloody uprisings in the nineteenth century: outnumbered by oppres-sors, fighting with bravery bordering on insanity for the cause impossible to achieve — freedom. So it was nothing new for Poles to fight and believe in victory when the odds were against them, and this time — when the cause was not *regaining* but *preserving* the freedom of a country brought back to life only the year before by the Treaty of Versailles — the spirit of fighting for a just cause was stronger than ever.

Polish units were pushing forward, with heavy casualties on both sides. Just behind the front lines, Red Cross hospital units were rolling; first aid stations for the slightly wounded (who were, of course, sent back to combat), operating rooms for emergency cases, while the severely wounded were sent by endless trains to the hospitals of Warsaw. Wounded prisoners had to be separated from wounded Poles.

Attached to her Red Cross unit, Sophie had moved all the way across the country from Warsaw to the eastern frontier. It was hard, high-strung and unmethodical work. One worked as much as one could without collapsing, and snatched some sleep whenever one could... the constant arrival of new casualties, sorting, attending, getting hospital trains ready for departure to Warsaw. And operations, operations! Head wounds, abdominal wounds, chest wounds, amputations... eight, ten, twelve hours a day. Sophie often left the operating room dizzy, unsteady on her feet. Not that watching operations affected her mentally — long ago she had become used to the sight of gushing blood, torn mutilated bodies and the stench of gangrene. She had been forced to build up an armor of indifference in order to preserve her sanity. But as a nurse-anesthetist, she inhaled chloroform and other fumes hour after hour, and this, together with the lack of sleep, made her feel weak.

Quite often she would go out and walk for a while, letting the cold wind penetrate her light nurse's garments. Her legs starved for exercise in the fresh air. It was as if she were trying to get rid of not only the operating room odor, but of all the suffering and misery she had witnessed during the day. How many "unfinished" operations had she witnessed when the soldier died halfway through the surgeon's efforts to save his life? Yes, she had grown accustomed to blood and pus, but not to death. To the wounds, but not to the suffering. Premature death... useless suffering.

"... Am I going to lose my leg, doctor?... Am I going to be blind?"

"Who on earth sent this soldier here?" cried Sister Julia in a highly irritated voice. "Are they blind? He is a Russian and belongs in the POW pavilion."

"It's no mistake, Sister," said one of the orderlies. "Sister Sophie sent him here with this card: emergency."

"Yes, that's correct," said Sophie, entering the room. "He is a shrapnel abdominal case, and if he does not get immediate attention, he will die. Get all these men ready for the operating room. The doctor says that we will start in half an hour."

"But this one is a *Bolshevik!*"

"I just came from the POW pavilion. They are so behind in emergency cases that he would not have a chance..."

"So, what do you care? He is a *Moscal,* Sister Sophie."

"He is a badly wounded man, that is all I care. Leave it to me, Sister Julie. I will talk to the doctor..."

"... It is against the rules, and you know it, Sister," said the doctor. "But what can I do? You are my right arm; if you are determined to have him operated on, what can I do? I guess I will survive this..."

"Your Russian protégé is lucky," he said later, finishing the operation. "Neither his liver nor his kidneys are damaged. With so many pieces of shrapnel in his guts, it is simply incredible. There. He is all patched up. If only infection does not set in, he might live."

"Do you believe in fate, Doctor...? I do."

"You mean, for instance, that if this man is meant to live, he will. If not, he won't, no matter what we try to do about it."

"Something like that."

"No, I don't. How can you be sure... how can you be a nurse and believe in fate? Is it not illogical? On the one hand, you fight to save lives; on the other, you believe in predestination?"

"I simply have an urge to do things for people. And I believe that I am part of fate, which can bring something good to their lives. *It is* unreasonable, I'll admit."

"No, Sister, I don't believe in fate. I know, for instance, that if drugs were invented for the prevention of postoperative infections, we could save many lives. And the same thing is true if we could do something about shock or the loss of blood... I feel not like a doctor, but like a butcher: cutting their limbs, pulling out their guts, and later watching helplessly for postoperative complications to kill what I tried to save…"

"You are not a butcher, Doctor. You are a priest, and through your hands fate speaks its will."

"I give up, Sister. You have to have the last word…"

"My name is Konstantin…"

"I know your name from the chart."

"They call me Kostya. And you must be Sister Sophie."

"I am. But why did you say 'must be'?"

"Because only someone with a face like yours could have done what you have done for me."

"_____?"

"Sister Julie told me that I would not be here and would not have been operated on if it were not for you."

"As soon as you are better, you will have to be moved to the POW section."

"What is your *otchestvo*, Sister?"

"Aleksandrovna"

"Sofia Aleksandrovna… I was sent to this war — I was told: go, kill Polish *burzhui*, they are your enemies. But I did not see any enemies. I saw soldiers fighting and dying for their country. I met a doctor who saved my life… I met a nurse who was kind and compassionate, as if I were not an enemy, but one of their kind. Something is wrong…"

"War is wrong. Hatred is wrong. I have to go now. Keep sipping water, will you?"

The doctor was doing hurried rounds: temperature? Pain? Can the stomach hold liquids yet? He stopped at the Russian's bed, lifted the sheet, and lightly pressed his abdomen through the dressings. "Does it hurt?"

"Yes," he grimaced.

The doctor told Sophie later, "I am afraid that your Russian protégé is not going to make it. His abdomen is swelling and his temperature is rising. By tonight he will be running a high fever. You'd better ask him about his relatives."

"Isn't there *anything* that we could do further...?"

"How many hours a day do I operate?"

"About three times as long as you ought to, Doctor."

"How many hours a day do *you* work and sleep?"

She did not reply.

"You work too much; you sleep not enough, isn't that true?"

She still did not say anything.

"Do I have the right to waste my time, your time, other nurses' time on one patient who with the best of care would have a *one-in-a-thousand* chance to live through peritonitis?"

She still did not reply.

"We operated on him — he had his chance. How many boys are waiting for their first chance?"

"You are.... right, Doctor."

When she came to see her patient later after her duties, his face was flushed with fever, and he appeared to be unconscious. She put a wet compress on his forehead, and after a while he opened his eyes. Sophie gave him a sip of water, but he soon spit it back.

"I love you... Sofia Aleksandrovna."

"Of course you do. All soldiers love their nurses," she replied, sponging his neck and face. "We are a symbol of your wives, mothers, sisters, sweethearts... or *whoever* you left behind."

"I did not leave anybody, Sister."

He spoke slowly and softly.

"I love you not because you are beautiful, but because you are good. Kiss me just once, Sofia Aleksandrovna...."

He fell into an unconsciousness, into a sleep from which he would never wake up.

She stood there for a while, then suddenly leaned over and lightly touched his hot, dry lips with hers.

Henryk came back from the army and enrolled right away at the Warsaw Polytechnique. He had been discharged because of a leg wound that had healed quickly. All that was visibly left — of what the Bolshevik invasion had done to him — was a slight limp. This soon disappeared entirely.

Sophie, on the other hand, came home in such a bad state of health that her mother asked Uncle Sigismund to come and see her. Uncle Sigismund had aged suddenly this past year. He and Aunt Juta had lost one of their sons in the Invasion.*

That is how it was referred to by the Poles: *the Invasion*. Not *a war with the Bolsheviks*. War happens in the history of nations, when both sides declare the war, not when one of the countries is brutally invaded without any reason or warning. Poland had — once again — rid itself of a ruthless invader, but how many of her youth were dead?

"How long has this illness been bothering you?" asked Uncle after examining Sophie closely.

"Oh, I did not have much chance or time to think about it. I have had bronchitis many times in my life, but this time it does not seem to be going away… and I have such a pain in my left side."

"No wonder. You have pleurisy, my dear. What hurts you is the fluid collected in your chest. You have to stay in bed until it is absorbed. After you get well, I would definitely suggest that you change your job. Forget about nursing; it's not for you. Your lungs are not in good shape. You need plenty of rest, regular hours of sleep. Get yourself an office job."

"I was thinking about becoming a country school teacher."

"It's a tough job, too. Our schools for peasant children are very primitive and overcrowded. But at least you will have fresh country air and regular hours of sleep."

"I already sent in my application. Thank you for coming, Uncle…"

---

* Władek

CHAPTER NINE — Letter from Lubyanka

"I have been thinking for a long time, Vlodek. Now that Russia is no longer at war with Poland, perhaps we could go back to Warsaw?"

Jadwiga and Vlodek were in their beds, staring at the dark ceiling, talking in whispers so as not to wake Tadyo. His bed had been moved into their bedroom, the only room they could call their own. All the other rooms had been occupied for some time by "supervisors," young arrogant communists without any training, experience or education in engineering. Niania now slept in the kitchen; they had to share the dining room with all the others.

"I have been thinking about it, too, Yadunya," replied Vlodek. "I know that *they* are keeping me here only as long as they need me: but these "supervisors" are learning fast. In fact, I have no executive powers of any kind. I do what I am told. The only difference now between me and the factory worker is that I know more about engineering."

"Then let's try to get out of here. I miss my family terribly, and you must be homesick for your family, too, aren't you?"

"Yes. But the question is: can we leave this country safely? Do we have the right — in the eyes of the Bolshevik regime — to leave? Is it safe to let them focus their attention on us? Things are deteriorating here; we see now that the Revolution has changed into a reign of terror by a ruthless clique. They arrest and kill people without right or method. To stay here is not safe, but to try to leave might be even more dangerous: we must consider the pros and cons and decide carefully which road to choose."

"Let's see. I was born in Warsaw, have Polish parents. Does this not give me the right to go there? You were born in Warsaw, too. Your father was Russian, but your mother is Polish. She lives in Warsaw and so do your two sisters. Does this not give you just rights to leave?"

"Don't be a child, Yadunya. Forget what is 'right' and 'wrong', 'just' or 'unjust' when dealing with the Bolsheviks. What counts with them is whether one is *useful* or not, or an enemy of their regime, or a collaborator. What they will think about my wanting to leave their heaven, I do not know. But tomorrow I will start carefully sounding out the possibilities."

Vlodek was surprised to find so much cooperation and understanding. His resignation was accepted and his plans to leave the country approved.

Now the day of departure was set. There was not much to do, except pack a few suitcases. The "supervisors" decided that all the furniture and other belongings should "gladly" be left to them by the departing *tovarishch*, so there was no question of trying to sell anything.

Jadwiga did have some money, though, withdrawn from the bank at the beginning of the revolution and kept hidden at home. She also had some jewelry.

"They won't let us take anything out of the country. They might even make a personal search. What shall we do? We will need the money and jewels badly in Poland until we settle down and I get a job." said Vlodek a day before departure.

"I know what I will do," said Niania, opening her suitcase. She took out a corset that she had not worn for years. "If an older woman like me looks a little stouter in the waist, nobody will notice. Let's sew all the money and jewelry inside the corset lining."

All day and into the late evening Jadwiga and Niania sewed, preparing the corset. Niania added her own savings, too, and the money she had gotten from selling all the silver spoons on the black market in Tula. They were the ones that Irene had been so shocked to find in her suitcase one day in Koslovka.

"We are all set," said Jadwiga. "It is our last night in Tula. With God's grace we will be in Warsaw in a few days. Is it not hard to believe?"

They went to bed happy, and exhausted by all the last-minute packing, soon fell asleep.

In the middle of the night Niania was awakened from a deep sleep by a pounding on the kitchen door. She threw a *shuba* hastily around her shoulders, thinking, though half-asleep: "some machine must have broken down at Zavod." But when she opened the door and saw several soldiers with carbines, her legs trembled. "God have mercy on us… They have come to arrest him," she thought.

The soldiers pushed her aside, walked down the long corridor, crossed the dining room and walked into the bedroom, opening the door with a loud *bang* that seemed to shatter the still of the night.

Niania, who had followed the soldiers, stood barefoot, wrapped in her shuba and shivering nervously. The "supervisors" must have supplied the soldiers with a detailed plan of the apartment. They not only knew where the bedroom was, but even found the electric switch in the dark without hesitation.

"What is that? What is it? Who is it?" cried Jadwiga, sitting up in bed.

"You… get dressed and come with us, *Tovarishch,*" said the leader harshly.

Jadwiga, seeing Vlodek getting out of bed, made a move, too, but, embarrassed, pulled the bedcover over her nightgown.

"Not you, just him," said the leader.

"You stay here and don't move… or say anything," whispered Vlodek, dressing hurriedly. Putting on his socks and shoes, he managed to lean over to Jadwiga and whisper further, "Leave tomorrow if they let you. Get Tadyo and Niania and *leave*. Remember, *leave!* Don't wait for me. I will clear this up and join you later. Do you hear me, Yadunia? *Leave* Tula tomorrow!"

He kissed her and Tadyo, who had slept through it all. Leaving the room, he gave Niania's shoulder a pat.

"Take care of yourself, Niania. Take care of them, too."

His voice was hoarse with emotion.

The soldiers left, this time by the front door. All was quiet. So quiet. Niania came and sat down on the bed next to Jadwiga. They sat like that, staring into the darkness without saying a word, until the gray dawn started to creep into the room through intricate designs on the frost-covered windows.

Niania and Tadyo left the next day for Warsaw, but Jadwiga decided to stay.

"I can't leave him, Niania. I just can't! Maybe I will be able to help him. You get Tadyo safely to my family, and give them money from the corset… if you manage to get through with it."

Day after day, Jadwiga went to *Zavod* asking about the fate of her husband. Nobody knew anything. "He does not work here anymore," was all that she was told.

She went to live with Kolia's mother. "I am trembling for my husband's safety, too" she said. "We are all going to be eliminated one by one by the Communists: we are *burzhui* capitalists. What can one do, Yadviga Aleksandrovna?"

After a few weeks Jadwiga managed to learn that Vlodek was not in Tula. He was sent to Moscow. "He is in the Lubyanka Prison," she was told.

So Jadwiga took her little suitcase and went to Moscow. There she stayed with Maria Ermeyevna, but all day, from morning until night, she kept a vigil at Lubyanka Prison.

She left papers at the prison office that she brought from Tula, certifying that she was the wife of a former chief engineer of *Tulski Zavod*. She also left her present address and a letter begging for an interview. Although she was told that she would be "notified" about the date of the interview, she went there each morning, walking along the dirty prison corridors or sitting on a bench in a cold, drafty anteroom that smelled of mahorka tobacco. She simply could not stand to wait for the news in Maria's house.

"If they see me there every day, maybe they will talk to me sooner," she said in a miserably uncertain voice when Maria tried to persuade her to stay each morning.

"You hardly eat or sleep, Yadviga. You can't go on like this."

"No, no. I am all right. You see, first of all I have to know for sure that Vlodek is in *butyrki*, and then I have to talk to them and tell them that it is all a mistake, that he is innocent, don't you see?" She kept saying this every day with the stubbornness of a maniac.

When she got too tired of waiting, and became dizzy from the mahorka fumes, she would go out and walk along Lubyanka Street, back and forth, back and forth. Sometimes it was snowing, and sometimes the sleet — pushed by the biting wind — pricked her face… a pale and tired face… and accumulated on her small felt hat and in the folds of her caracul fur coat. Long after sunset, when the cold became more severe, she would go home, where Maria would be waiting with a hot samovar. Jadwiga would drink a few cups of tea, hardly touch any food, and exhausted, she would go to bed. The next morning, the same vicious, hopeless circle of daily activities would begin again.

After a few weeks, Jadwiga became so tired and so used to this schedule that it seemed to her that nothing existed in the whole of Russia, nothing was happening in the entire world, except what was going on inside Lubyanka Prison. A year or two later the highly organized police system would not tolerate what was happening in these days... what happened that particular afternoon. But the aftermath of the Revolution was still fresh, and the Communist system was working in a hodge-podge manner... Jadwiga began to recognize the faces of officials and workers within the prison building. Some crossed corridors with papers, opening and closing doors, appearing and disappearing, and drinking *chai* as in any office building. She recognized the old man with a broom who swept up cigarette butts and emptied the spittoons.

Among the faces now familiar to her, she recognized more than the others a man in his thirties, not bad looking, though his appearance was far from that of a high class, well-bred Russian gentleman. But he was typical of the new class that had emerged after the Revolution.

"He must be one of the top men here," thought Jadwiga. He never carries papers to the other rooms; they are brought to him. When he leaves his office, it is probably for a conference, a hearing, or to go to the washroom. If I could stop him and talk to him..."

But she did not have enough courage to do it. He walked briskly, with that artificial, built-in authority that men suddenly acquire when they rise in position.

Around four-thirty that afternoon when Jadwiga was walking in front of the prison, she saw him come out. He took a streetcar, and she took the same. When he got off, she did the same.

"Izvinitye menya..." ("Excuse me...") said Jadwiga, catching up to him. The man turned his head abruptly, thinking that he was being approached by a prostitute, but seeing a tall, svelte woman without makeup in an expensive sable-collared fur coat, he stopped with a puzzled expression on his face.

"Vy chto khotitye?" ("What do you want?")

"You work in *butyrki*, don't you?"

"What if I do?"

LETTER FROM LUBYANKA

"I go there every day. You see, my husband was arrested a month ago, and he is there — so I was told..."

"If he is there, he apparently deserves it. What is it to me?"

"No, he is innocent. He was an engineer in Tulski Zavod, a very good engineer. Then, we wanted to leave the country, and he was arrested. I left my papers at the prison, asking for an interview, but I have not heard anything for weeks. I thought, perhaps... you would be kind enough to see what could be done... to call me for a hearing... as soon as possible."

They stood now under a lamppost in a circle of light — two isolated figures on a deserted street. He was watching this young, pale woman with enormous, luminous eyes looking at him so imploringly. She had a strange, unearthly and intense beauty. It reminded him of when he was a child: there was an ancient icon in the *tserkov* of his home town, and during services he use to stare into the face of the Mother of God...

"I live here. Why don't you come in and tell me about it?" All the rudeness in his voice was gone...

"You are home? It's Misha..."

An elderly woman appeared in the hall when he opened the door, but seeing a strange woman coming in, too, quickly disappeared.

'Eto moya mat'. Moya zena umerla." ("That's my mother. My wife died.")

He opened the door to his bedroom, lit a lamp on a bedside table, let Jadwiga in, and closed the door. Apart from a few pieces of furniture, there was a large bed in the middle of the room on which there were soft, square pillows.

Misha sat on his bed, listening intently, while Jadwiga, sitting stiffly on the edge of a chair, told him about Vlodek.

"... What I would like to know is whether he is in *butyrki*, and to let him know that I am here in Moscow waiting for his release — and I would also like to be able to talk to someone about him to speed up his trial," she finished. Her face was no longer pale; it was flushed with excitement, and also from warmth as she was still wearing her coat.

"I will do what I can," said Misha. "You write a short letter to your husband, *in case* he is there. Give me a few days to check up — we have a lot of prisoners there, you know — and I will also try to arrange your hearing soon. But don't expect miracles. I can't act too conspicuously, or I may find myself where your husband is now," he laughed cynically. "But take off your coat. It is warm in here."

"No, thank you. I have to go."

She wrapped herself even more tightly in her fur coat.

"You are not going yet. You will write a letter to your husband first, ah?"

"Oh, yes. Of course."

"You write now; I will bring some tea," he said, pointing with his finger at the small table where there was an inkpot, pen and some paper.

She wrote:

> Dearest: I am in Moscow, staying with Maria. I tried for a long time to contact you and to get an interview with officials in the prison to clear up your case. After so much waiting I hope to be able to see you and help you. Please write me a short note letting me know how you are. Did you have any hearing or are you still waiting for your case to come up? Niania and Tadyo left as scheduled. I love you and hope to be with you soon. I miss you so much!
>
> Jadwiga

She was folding the letter when Misha came back with a tray. He brought glasses of tea, a plate with slices of bread and sausage, and a bottle of vodka. He made her take off her coat. She felt so tired and weak from lack of food and sleep that she felt that she would faint.

"We will have a bit and a little vodka, eh?"

"No, thank you. But I will have a glass of tea."

He leaned over her, placing a glass in front of her. A faint odor of perfume, which Jadwiga used to apply to her sable collar, hit him in the nostrils. The scent of the perfume mingled with the scent of a woman's warm body. Blood rushed to his face. He pulled her up by the arms and kissed her.

"*Nyet!*" she cried, running toward the door. But he was there first, blocking the door. He swung around, pushing her toward the wall.

"*Nye nravitsya?*" ("You don't like it?")

"If I slap him and try to run away, he will not help Vlodek. He can ruin him. He can get *me* arrested." All this went through her mind in a flash.

He kissed her again. "*Nye nravitsya?* Ah? A few years ago you would not even talk to me… *barynya* ('lady'). Well, now you not only have to talk to me, but kiss me as well."

She could see the bloodshot eyes near her own eyes, the strong cheek bones, the uneven, widely-spaced teeth. His body was pressing her body against the wall. She was out of breath, and feeling weaker and weaker, until a black veil of unconsciousness enveloped her body.

When she came to, she found herself on the bed, half undressed. Misha was trying to make love to her.

"Don't get hysterical," she said to herself. "Don't scream. Don't think. It's for Vlodek, do you understand? For Vlodek. To help him get out of *butyrki*. Don't scream. Think of Vlodek, Vlodek, Vlodek…"

But it was no use. That heavy, unwashed body, full of sweat and belonging to a strange man, made her stomach turn. It was an empty stomach, as she had not had anything to eat since morning, so she did not get sick. Instead, a strange sound came out of her throat, something between a moan, a scream and a gag.

Misha stopped for a moment.

"*Nye khorosho?*" ("Not good?")

What did he mean by that? "Are you not well?" or "Don't you feel any pleasure?"… She did not know. With body and mind devoid of any feeling, her lips kept repeating:

"No, no… very nice… *khorosho, ochen' khorosho…*"

"I am so worried about Yadviga," Maria said to her husband, clearing the dishes after dinner. It is forty-eight hours since she got home from the prison, and she has not gotten out of bed since."

"Did she say anything special? Maybe she got bad news about Vlodek."

"No, to the contrary. She said that she was able to write to him and that she was supposed to come three days later for information about him, and to have a date fixed for an interview."

"Well, you see, there is nothing to be worried about. She is probably catching up on some sleep and rest. People usually can stand tension caused by unhappiness for a long time, but when the tension is relieved by a happy event, a physical and often mental reaction occurs."

"I hope that you are right. We will see tomorrow, when she will have to get up to go to Lubyanka."

"Did she eat anything?"

"Yes. I had to feed her like a baby, though. She would make no effort to feed herself."

The next day, Jadwiga got up at noon, washed and dressed herself meticulously. She had a strange, faraway look in her eyes, as if in some hypnotic trance, but otherwise she acted normally.

"I am glad that you are better," Maria said. "You have to get some strength."

"I have to get some strength," she repeated.

"Why are you going so late?"

"I have to be *there* after office hours. Goodbye, Maria."

"I wish you luck with all my heart, you know that."

Vlodek was sitting on the floor, holding a short, worn-out pencil and a small piece of paper — two precious things given to him by a guard. From time to time, he took Jadwiga's letter from his pocket and read it again. He knew it by heart now, but he still followed avidly with his eyes every word, every letter written by his wife's hand. He had lost much weight, and his suit, which he had not taken off day and night for the past five weeks, was hanging on his wasted body like a crumpled sack.

In a cell the size of an average room there were thirty-one other men sitting, standing or crouching on the floor. Except for a bucket in the corner, which served as a *pissoir,* there was nothing else in the cell; there was no room anyway.

"What shall I write to you, Yadunia?" he thought. "That I feel hopeless and discouraged. That every time a prison guard comes, we all tremble, afraid that our name is going to be called? That those whose names are called never come back again? That new people keep coming and coming? That one of my cellmates has been here six months because his papers got lost somewhere, and he is not on the list but afraid to bring it to the attention of the guard? That I have no alternative but either to rot here, eaten by vermin, or to be shot? That at night we hear shots coming from the prison yard, which we all know means only one thing: death again for someone else?"

He tried to find a smooth place on the wall, or enough room on the floor, where he could write. He finally had to creep toward the door, and on his knees, pressing the paper against the rough wood, started to write:

LETTER FROM LUBYANKA

Yadunia, dear:

Your letter brought so much happiness to my life. I was dismayed to realize that you did not join your family, but I cannot hide, selfish as I am, how much it means to me to know that you are here. Don't worry about me. I am all right except for losing a little weight, but as I was such a husky man, I can take it. I did not have a hearing yet, but maybe they proceed by alphabetical order, so my name might be at the end of the list.

Next fall ~~would be~~ <u>will be</u> our tenth wedding anniversary. I want you to know how happy my life has been with you. I was hoping that we would see our son grow up to be a man, that we would face old age together; maybe we will. If not, I will still die a happy man, because I had you in my life. Tell Maria and Boris how much I appreciate their true friendship. I love you.

Vlodek

CHAPTER TEN — Class Enemies

She was holding Vlodek's letter in her trembling hands, standing in the middle of Mikhail Ilyich's room. She folded it carefully, as if it were a thousand-year-old museum manuscript, and put it inside her pocketbook.

"Well," asked Misha, "did I not keep my side of the bargain? Ah? You write him, he writes you."

"Thank you. Thank you very much."

"I also spoke to Comrade Razinov; he will see you next Monday at nine o'clock."

She forgave him everything. She forgave him the rape of her body, the torment of her soul. How much would her miserable body be worth if she were unable to save Vlodek?"

"I am grateful to you."

He came toward her. "Do I get a little kiss for that?"

She stood quietly with her eyes closed and let herself be kissed. Suddenly, he fell to his knees, put his arms around her waist, and pressing his head into her body, cried in as strange, ridiculously dramatic voice — like a third-rate actor in a Shakespearean play:

"Moya prekrasnaya koroleva!" ("My beautiful queen!")

"What am I going to say?" Jadwiga asked herself in panic while looking at the clock hanging on the mustard-colored wall. The small hand was on the nine, the large hand was moving toward twelve.

"What *should* I say? How to begin?"

For weeks she had rehearsed in her mind, going over and over what she was going to say to the interviewer, but now, as the hour drew near, her mind went completely blank. Her tension grew, when hour after hour she sat there and was not called in. Ten, ten-thirty, eleven, twelve. Tea and food were brought to Tovarishch Razinov's room. She sat there, numb, discouraged and tormented in turn, then numb again.

Suddenly Misha appeared and passed the anteroom. He saw her but pretended not to recognize her. He stopped at Razinov's door, hesitated for a moment and entered. A short while later, after he left, Jadwiga was called in.

Razinov's office had the same dirty, mustard-colored walls and shabby, dusty furniture as outside. He did not ask her to sit down, so Jadwiga stood, clutching her bag to steady her trembling hands. Razinov was sitting comfortably with arms outstretched on the desk, pretending to read some papers. He was trying to get rid of food particles stuck between his teeth with a sucking, sometimes whistling noise. He was a man in his forties, with a pale, sickly face and unkempt beard.

After a long pause he suddenly lifted his eyes, stared at Jadwiga for a while, then began to read: name, so-and-so, wife of so-and-so, lived in Tula, present address at so-and-so. Jadwiga replied "yes" each time.

"What do you want?"

"My husband was an engineer in Tulski Zavod from 1914 until six weeks ago. He was performing his duties with competence and experience, doing more than his share, working overtime, especially during wartime when armament production had to be greatly accelerated. He served this country well. He asked permission to resign and leave for Poland where we both have relatives. The permission was granted, yet just before our departure he was arrested without reason..."

"What do you mean, *without reason?*" interrupted Razinov. "When *we* arrest people there is always a rea—son!" he shouted angrily.

"What I mean is... if the reason for his arrest was to check up on his background, or his right to leave the country, he should be allowed to speak for himself and be given the right to defend..."

"You are telling *me* what we are supposed to do?" interrupted Razinov, sucking his teeth louder than ever, and passing his tongue from one side of his mouth to the other, checking on the remnants of sausage that were bothering him.

"I am doing it all wrong," thought Jadwiga. She said aloud, "Of course not. I do not question the efficiency of the People's

Government. I came here to... to beg you to bring my husband up for a hearing."

Comrade Razinov, concluding that sucking would not remove the food from his teeth, now put two fingers into his mouth, pulling several times at spaces between his teeth and looking at the tips of his fingers to see what he had removed.

"... I am sure, if you would only be so kind as to talk to him..." continued Jadwiga ("He is not even listening to me," she thought in desperation) "... you would find out that he is innocent."

Razinov still was pulling out food and staring at the tips of his fingers.

"I am doing it all wrong. Where is my gift of persuasion?" she asked herself. Vlodek once said that she ought to have been a lawyer... that she would never lose a case.

Suddenly a blind anger and desperation possessed her. Anger and hatred for that disgusting man, picking at his teeth.

"Is it such a crime..." she shouted, "is it such a crime to want to go back to one's own country, to go back to a place where one was born?!"

Razinov got up suddenly, half-opened the door and mumbled a few words to the soldier standing by the door. Jadwiga stood, clutching her bag. "Maybe I did convince him after all? Maybe they will bring Vlodek here, and I will see him. Maybe they will let him free right now..." She thought of all this with a painful intensity.

But when two armed soldiers came and told her to follow them, she knew what it all meant. The battle was over.

"Your luck has run out on you, Jadwiga," she said half-aloud, as if talking to someone. She felt as if her soul did not belong to her any more, as if the woman walking uneven steps between the two soldiers down the soiled, mustard-colored corridor was not she... but a stranger.

Razinov came into Misha's room and sat on the edge of his desk.

"I have arrested that woman you sent me. She is a *nastoyashchaya burzhujka* ('genuine class enemy')."

"You arrested her??"

"Yes. By the way, how come you know her? What is she to you?"

Misha's face turned white as a sheet.

"She is… nothing to me. I don't know her."

"Then, why did you ask me to give her a hearing?"

"She was… pestering me a few times on the street. I thought that I would send her to you. I knew that you would take *proper care* of her," laughed Misha.

"Aha."

Razinov left the room, thinking what Mikhail Ilyich had said — and that he had laughed somewhat too loud when asked about the woman.

"If I had the time, I would have to check on him," he thought, sitting down to his desk once again…

Maria was mending socks in the dining room. Her husband was at an evening "indoctrination" meeting that would be dangerous for him *not* to attend. Yura was in his room doing homework.

Two weeks had passed since Jadwiga had gone for the hearing at Lubyanka and had never come back. What had happened to her? Maria never found out. She was afraid to go there and ask. She was involved enough, as her address was on all of Jadwiga's papers. She had no right to endanger further the lives of her husband and son. In the still of the evening, the ticking of the clock reminded her more than ever that every passing second brings one closer to death.

The doorbell rang. Maria opened the door and saw a stranger, a young man who walked in without being asked. Without introducing himself, he handed her a small package.

"I used to know your friend Yadviga Aleksandrovna," he said. "These are her wedding and engagement rings. I thought maybe you would like to keep them. She died yesterday."

Maria's throat tightened. She barely managed to say:

"Was she…?"

"No, she died of pneumonia."

"Ohh…"

"I was thinking, maybe you have a picture of Yadviga Aleksandrovna you could spare for me?"

She went to the next room and brought back a picture in a leather frame. Taken a few years before, it showed Jadwiga wearing a light summer silk suit and a large, flowery hat. Standing with a parasol, she was smiling coquettishly.

The man held the picture and looked at it for a long time.

"Who is this man with the face shrunken in pain who cared to have Jadwiga's picture," thought Maria. "Did *you* help her get news from her husband?" she asked.

"Yes."

"Why?"

He did not reply, still staring at the picture.

"And her husband, what about him? Can you help him?"

"Her husband was shot the day she received his letter through me."

"You knew that he was dead and yet you arranged an interview for her in spite of it? Why?"

He did not reply.

She looked at his tormented face, and suddenly understood.

"... You have been using her! You sent her to a hearing, knowing that she could not save her husband, but you sent her... so that she could be grateful to you! Is that not it? Is that not it?"

"Ostanovitye eto! Mnye i tak tyazhko na dushe!" ("Stop it! There is such a heavy burden on my soul!")

Maria tore the picture from his hands.

"Get out! Get out of here! Get out!" she shouted half-hysterically... "Get out!"

Even after he left, she was still pounding at the door with her fists, as if it were not a door, but a living thing, a repulsive monster that she was trying to destroy.

"Why aren't you eating, Misha? If you keep drinking vodka without any *zakuska,* you will get drunk."

"I want to get drunk."

"What happened? *Nyepryatnosti?"* ("Any trouble?")

"No. Don't worry. Soon I will be on the very top of things."

"You *must* have had some trouble at the office."

"The trouble is... do you know... in the Bible...?"

"The Bible? I thought you did not believe in God any more, Misha."

"I don't. But remember the night Christos was caught and brought to trial, one of his disciples was asked three times if he knew him, and three times he said: 'I do not know this man.' And he did not help Christos — because he was afraid, because he was a coward."

"So, what is that to you, Misha?"

"I am a coward, too. I was asked if I knew someone, and I said no, and I did not help... because I am a coward."

"Everybody is a coward at some time, my son."

"I am not your son! I am a *sukin syn!*" ("Son-of-a-bitch!")

Misha's mother did not have any idea what he was talking about. "You are getting drunk. Eat something!"

"Leavemealone... leavemealone..." He lifted up his glass of vodka and mumbled: "Long live Mikhail Ilyich... *sukin syn* and coward."

He dropped the glass, and with uneasy steps walked into the bedroom. He fell on his bed and buried his head in a pillow, trying to trace the faint odor of perfume.

CHAPTER ELEVEN — Magdalena

Spring invaded the country early. One night in February came a violent storm and torrential rains, which washed out all the snows of the winter.

"Peasants believe that everything starts with the first thunder," said mother. "You will see. There will be an early spring this year."

She was right. In March, usually windy and cold in this part of Europe, heavy clouds would race low in the sky, shedding rain mixed with snow. The sun would occasionally come out, embracing the shivering earth and stirring life, and the warm air would suddenly bring out the smell of the awakening soil, almost fragrant with its unborn flowers. Such sunny days, occasional to be sure, were called "pre-spring" and were cherished by many — even more than spring itself. But soon the clouds and wind would take over again, and winter would reassert its hold on nature.

Not this year, however. This year the month of March was warm and mellow, as if someone had torn off a page of the calendar, and one winter month had become lost and forgotten.

"There was a letter from Sophie today," said mother one day when the girls came back from school. "She wants you to come up to Kłosowo for Easter vacation."

"Why is she not coming home for Easter?" asked Janka.

"She says that she has a cold and has to catch up with her correction of the children's papers, but the truth is probably that she wants to avoid a long trip after her illness. What do you think about going, girls?"

"I would love to!" cried Irene. "I don't know that part of the country, and I want to see Sophie's school, and... anyway spring is so early it must be beautiful up there!"

"I guess I would like to go, too" agreed Janka.

The doorbell rang and Janka, who opened the door, brought in a small, registered-mail package that was addressed to mother. Mother opened it. Inside there was a letter, folded many times, and when she unfolded it, two rings fell out — Jadwiga's rings. Mother's heart was pounding, and her hands trembled. She put on her glasses and began to read aloud:

Dear Zofia Marcelevna:

It is with a heavy heart in sorrow that I have to announce the death of Yadviga, who died of pneumonia on February 27th. I am sending this letter and Yadviga's rings through someone who expects to be in Poland soon. You will know better than anybody else how beautiful, charming and gifted Yadviga was, and how she was loved by everyone who knew her. But what you do not know, Zofia Marcelevna, is that before she died she reached the sublime heights of heroism and love. No suffering was too hard, no sacrifice too great for her to endure for Vlodek.

In the end God took everything away from her, but he spared her at least the knowledge that her sacrifice and suffering had been in vain. She did not know that Vlodek had been shot, so maybe she died happy. I don't know because I could not be with her when she died. I will always remember Yadviga.

Affectionately
Maria

"Poor, poor Jadwiga," wept Janka. "She was always so lucky, and yet she had to die so young."

Mother started to weep, too. "How am I going to tell it to Tadyo? How do you say things like that to a little boy?"

Tadyo, who had arrived safely with Niania the month before, now lived with Vlodek's family.

"Don't cry, Mother," said Irene. "Sophie once said that maybe it is not important what we did in life, but what we *were trying to do*. Maybe Jadwiga died happy."

The train stopped. The long sign read: ALEKSANDRÓW KUJAWSKI. Irene jumped out first, then Janka, carrying a small suitcase.

"Let's see," she said, looking at the drawing Sophie had sent by mail. "We are supposed to cross town, pass the church, take the main country road past the cemetery, turn left and walk along the side of the road until we reach the school."

"Sophie wrote that as soon as we leave town, we will be able to see the school building because it is standing all alone in the middle of the fields."

"I wonder why the school is not in some village."

"Maybe it is easier for the children from several communities to reach it."

As soon as they left the town and took the country road, they found themselves in the middle of endless fields and meadows. Some were green with growing rye, others dark with fresh, upturned soil. It was warm and sunny, and the breeze was whistling gently in their ears. They stopped and started to dance, like two little children playing "ring-around-the-rosie."

"Aaaah! That fresh air!"

"Listen to the meadowlarks! They have already come back!"

The district of Kujawy in the north was one of the richest parts of Poland; it was wheat country, with many large estates belonging to Polish gentry. As to the peasants, some owned land and were able to get along well, and some were poorer. Some had no property at all, working on big estates as hired hands.

Like each separate district of the country, the peasants had their own folk costumes, songs and music, and a famous dance called the "kujawiak." It was as popular as other Polish dances, like the "mazurka," "polonaise," "oberek" or "krakowiak," many of them immortalized by Frederick Chopin, who had spent his childhood in his native land. These simple folk tunes, interwoven with his genius, became part of him, and they haunted him until his death.

"There... there is the school," Irene cried suddenly. "I can see Sophie. She is coming to meet us!"

Soon they met half-way, greeting each other warmly. Sophie looked taller and thinner, and she had a bad cough.

"Did you get Mother's letter about Jadwiga?" asked Janka.

"Yes. Let's not talk about it."

When they reached the school, Irene understood why her sister did not want to spend the holidays alone. It was a dismal, lonely place. Even on that beautiful, spring day it looked spooky, abandoned and drab. How it must have been through those long winter months, through the long winter nights, with snow around and winds howling outside the window!

"Are you not afraid to live here all alone, Sophie?" asked Irene, dismayed by what she saw: two primitive schoolrooms built out of wooden planks, and a lean-to consisting of one room — Sophie's home. It looked like a nun's cell: a simple country bed made of wood, a table, a chair and a small peasant-style wardrobe. A black, iron potbellied stove kept the room warm, and on it Sophie boiled milk and brewed coffee.

"You must be terribly lonesome here!" cried Irene. "If at least you had a piano!"

Sophie smiled sadly, and her shoulders moved slightly in a gesture of hopeless indifference. "Someone has to teach these children, and I like it. It is not so bad. First of all, for the greater part of the day I am with the children. Milk and bread is brought to me in the morning by one of them. After school I eat dinner with the principal and his family. He is a rich peasant and lives in the village of Kłosowo. At night I correct papers and read books. Sometimes I go to Aleksandrów to get books from the library. I met a very nice woman there who invited me to come and play the piano in her house any time I like. Her daughter, Magdalena, is studying in Warsaw's Conservatory of Music, so the piano goes to waste, so to speak."

"Still, I think it must be awful to live here alone," Janka insisted. "I would not do it for all the money in the world."

"Now, with the school closed for the holiday, I feel more alone. That's why I am grateful that you came. A peasant will bring some straw in the afternoon and fill these two bags, so you can sleep on the floor."

"We brought our blankets with us," said Janka.

"Good. We will cook morning and night meals here, and we will eat our afternoon dinners with the principal. I arranged that."

"Tomorrow is Holy Thursday. Are we going to visit any churches?"

"There is only one church in the vicinity of the *wieś*, the one that you passed. We will go there, of course. If you wish, we can also go to the church at Aleksandrów."

Occasionally, a peasant's son would show an unusual gift for studies. If he was a child of not very poor parents, they would somehow scrape together the money, or sell a few head of cattle, and send him to the secondary school in the city, or even to study at the university. Two occupations were most sought after, because they brought so much prestige: medicine and the priesthood. If the child was not bright enough to be able to go through advanced studies, he would be satisfied with a third choice: teaching. This required only a secondary school education, yet brought enough prestige to keep a peasant apart from, and above, the rest of the community.

The principal of Sophie's school was such a teacher. He was glad when the prior fall it was decided that there were too many children for him to take care of alone, and he was allowed to hire another teacher. He built the lean-to with the help of other peasants and warmly welcomed a young and pretty "city girl" who came there to teach. Simple and ordinary as the principal and his wife were, they fell under the spell of that delicate, fragile-looking girl who had chosen a life of hard work and loneliness. There was not a thing that they would not do for Sophie, and they cared for her like they would for their own child.

"Mama sends you her greetings and this *placek* (crumb cake)," said a girl knocking at the door. She brought milk and bread, too, and seeing two of "Mrs. Teacher's" sisters in the room, bashfully with-drew. One could hear the sound of her bare feet as she ran away.

Leaving for church at about noon, they saw a flaxen-haired boy waiting outside with a big wicker basket that was covered with a hand-loomed, linen napkin. He approached Sophie timidly and, handing her the basket, said:

"I brought you *Święcone*, Missus Teacher..."

Święcone means "blessed." It is an assortment of foods that the peasants bring to church on Easter Sunday to be blessed by the priest and sprinkled with holy water. Depending on how rich you were, you could have many things in the basket, but two were a must: bread and salt. This, even the poorest peasant could afford. Wealthy people had long tables set with fancy food, and the priest whom they invited to their houses blessed them and later participated in the feast.

Sophie lifted the napkin: there was bread and *kiełbasy*, eggs, *babka*, country cheese in the shape of a heart, and salt in a hand-carved bowl. She knew that the boy was poor and that he could not have brought it all from his house.

"Where did you get it, Marek?"

"Oh, we... sort of... everybody gave something. But *I* brought you the salt and cheese!"

He was squeezing in his little hand a bunch of short-stemmed spring flowers from the woods, yellow and white. The woods were quite far away, and Sophie knew that he had made a special trip there.

"Thank you, Marek. They are lovely. Thank you for the Święcone, too. You are my great friend," she said, patting his head. Marek grinned happily, turned away and started to run toward Kłosowo.

"You see, I am not as lonesome as you think," Sophie said. "It is not a question of all the food I get, but the intentions of these people. I always wanted to be with people of simple deeds and emotions. Maybe it's because *I* am such a simpleton myself."

As was customary, the tomb of Christ was the center of attention. The front part of the altar had been removed, and the statue of Christ was lying in the nook, surrounded by living plants. It was a simple country church, and everything in it was simple. The tombs of big churches in the cities, great and impressive in their Gothic, Renaissance and Rococo splendor — and hothouse flowers — were beautiful, but they had the atmosphere of an artificial theatrical stage setting. Here, the statue, surrounded by sprouting willow branches, witch hazel, evergreens and bunches of wildflowers, was Christ — a god but also a man, a friend of the poor. Death was not just a sleep; it was a rest after a long, hard struggle.

"I never saw such a beautiful tomb as this one," whispered Irene, standing enchanted and listening to the silence of the church. "I wonder how it is going to be in the town?" she said later, walking with her sisters toward Aleksandrów.

"I am afraid you will find signs of civilization there that strip everything of its natural simplicity, even in the churches," Sophie replied.

It was true, so they stayed only a short while in Aleksandrów, and they were on their way back when Sophie greeted a passing woman. They stopped, chatting for a while, and Sophie introduced her sisters to her. She was about fifty, with a strong, energetic face. In spite of the warm day, she was wearing a long, fur-lined *shuba,* and she spoke with the sing-song accent of the eastern frontier gentry, with charming diminutive alterations of words (as in Russian), which was so alien to the classic, sober language of central Poland. She called Sophie a...

"Little laaady deee-aar! Little lily-of-the-valley flower!"

Yet, despite these regional peculiarities, one could see the grand manner and behavior of a person of high breeding and culture.

"I am glad to meet you. Please come Sunday for *Święcone*. Like in every provincial town, everybody visits everybody else. We will have guests dropping in all afternoon. You know: the priest, the doctor, the druggist and the librarian... the judge and the teachers, and so on..." She laughed and walked away.

"What a character," said Janka.

"Oh, she is a grand lady. They had a big estate in the Western Ukraine, and of course they lost it to the Bolsheviks. Her husband was a great horse breeder and as a hobby took veterinary courses at the University of Kiev. Little did he know that one day he would make a living as a veterinarian. He is now head of a department for the whole district of Kujawy. You know: prevention and cure of cattle disease, inspection of pork for trichinosis, and so on."

"Is it in her home where you go to play the piano?" asked Irene.

"Yes. That was Magdalena's mother."

With what silent, treacherous steps does fate creep into a person's life! Even Sophie, endowed with a gift of intuition and an occasional premonition of the future, had no idea that a simple meeting with a woman one day in the library would change the course of the lives of so many people around her.

> "I hope that you will forgive me, stranger as I am, for writing you this letter, but I met your charming daughter, Miss Sophie, some time ago, and during the past holidays. I also had the pleasure of meeting your two other daughters. I heard that you have two more, which I hope to be fortunate enough to meet some day.
>
> Miss Sophie comes to see me sometimes and plays the piano at my home. She plays very well, very well indeed, and that is a lot to be said by a mother whose daughter is a student at the Conservatory of Music in Warsaw! It is about my daughter, Magdalena, that I am daring to write you. As we don't have any relatives in the City, she has to live in a rented room. So far, she has had no luck. She has changed rooms several times, but it seems that nice, cultured people do not rent rooms.

MAGDALENA

It has been miserable for Magdalena to live surrounded by people of the petit bourgeois type.

I was thinking, perhaps, with so many daughters one more girl in the house would not make much difference. Magdalena spends most of the day at the Conservatory. She would be satisfied with the smallest room and is not fussy about food. Also, I know that you have a piano that she might use for practice.

Would you mind very much if she dropped in sometime so that you could meet her and see if you would like to have her in your home? I hope that you will say 'yes.' Would the price for room and board of…"

"With so many daughters…" There was no mention of *a son* in the house, of whom Magdalena's mother must have heard from Sophie. But mother did not think for a moment that a strange girl, living under the same roof as her son, might cause any problem. Henryk was a quiet, studious boy, up to his ears in engineering.

"We could use that money," thought mother. "Even with my pension, and Sophie's and Stefa's help, we can hardly make ends meet. Henry will simply have to share a bedroom with the younger girls. Magdalena could have his room."

When Magdalena came to introduce herself one afternoon, mother's mind was already made up.

"You can move in any time you wish my dear. You are welcome here."

Everybody fell under the spell of Magdalena's charm. Tall and strong, with straight dark hair reaching almost to her shoulders, she looked like one of the handsome youths in Renaissance portraits. But if her face was handsome in a masculine way, her figure was perfectly formed in a feminine way.

She had a tremendous vitality and temperament, typical of young people used to horseback riding and the outdoor life, and self-assurance, coming from years of an easy, happy home full of servants. Apparently her parents' loss of their estate and the move to Aleksandrów had not changed Magdalena's disposition. With a sense of humor she showed vigor, energy and an unmatched adaptability to this new kind of life.

She fit into her new home as if she had lived there all her life. Mother liked her, perhaps because she reminded her of her sisters and her childhood; the girls because she was so different from them. As to Henryk, he seemed very embarrassed and bashful in her presence. The evening meals were now happy family gatherings, with jokes, wit and fun sparkling and bubbling like champagne. Magdalena sat next to Henryk and teased him constantly, which made him blush.

Even if she had not been so attractive and full of vitality, Magdalena would have kept the whole family under her spell because of her talent for music. With their taste and appreciation of music, they knew immediately that here was not just an average student of the Conservatory of Music, but that her talent placed her among the chosen few, with a great future as a concert pianist.

Asked to play after supper, Magdalena never refused, even seemed to enjoy it. They all sat around the dining room table and listened, enchanted and grateful for what she had brought to their drab lives. Irene simply worshipped her. She cleaned her room and polished her shoes.

"You should not do that," said Magdalena. "I am supposed to take care of myself."

"Oh, but I want to!" cried Irene. "You have such beautiful hands; they belong to the piano, not to simple chores!"

Early in the afternoon Magdalena practiced, playing études over and over again to improve her technique and keep her hands in condition. These hours seemed to Irene as precious as if she were attending a concert. Sometimes Magdalena would practice part of some concerto, playing a short passage — or one line, or a few notes — over and over again, because she thought that she used the pedal a fraction of a second too long or too short. To the average listener it would be dull or even distressing, but not to Irene. She was overwhelmed by that striving for perfection. When finally Magdalena would play the whole part for the last time, overcoming the difficulties, Irene shared with her the final moment of victory as if the torment and effort of having created something perfect belonged as much to her. Irene sat there, turning the pages of her book slowly and silently so as not to make the slightest noise.

All seemed perfection itself on the home front until mother noticed that Henryk, instead of spending the evening on studies or working on blueprints, began to sneak into Magdalena's room after supper. She, too, seldom stayed longer in the dining room than was necessary and seemed not as willing to play the piano for their pleasure. One night, mother got up abruptly from the table where she was reading, knocked on Magdalena's door, and without waiting for a "come-in," walked into her room. She found Magdalena and Henryk on the bed in a position described by Ovid two thousand years before in his work *Ars Amatoria*. Mother withdrew hastily. She came back as white as a sheet, with disgust visibly on her face.

"As old as I am, and the mother of ten children, I did not know *such things* were being done," she said.

The next day Henryk told them that he and Magdalena were going to be married in a few weeks, as soon as vacation began.

"Do you realize what you are doing, son?" mother asked. "You can ruin your studies, your career and your life. You just started your studies. How are you going to take care of a wife?"

"Magdalena will be getting the same amount of money from her parents as before. She will be paying you for her room and board as before. Nothing will change, except that she and I will share the room. Don't worry. I will get through my courses at the Poly-technique, and so will Magdalena at the Conservatory."

It seemed reasonable. What more was there to say? What could mother do? Maybe the girl was pregnant? How could mother object to the marriage? An instinct was shouting within her that things would not turn out so well, that life is seldom as uncomplicated as we would like it to be. But she did not say one more word.

While Henryk and Magdalena were spending their honeymoon in Aleksandrów, the girls spent the summer preparing the newlyweds' bedroom. It was all Irene's idea.

They painted and scrubbed and varnished everything in sight, polished their parents' old bedroom suite and moved it into Magdalena's room. On the day of their arrival they even spent money on flowers, which they put in a large vase on the bedside table. But Magdalena did not seem to notice either their enthusiastic greetings or the room's attractive changes. She did not even thank them for the flowers, as if all these things were expected and normal courtesies, not worth a mention.

Mother and daughters stood around the room, trying to pick up the dying conversation, still craving for news, for interaction with their only son and brother, trying to spill out from their hearts the warmth and love that had accumulated in the long wait for their arrival.

"I am starting classes tomorrow morning, and I am very tired," said Magdalena in a voice hardly disguising irritation. "Would you all mind leaving the room?"

"She has changed, has she not?" said Stefa in a voice more filled with wonder than disappointment. It was as if she expected someone to deny it. But none of them did.

CHAPTER TWELVE — The Sleeping Giant

An atmosphere of polite hostility now reigned at home. No unpleasant words were exchanged, but both sides felt justified in being critical and irritable about the behavior of the other.

It seemed inevitable that one day the least important occurrence would become that last drop in the bucket which would spill over the top, a tiny spark that would start an uncontrollable fire.

One day into this stormy atmosphere plunged a starry-eyed Helena, back from her summer job as a doctor's aide at the veteran's hospital. One of the leading families of the Polish aristocracy of the District of Kielce had opened one whole wing of their palace as a convalescent home for wounded soldiers who required longer periods of care and rehabilitation. For Helena it was not only a great opportunity to gather experience as a young medical doctor and to earn money, but also to spend time after work on a magnificent estate as the personal guest of her hosts: the Count and Countess.

Among the guests and neighbors whom she met that summer, there was a young man, fresh out of the College of Agronomy. As a rule, Polish gentry, to avoid subdivision of smaller estates, kept them intact in the hands of the eldest son. The younger brothers, becoming industrialists, judges, lawyers, doctors, and so on, often drifted to the large cities, forming the top class called "the intelligentsia." Some of them, however, who liked country life, would become superintendents of great estates until they eventually married an heiress, thereby getting an estate of their own.

Janusz, with whom Helena instantly fell in love, was the superintendent of one of the estates in the neighborhood. To him, that young woman physician, talented, intelligent and vivacious, was so different from the country girls that he knew that he was attracted to her from the first moment that he met her. To her, the tall, elegant and handsome young man was like a movie actor or a hero from a romantic novel. In her spare time he taught her to ride a horse, and at night he helped her entertain the patients. By the end of the summer, they were engaged.

"I am in love! I am engaged!" Those were the first words Helena uttered when she got home.

Helena showed everyone Janusz's picture. Irene decided that she did not like him but kept it to herself. He was definitely handsome, but he had that over-bred look — with too small and too flat ears... that "little boy" look. "He will have that nice-little-boy look at forty-five," she thought, "with a few wrinkles... and the same look at sixty-five with a few more wrinkles." Even at the age of thirteen, Irene did not care for that type of man.

"He is coming next week to meet you all," declared Helena. "Pleeese make the house presentable..."

So they took out the old Baccarat crystal glasses, filled the decanter with sherry, and polished the silver. When he came, the table was set with mother's best linen, still beautiful despite years of use; dinner was simple but elegantly served and good. Janusz took one look at the modest apartment, noticed the absence of servants, and made a note in his mind of the aging widow and the younger sisters of Helena, two of them still in school. Coming to their home, he had hoped that perhaps Helena's father had left enough money in the bank to be used for the purchase of land.

"My Lord!" he thought. "Let's get out of here, quick! I could not expect anything from here. I would have this family hanging on my neck for the rest of my life. I can wait... I will wait even ten years if necessary to get the *right* wife."

He left hurriedly the next day, saying that he would come back soon, and in the meantime he would write. For a week Helena looked for a letter that never came.

"Maybe he forgot the address?" she tried to persuade herself. So she sent a postcard with a few words, something like: "I am still alive and my address is..."

When another week passed without news from Janusz, she took off the ring and sent it back by registered mail. She was still hoping that he would return it with a letter: "What did you do, you silly girl? Put that ring back on your finger where it belongs! I did not write because I was ill…"

But nothing came. Helena did not get up from bed. She did not get up the next day, or the next. She did not wash, comb her hair or take any food, except drinks of water. Mother was suffering also. To Irene it was even more heartbreaking to watch mother's great unhappiness than Helena's. Maybe it was because Helena was in bed with her head buried under pillows, and though you could feel her grief, you could not see her face. But you could see mother's face.

Sometimes Irene would come to her room with a bowl of soup or a glass of coffee.

"Please, Helen, have something…"

"I don't want-anything-please-leave-me-alone," would come the muffled answer from under the covers.

"She doesn't want anything, Mother."

"How could she fall for someone like that?" cried Stefa.

"God knows why, God only knows. She was so wrapped up in her medicine all these years; nothing else seemed to matter."

"But we can't just let her die of suffering and starvation in that bed, Mother!"

"What can we do? What can we do?"

But on the eighth day, a Monday, Helena got up, washed and dressed. She came into the kitchen where mother was making tea and boiling milk.

"Are you all right, Helen? Is there anything I can do?" she asked gently.

"I am all right, Mother. You don't have to be evasive or subtle about it. I can talk about him. I had to burn it out of my system, and I did. Just like I will burn this…"

She lifted the tea kettle and put Janusz's picture on the burning coals. She watched for a minute or two as the picture of a man in a riding outfit — his body twitching convulsively on hot coals as if consumed by the damnation of hell — disintegrated quickly into ashes.

She put back the tea kettle.

"Let's eat, Mother. I'm very hungry."

Helena had changed. She looked, dressed and acted like she did before, yet she had changed. It would be hard to actually describe what it was. She did not give the impression of being spinsterish — she was only twenty-three years old — or over-masculine like some lesbian women are, or asexual like nuns are. Yet it was as if these three characteristics were somehow mixed in her personality. She described it best herself one day: "I am a woman doctor, but I am more a doctor than a woman."

At this time Helena and three of her friends were deciding on choosing a particular branch of medicine. Tola was to be a skin specialist, Marta an internist, Stella a gynecologist, and Helena decided on pediatrics. She was thrilled at being accepted on the staff of the Children's Clinic, which was only loosely connected with the large Children's Hospital. It was more of a research center that dealt with unusual cases: premature births, defective births, nutritional disorders, allergies, and rare and incurable diseases. Helena was learning so much and was so completely wrapped up in her work that she was unable to talk about anything else. A premature infant kept alive was to her a personal victory. An infant, born with a defective esophagus and successfully operated upon was a source of triumph. And the fight to save a child dying of a tetanus infection was her personal fight with death, her very own tragedy in failure.

Besides the Clinic, Helena's day was filled with other work: routine postoperative cases and diseases of childhood at the Hospital, and also some work at the "Care for Mother and Baby Station." But the Clinic was the center of her work, her interests and her efforts. It was the essence of her life.

"Miss Sophie is very ill," wrote the principal from Kłosowo to mother. "It looked like bronchitis, which she said that she had many times before, but one day she had a hemorrhage. I called the doctor and he said it was an advanced tuberculosis. She is a little better now, but quite weak. I am waiting a few days for you to get this letter and to make proper arrangements. I will put Sophie on a train to Warsaw on Sunday. Please meet her at the station at six-thirty. Doctor says that she should be taken to a sanitarium without delay. I am so sorry…"

Neither Helena nor Stefa could be away from work, and Janka did not want to miss school, so mother could count only on Irene's help.

"Someone has to be with me. I don't know how weak she is, and I want to take her straight to a sanitarium at Zakopane. That means waiting at the station and moving her suitcase from one train to another. Irene will you come with me?"

"Of course, I will. I can miss school for a few days. I will catch up easily, you know… Don't worry, Mother. I will take care of Sophie's baggage."

Even that sad trip, accompanying her sick sister, appeared thrilling to Irene. She always dreamed of seeing mountains, which she knew only from pictures and postcards.

"Where are you going to find money for a sanitarium?" asked Janka, already jealous that someone was going somewhere and sorry, after all, that she had refused to go.

"There is a large state-owned sanitarium at Zakopane, I know. It should not cost anything," replied mother.

She was thin and pale when she finally appeared at the door of the compartment, after all of the passengers had spilled from the train. Irene took a suitcase, mother a small bag. Mother tried to get hold of Sophie's arm, to support her in her walk, but Sophie refused. "I am not that helpless, yet," she said. There was something new and differ-ent in the tone of her voice: bitterness, sarcasm, defiance, all mixed with dry humor. A few remarks that she made about the trip: the passengers, the weather, all had that new, macabre tint, so alien to the Sophie they had known. She walked very erect, but you had the feeling that she would rather let her shoulders droop, her chest sag, her spine curve. She walked the way old or blind people do. Each step was not a mechanical function; it was a careful exploration of space.

"We have nearly an hour until the train for Zakopane, Sophie. I thought it would tire you less to make the trip right away, instead of being dragged home and back to the station tomorrow. We will make you a comfortable bed on the train for the night. Let's go to the station restaurant. You need a good dinner after the all-day trip."

How many times had Irene seen that look on mother's face, the slightly trembling hands, or heard that muddled voice reflecting suffering and despair? How many times during the past five years?

Mother ordered dinner for Sophie. "Irene, would you like something, too?"

Irene knew that mother had very little money for the trip. "I could not eat anything, thanks. Anyway, we have our sandwiches. If I get hungry, I'll have one on the train."

The train was half empty. October was not a tourist month; the summer season was over, and skiing would not begin until December. The conductor lifted a bed for the night. It was almost as comfortable as those in the sleeping car, except it did not have bedding or sheets.

It was noon on a gray, cloudy day when they arrived. They bought some coffee at the station and ate their sandwiches. Afterward, mother hired a mountain dweller with a horse and buggy and told him where they wanted to go.

Zakopane is a notch high up in the Tatra Mountains. Originally a settlement exclusively for the local mountain people, it was "discovered," first by climbers, writers and artists, until it became a popular health and tourist center. The mountain dwellers, with their colorful, handspun and hand-embroidered woolen clothes, handmade moccasins, their regional language, folk music, dances, art and sculpture, were a constant source of exploration for scientists, artists and tourists alike. Their furniture, the walls and beams of their houses and the kitchen utensils were exquisitely hand carved. Their primitive paintings on glass, found in many homes, had museum value.

These talented, brave people, hardened by the elements, had their own history. The stories and legends, told by father to son and by storytellers, were as rugged as the people. The most famous character of legend was Janosik — an audacious hero-brigand whose superhuman exploits had grown with the years, very much like the Robin Hood of British lore.

Irene looked at the young, lanky highlander standing near his buggy. He looked just like the men on postcards, or just like the little doll-figures sent to her from Zakopane! He wore well-fitted, natural wool pants, embroidered at the bottom and on the pockets; a leather vest with colorful beads and wool-stitched colorful designs; and a jacket, made of the same wool as the pants, thrown on his shoulders cape-style and held under the chin with red and black wool ribbons. His round, black felt hat was decorated with a string of tiny white shells, with an eagle's feather sticking boldly on one side. His dark hair was long, not unlike that of an American Indian.

Where did the shells on his cap come from? For centuries, millennia perhaps, traders from the Mediterranean shores had come north, bringing shells and corals in exchange for wool and ornamental amber. No matter in what part of Poland or on what regional costume, all Polish peasant women wore strings of coral. Inherited for generations from mother to daughter, one could estimate the wealth of a peasant or highlander by the number of coral strings on a woman's neck.

Besides the great notch of Zakopane, there were countless smaller notches around, ideal for the raising of sheep, with gentle abundant green pastures. Always independent and self-supporting, with tourists growing from year to year, the local people became even more prosperous without losing any of their customs or changing their manner of dress.

The man put their bags in the front seat, and after seeing that his customers took their places in the back, jumped in. They drove in silence. Sophie was tired, mother sad. Irene was overwhelmed — almost crushed — by the power and beauty of the mountains.

Irene was searching among the towering, granite peaks — almost black on that dreary, late autumn day — for the tallest mountain, the Giewont. She knew its contour from her early childhood. It looked like a giant body, lying down, the bold profile of its head tearing at the sky. Giewont, called "the sleeping knight," about whom there was a legend as well, was referred to as "he" — not "it" — by everyone. Irene was looking for the sleeping knight, but he was wearing a "cap," as the natives would say: the soft, white clouds, high in the sky, were hovering jealously, like professional mourners, hiding the top.

How different the mountains looked from what she had imagined! In pictures they gave the impression of being two-dimensional, like a drop in a stage set for the opera *Carmen*. Here, she felt the overpowering force of the three-dimensional mass. The peaks, disappearing among the clouds, seemed infinite, like the *finished* Tower of Babel, reaching the sky, reaching God.

The buggy, moving along the deserted roads, passed houses which popped up here and there among tall pine trees. Built of wood, with carved doors and fronts, highly sloped roofs to shed the heavy winter snows, they stared silently with their closed windows at these intruders who were disturbing their autumn sleep. Around Christmas this place would be crowded with skiers, noisy with human voices and the tinkling bells of sleighs. Not now.

The driver stopped in front of a large, three-story brick building. Wide, flat-roofed, it looked out of place among the high mountains and scattered houses of varied design. The man took out the bags, put the money that mother gave him into a crumpled, colored handkerchief, and drove off.

"You will have to stay in the waiting room until I talk to someone in the office," said mother.

"I would rather wait here, outside," said Sophie, sitting on a bench.

When mother went inside, Irene put blankets around Sophie's shoulders and legs, and sat next to her sister. It was so easy to breathe that thin air, fragrant with pine needles!

"What are you thinking about, Sophie?"

"Nothingness."

"You mean the nothingness that a Hindu believes in?"

"Yes. To me Nirvana means not the 'return to Nothingness' but the 'return to Nonexistence'. We did not exist before we were born, yet we did not come from Nothingness. I believe in God. I believe we return to what we were before — part of God."

"Mountains make me feel I'm part of God — more than anything else. Do you feel the same way, Sophie? Is that why you thought of Nirvana?"

"Perhaps. But mostly because I know I have to die soon."

"Don't say that, Sophie. You are going to be well…"

A middle-aged woman was typing at a small table near the window, when mother knocked at the half-open door.

"Yes?" she said, without hesitation.

"I would like to see someone who is in charge here," mother replied.

"Do you have an appointment?"

It was not good policy to admit that she did not.

"I came all the way from Warsaw," she said evasively.

The typist went to the next room and shortly reappeared.

"You may come in now."

The woman, sitting at a desk, was about forty, with a pleasant, alert face. Her dark hair, parted in the middle, was arranged in a low, flat bun that made her look as if she had her hair cut short.

"What business brings you here?" she asked in a pleasant but official tone of voice.

"I brought my daughter here. She has advanced tuberculosis, and a few days ago she had a hemorrhage."

"Do you have with you a copy of your application?"

"What application?"

"The application necessary for your daughter's entry into the Sanitarium. What is the date of her evaluation? What is the case number? It will be easier for us to find it in the files."

"I... I don't have any application. I did not know we needed one."

"You mean that you are not on the waiting list?"

"No. You see, she became ill quite suddenly. That is... she was ill for a long time, but we did not know that it was tuberculosis..."

"Do you know that we have a waiting list many months long?"

"Do you mean there is no room for my daughter here?"

"Absolutely not. If you qualify for the free State Sanitarium, and make the application now, you might get a place, say... in three or four months."

"Oh, but I can't take her back! Have pity on her! She was on the train all day yesterday to Warsaw from the place she used to work. She was all night on the train coming here. She is so exhausted it would... kill her if I were to drag her back again."

"Try any of the private sanitariums here. I'm sure they have room for an extra patient."

"I... can't afford to pay for her. I am a widow with six children, some of them in college and unable to earn money. She was helping to support the family. Please have pity on her!"

Mother's eyes were dry, but her voice was faltering and thin, as if on the verge of tears.

There was a short silence, during which mother was trying to control herself, and the woman was thinking.

"Where is your daughter now?" she asked, getting up from her chair.

"She is outside on the bench with her youngest sister."

The woman went to the window. She saw a pale, thin young woman covered with blankets, and a slender schoolgirl sitting next to her, trying to cover her long legs with the bottom of her short winter coat. She looked for a while at these two little gray figures — so small and helpless in the emptiness of the big yard, with dark mountains towering above them as if threatening to crush them.

"Wait here, please. I will see what we can do."

She left for what to mother seemed an eternity. It seemed to the girls sitting outside an eternity, too. Irene was getting numb with cold; Sophie felt weaker, dreaming about a bed into which she could sink her fatigued body.

Finally the woman came back, accompanied by a nurse.

"We managed to move an extra bed into one of the larger rooms," she said. "You can bring your daughter in."

Afterwards, leaving Sophie behind in the room, they sat outside on the bench — mother and daughter — and ate some leftover, stale sandwiches.

"I feel as if a big stone has been removed from my chest," said mother. The air is so fresh here; Sophie must get well. Come, Irene. We will have some hot tea at the station. We have to take a train back soon."

They walked all the way to the station — a long way.

Just when they were about to reach the station, the clouds dispersed, and suddenly the tops of the mountains appeared in black contours on the gray sky. There he was — Giewont — the sleeping knight, felled by death, yet powerful and defiant, tearing with his proud face at the sky, at infinity, unconquered even by death.

"How beautiful, how beautiful he is... Oh Mother, even death can be beautiful!"

"What made her think of death?" wondered mother.

A big, soft cloud drifted in and enveloped the tops of the mountains. It covered the face of the sleeping knight, like a merciful hand pulling up a sheet over a dead man's face.

CHAPTER THIRTEEN — Rachmaninov Concerto

There were three causes of irritation between Magdalena and the rest of the family… or rather symptoms of perpetual hostility.

One of them was dinner time. Either Magdalena was a little late coming home from the Conservatory — and mother would not wait but would serve dinner and greet Magdalena with a somber expression (she showed an equal lack of enthusiasm while eating the cold dinner) — or she would come earlier and show impatience because the meal was not ready.

The second cause also seemed ridiculously trivial: when Magdalena would practice one particular piece of music, naturally it would stick in everyone's mind, and sooner or later, someone would start humming or singing the most melodious parts. As the girls — except Irene — had a poor ear for music, the result was far from artistic. They would hum in a simplified or distorted manner, "making up" in a few places when they did not know exactly how it went. It was highly distressing even to Irene's ear, who not only remembered every note, but also the rhythm and tempo of the music. What it must have been to Magdalena, to listen to a concerto by Rachmaninov, Chopin or Grieg as "um-ta-ta-ta-um-pha-umpha-um-ta-ta-ti-tra-tra-la-la" is easy to understand. Even if she was not in the same room with the person humming, she would come out of her room and in a whispery voice vibrating with rage ask — whoever it was — to please stop.

The worst offender was Janka, who usually did not sing, but whistled off key. This would not be very good even with modern compositions, but with classical music it was sheer murder. On top of it, Janka would forget not to whistle soon after she was told. Maybe she did so anyway just to spite Magdalena; she would, in fact, whistle even louder.

The third cause also had something to do with music. The piano was in the dining room, which connected the bathrooms and kitchen with the rest of the house. Naturally, there was considerable traffic through such a room, no matter how hard you tried to avoid it. But when Magdalena practiced, she expected not to be disturbed or interrupted in any way. The only person allowed in the room was Irene, maybe because she still worshipped Magdalena, and in spite of everything still cleaned her room and polished her shoes.

Naturally, everyone tried not to bother Magdalena, but it did not always work out so well. Sitting at the dining room table and reading a book, Irene was always full of tension: "Don't let anyone come in the room, oh God, let nobody come in the room now," she would think to herself.

But that particular day, God must have been busy with something more important than regulating traffic in their household. Magdalena had come home from the Conservatory quite early, and she decided to practice for an hour or so before dinner. She closed all the doors and began to play. It was a Rachmaninov concerto, and today she was concentrating on the *pianissimo* section. She was not satisfied with the way she was using the pedal, and the tempo was not fast enough. Then the tempo was right, but the passage sounded blurry rather than crystal clear. Now and then, she would stop, shak-ing her head in a negative way, inhaling air, making a slight hissing noise through her teeth. Then she would resume the section. Irene, who was doing homework at the table, was almost afraid to breathe, or to turn a page. Mother was preparing dinner, and there was no one else in the house.

"It is going to be all right today," Irene thought.

Just then, mother opened the door (which during the *pianissimo* seemed like a shattering noise), took something out of the breakfront and returned to the kitchen. Magdalena, ostensibly interrupted, then resumed playing. Just then, Janka, coming home from school, slammed the front door. Not realizing that Magdalena was practicing, she decided to go to the bathroom.

Bang! ...the door opened ...Janka crossed the room, opened another door. After a few minutes she came back, opened and closed the doors again. Each time Magdalena stopped playing, each time making that hissing noise while inhaling deeply.

"It will be all right, now," thought Irene. "No one else is coming until dinner time."

But mother came in again. She pulled open two drawers, looked for some pieces of silver: *dink, dink, dink!*

Magdalena jumped to her feet, and slammed the piano top. She did not slam it hard, but the quick, firm movements of her body were obviously showing what she wanted to show.

"You don't have to be so sensitive about your practice," said mother. "After all, you can't expect us all to change into butterflies."

The girl did not reply and started to cross the room.

"Maybe you don't think that I am doing enough to keep you comfortable in this house," continued mother.

"Did I say anything?"

"You don't have to say it with words. I don't have the skin of a rhinoceros... though you are probably of a different opinion." Mother's voice rose in pitch, though it did not rise in volume. It was irritable and querulous.

Magdalena obviously did not want to argue and had her hand on the doorknob, trying to leave the room. But mother tried to stop her with a further tirade:

"I am fed up with your queenly manners," she said. "Just because you were brought up on a big estate where servants are treated like slaves, you don't have to carry on like this *in my house!* I was brought up on a big estate, too, and my family crest is not inferior to yours. If you do not wish to treat us as members of the family, that is your privilege, but keep in mind that we are not your servants..."

Magdalena left the room, closing the door quietly but firmly.

"Oh, Mother, why did you have to say all that?!" cried Irene.

"I told her what I should have long ago."

"Oh, but she is so sensitive — she is an artist."

"What difference does that make?"

"Don't you see? It makes all the difference in the world!"

The dinner was eaten in gloom. Henryk was silent, and Magdalena did not show up at all.

The next morning, after everyone had left, mother went to her daughter-in-law's room and found all her things packed.

Early in the afternoon Henryk came to take their suitcases.

"What is it? What are you trying to do?"

"We rented a room."

"Where are you going to find the money for it?"

"Whether Magdalena pays you for the room or someone else, it is the same money."

"But where will you find the money for food? Who is going to take care of your laundry?"

"I am going to take a job."

"A job? With your engineering courses? You know better than I that your classes, studying and drafting table take up all your time!"

"Don't worry about me."

"Who is going to take care of you when you are sick?"

He did not say anything. By then all the bags were outside, near the elevator door.

"Son, don't do it to me! Don't do it to yourself! Life is give and take. I will give a little, Magdalena will give a little. We can straighten things out!"

He did not even say goodbye. He closed the door. She could hear the elevator door slam and the whining, humming noise of it descending. She stood in the hall and listened. Somehow she was hoping the elevator would come back up, and he would get out, come in and start unpacking...

A little boy in a little coffin. He was sick only three days...

A seventeen year-old youth in a coffin, lips burned with poison... And now her last, her only son had walked out of her life.

She never expected him to repay her for the years of love, care and anxiety when he was ill or at war. All she cared was that he would be somewhere around... that someday, perhaps, she would be able to hold his little child in her lap... Oh, but he can't just walk out forever. He is an impetuous young man, influenced by a wife... but it won't last. They will find out how hard and expensive it is to be on their own... cleaning, laundry, meals in some cheap cafeteria. Of course they will come back. They have to!

> "Next week it will be three months since your daughter was admitted to the State Sanitarium. Since this is the limit of time that a patient can stay here, as we must make room for other patients on our waiting list, we therefore ask you to please make the proper arrangements..."

This time Helena found a place for Sophie in a private sanitarium not too far from Zakopane in Rudka, through the courtesy of the Director of the Children's Clinic. Sophie was accepted free of charge, even though it was the best and most expensive of all private institutions of its kind.

"She will get the best care there," said Helena upon arriving home after settling in her sister at Rudka.

But in less than two months mother received another letter. It was from Rudka. By now, even before opening it, she knew that the news was bad. Any letter that she had received contained bad news: about Jadwiga... from the principal at Kłosowo... from the sanitarium at Zakopane.

> "It is the firm policy of our institution not to keep incurable patients here. Since your daughter does not respond to treatment, we consider keeping her here any longer a possible cause of an undesirable atmosphere in our institution. We regretfully ask you to take your daughter as soon as possible..."

There was, among the City Hospitals of Warsaw, one with a tuberculosis ward where the regulations <u>did not specify</u> that the patient was not allowed to die...

So, at the age of twenty-one, Sophie was brought one day to the city where she was born... to die.

CHAPTER FOURTEEN — Phlox

Stefa, who finished her courses at the School for Librarians and for some time had held a job at the Public Library, was now working as a librarian at the Belvedere Palace, official residence of General Piłsudski. "Chief of the Nation," as was his title, he was actually the first president of Poland.

The new nation, after nearly one hundred and fifty years of division and occupation by Germany, Russia and Austria, now faced immense problems (among others) of revising and uniting the penal code, drafting a new constitution (the first and last had been proclaimed in 1791 under the last king of Poland, King Stanislaus), and putting in order the National Library.

The beautiful and immense King's Palace near the Vistula River was in the process of restoration and renovation, and the smaller Palace of Belvedere was chosen by General Piłsudski as a temporary residence. It was situated next to the Lazienki Palace, which had been built by King Stanislaus in the middle of one of Warsaw's largest parks. It was dotted with magnificent old trees, ponds and an outdoor theatre with artificial Greek ruins as the décor for the court's entertainment.

The park and the Lazienki Palace were open to the public, but a part of the gardens near Belvedere Palace was separated from the public and under guard — but not the very strict security guard that heads of other governments usually had for protection. General Piłsudski, an austere man of moderate pretensions, did not care for pomp or attention.

In these surroundings, then, Stefa was busy organizing and cataloguing the huge Library of Congress, as well as all other books that were government property. Irene came quite often after school and walked tiptoe through the rooms full of books. There Stefa, a few lawyers and other employees were working at small desks in front of the big French windows that provided a magnificent view of the old Lazienki Park. On entering, Irene took the same entrance as did the "Chief of the Nation"; the private apartments were to the right of the great hall, while the library and the offices were to the left. Sometimes, when the weather was nice, Irene would go out through one of the French doors into the park. It had been left in a state of wild growth, completely unattended — unlike the rest of Lazienki Park, which was meticulously kept in the best tradition of French and Italian formal gardens.

At the closing of school in June, Irene's life suddenly changed in every respect. Stefa was given a month's vacation and, as an employee of Belvedere Palace, could spend it free of charge (except for food) in Spała, the former residence of the Russian tsars south of Warsaw, which now belonged to the Polish government. Stefa decided to take her two younger sisters. She bought some cotton and linen remnants, which Helena turned into summer dresses for the girls. They also got light-colored stockings and pumps for the first time (no more high-laced shoes, thank God!).

At thirteen, Irene had suddenly caught up with Janka. They were the same height and weight, and although their faces were not alike, when they dressed alike they looked like twins. Janka had grown into an attractive girl. With a good figure, nice teeth and complexion, and a red shapely mouth, she was far from the homely child that she had been. After all, what girl, unless unusually ugly, is not good-looking at sixteen?

They seldom spoke of, or even thought about, Sophie that summer. When one goes through so much misery — as the girls had those past few years — one is glad to push any unpleasant thoughts far into the subconscious. Anyway, they could not do anything about Sophie; she was dying, and that was that.

The palace in Spała was a large but unimpressive mansion, built and occupied by the Russian tsars and their court.* It was beautifully

---

* The mansion no longer exists, having been destroyed by fire in 1945.

situated on a hill, with a park descending in terraces to the Pilica River. The immense government-owned forests, rich with game (including wild boars) were used by the tsars mainly for hunting. The interior of the mansion did not impress Irene very much, maybe because the furniture was covered with white slip covers. Perhaps with lights and music, bemedalled court officials, colorful imperial guards and the glitter of parties, it would be impressive and beautiful. However, devoid of all that, it did not possess the true immortal beauty of real *objets d'art*, like Greek and Roman ruins or old Italian and French palaces, which are beautiful even in a state of utmost abandonment. The only thing that "impressed" Irene was the tsar's bathroom, with its carvings of ebony wood and solid gold faucets.

If in daytime the palace was unimpressive, on a moonlit night from the large terrace it provided a view of breathtaking beauty. Down below, reflecting the moonlight, the curves of the river appeared and disappeared between the trees and shrubs... a forest of colors nonexistent on nature's palette: neither black, green, gray, silver nor gold — none of these, yet all of them — the secret hues of nature on a moonlit night. The air, pungent with the resin of pine and fir trees, vibrated with silence, interrupted only by a nightingale's song. The sky now and then shed a shooting star... a tear of cosmic joy.

Besides the Palace, there were two other mansions that had been built for the Imperial Guards, guests, and so forth. The girls occupying two rooms in one of the mansions certainly were not the only guests in Spała. A professor from Warsaw's Polytechnique, who was head of the Conservation Department of the king's palace and other museum buildings, was there with his two sons and daughter. There were two young engineers, doing surveying of Spała and the vicinity for the drafting of new maps of Poland, and their brothers. Also, there were two Justices of the Supreme Court, working on revisions of the penal code.

All in all, about two dozen people sat at meal time at the long, banquet-style table in one of the dining rooms. They shared the expenses of the food, prepared by the cook and served by the head butler and his aides. They were served on very old and heavy china, with a two-headed Russian eagle monogrammed « A II » for Tsar Alexander II. Apparently, the later china of the next two tsars was considered by the butler as too good for daily use. The butler, wearing the livery of a footman, with a moustache and beard trimmed à la Tsar Nicholas II, was the only member of the court's household still remaining in Spała. He served not only under Nicholas but started his apprenticeship as a footman during the reign of Alexander II, and of course continued to serve Alexander III. He was now about seventy years old, a quiet, distinguished and impeccable servant, proud of his long service under three tsars, even though he was not a Russian but a Pole.

A whole new world opened up to Irene. True, she had grown up in home at a time when family tradition was kept alive, when books, museums and music were part of daily life, where in spite of the hardships of war and the estrangement brought about by the torment of hunger, never a harsh or foul word had been spoken to her. Irene's cultural background had been rich, but her contact with people had been very limited thus far. Except for Jadwiga's friends in Moscow, some of Helena's friends, and students and teachers at school, the only other people whom she knew were relatives. Now, she was in daily contact with brilliant, talented and unconventional people. The conversation at the table was original, stimulating and unusual.

In spite of the fact that Irene was so young and handicapped by the physical and mental changes that come with the age of puberty, in spite of the fact that nobody paid special attention to her, she was nevertheless a part of this exciting life in Spała.

One of the architects was also a talented painter; another guest, a capable musician. And one of the professor's sons, a student at the University, was a witty, talented writer with a tremendous personality. The evenings were spent on painting, listening to music, organizing *ad hoc* witty, amusing shows, or sitting on the terrace in silence, watching the shooting stars. Besides Stefa and her sisters, the only other girls present were the professor's daughter and her friend, both students at the fashionable School of the Ursuline Sisters in Warsaw. This private school for girls of noble origin had a reputation for impeccable manners, good French conversation, and a good general education. What the poor Ursuline Sisters did not know was that the girls, fed constantly with proper manners, French conver-sation and daily Mass, needed an outlet from their boredom, hidden defiance and disguised hostility.

There was not an adult, "forbidden" or pornographic book — English or French — that was not read right under the noses of the pious Sisters. There was no daring exploit that was not undertaken by the girls, including sneaking out for dates with boys at night after the lights were out. Julia and her friend were, in comparison with Janka who was about the same age, sophisticated grownup women. Their easy, outgoing manner toward the young men was a constant source of envy to Irene. From a non-timid, resolute young girl, she had changed into a bashful, blushing young girl. The more she blushed, the more bashful she became... and that made her blush even more. It was a vicious circle. At meals, sitting at that long table, she was mortified by the thought that every time someone would speak to her, she would blush.

"I must look as red as a *beet*," she thought, mad at herself and near tears.

The two elderly Justices of the Supreme Court, feeling like fauns among the nymphs, often teased the young girls — including Irene, who wished that she could crawl under the table and hide there for the whole meal. A centerpiece of wildflowers on the table gave Irene an idea one day; if taller, thicker plant material were used, it would hide her face from the men sitting across the table and protect her from the teasing.

Not far from the Palace there was a clearing in the woods, heavy with underbrush, weeds, tangled raspberry bushes and wild phlox. The girls went there often to pick the berries, which were unusually large and sweet.

"Come with me, Janka. I want to pick phlox at the clearing. I want to make a huge arrangement for the table to hide us from the Judges," said Irene.

"That's a good idea," cried Janka. "They are bothering me, too. I feel so embarrassed, I could die."

It worked! Even though the Judges still peeked through the arrangement, the big bouquet made Irene feel less conspicuous and less self-conscious. Now, she went every day to pick fresh flowers, jumping from one hill to another, looking for berries and eating them by the handful, her feet sometimes catching in holes and crevices among the overgrown vegetation.

"Where did you get those beautiful flowers?" asked the professor.

"They are growing in the woods," replied Irene.

"Strange. Phlox is not a woodsy plant; it is a garden flower. Even if it grows wild and re-seeds, its origin is not wilderness."

"You would be surprised how far wind and birds can carry seeds, Professor," observed one of the judges.

"That's true. But these are unusually large and fragrant flowers, as if fertilized and tended by a gardener."

"The soil must be exceptionally rich there, because the berries are of unusual size and flavor," said Stefa.

The next day Irene went with Janka again to bring flowers from the woods. As usual, they ate a lot of berries, and carrying big bunches of phlox, they were jumping through the underbrush on the way back. Suddenly, Irene's dress got caught and tore on a rusty nail that was sticking out of a long, flat piece of wood.

"Oh, dear! I ruined my dress!" exclaimed Irene. "Where on earth did that nail come from in the middle of the woods?"

She picked up the piece of wood and saw another piece lying nearby. Put together, where the nail was protruding, they formed a cross! Irene looked around. Those small mounds, those wide crevices hidden by weeds and bushes… the rotten wood breaking under their feet… this was a burial place!

Looking more carefully now, she could distinguish long, straight rows of gentle hills, washed out by rains, evened by heavy snows and trampled by animals. But they were graves; the whole clearing was a graveyard! All the crosses, washed out by the heavy rains, had fallen and were buried in the soil, covered by weeds.

"Janka! We are standing on a cemetery lot! It must be a soldiers' graveyard from the last war!"

"There must have been a bloody battle here. The graves were hastily dug and the dead buried," said Janka, looking around as if she were in a trance.

Someone must have brought phlox there that later spread all over the lot. Forgotten and unattended, this cemetery, invaded by underbrush from the nearby woods, had ceased to exist.

Suddenly an awful thought struck Irene. "We have been jumping and stamping all over them!" she cried. "We have been eating berries fertilized by human flesh, picking flowers whose roots were touching their rotten bodies!"

She began to retch, throwing up the berries. Janka became ill, too. Pale and trembling, with tears in their eyes, they began to walk back to the palace grounds.

"Do you remember how sick we were in Baranowicze in that outhouse full of worms?" asked Janka later.

"Yes. But *this* is different. I feel like I've committed a sin, like desecrating a church, though God help us, we did not know!"

They knelt down and said a silent prayer.

"I wonder, Irene, whether they were Polish, Russian or German soldiers?"

"Maybe all of them," ventured Irene. "How sad, that only death could bring them peace — or maybe even death did not unite them… how do we know?"

"Where are all your beautiful phlox?" asked the professor the following day, seeing only a small bouquet of field flowers on the table.

"There aren't any more," replied Irene.

Somehow she did not want to tell anyone about the graves of the young men who had died there years before; violent, premature deaths… of men who now slept in rows and rows of shallow graves, with fragrant, colorful phlox above, with the wind whistling in the nearby woods… of men, grinning pathetic smiles, watching the sky with unseeing eyes, asking "why?"

CHAPTER FIFTEEN — Mrs. Teacher

The dark, bare branches were swaying in constant agitation behind the window. Sophie knew these trees, every contour, every shape of each branch to the smallest detail. When a gust of wind would disarrange the pattern for a while, it would soon come back to the original design.

It was November now. She had been brought to the hospital early in March. The trees had been bare then, too, but there was that certain dormant vitality, the expectancy of life in the swelling buds. Quite often the sparrows that nested on the southern wall among the hardy vines would sit on the branches, chirping and quarreling, or cleaning their little beaks. Sophie's bed faced the window, so day after day, all she could do was to watch the trees, the sky and the birds.

Sharing the room with three other patients was a harrowing experience… the cough, the spitting, the bedpans. It was enough to be hopelessly ill and not be able to forget about one's own body, but the constant pressure of other sick people was hard to endure. The Sisters of Charity were very efficient and kind, but were busy from dawn until midnight and could not spare much time for extra kindness. Anyway, to them sickness was sent by the Lord. It was not treated as a curse, but as God's will… and death was a welcome communication with God.

"Pray." This was the only advice and consolation that they were able to give to the sick.

But what if someone was unable to pray? It was not that Sophie did not believe in a Great Power governing the Universe. She always had a feeling of being a part of His creation, proud to be alive, to be unique. But now, knowing that she was near death, a feeling of strange emptiness, of emotional detachment possessed her soul. Her only contact with God was not through thoughts and prayers, but through a small part of his creation — the trees and a patch of sky beyond the window. She had watched the branches first swell with life. Then one day, tiny, fuzzy flowers appeared by the thousands and enveloped the trees in a soft, golden hue. After that came leaves, small, pale and shiny at first, growing and darkening into deep greens later on. The windows were kept half-open during the summer. Sophie could feel the healthy, robust breeze, smell the fragrant wetness of the leaves after a summer storm, and one could hear the quiet murmur of the wind among the trees at night. It was good.

Weeks passed. One patient was better and went home. Another became worse and was taken from the room. Two new ones came and began telling their life stories, like the others had before them. One had to listen whether one wanted to or not. Sophie couldn't talk anymore; only a hoarse whisper would come out of her throat. The sickness, having destroyed her lungs, was now choking off her throat.

One day the trees turned into colors, seemingly overnight. It was a lovely sight. Sophie could not swallow any food. Sister Teresa would come a few times a day and feed her clear, cold broth or tea, by a spoon. Even that was hard to swallow. As if to reward her for the lack of food, the Creator gave Sophie a feast for her eyes. The golds, the coppers, the bronzes and carmines of autumn were now in front of her tired, dying eyes all day long. Then came rain and heavy winds, and one morning all the leaves were gone. One lonely, stubborn leaf was clinging desperately to a branch, making the picture even more desolate.

That day, two orderlies came and wheeled Sophie's bed to a private room. She knew what it meant. Nobody was allowed the luxury of a private room — except those who were soon to die... "In order not to disturb other patients..."

Although in a different room now, Sophie could see the same trees, as she was still in the same wing of the building. The first snow fell that day. Sister Teresa came with broth and tried to feed Sophie, but she did not have the strength to swallow. The liquid spilled from the corner of her mouth and onto the pillow.

"I want a mirror, Sister. I want to see myself, please," she whispered.

"May God forgive me, but I cannot let this girl see her face!" thought Sister Teresa. "Sorry, my dear, but we have no mirrors."

"Don't let my mother see me today. Don't let anybody see me after I die."

"Now, now, you rest my dear…"

"She went away… how good it is to be alone. It's snowing. Strange… my body is so weak, yet my brains are still working… for how long…?"

"I don't love you Sofia Aleksandrovna because you are beautiful but because you are good. Kiss me just once, Sofia Aleksandrovna…"

"Why do I have to die? I did not want much from life; neither to be rich, nor even to marry. Just to teach peasant children, whom so few people want to teach…"

"Why aren't you going home, my child? The classes are over.

All the other children have left, taking their crumpled

Reading books and writing tablets. Why aren't you going home?"

"I don't want to go home, Mrs. Teacher. I want to stay here

In this room. My home has a very small window, my home has a

Bare earthen floor. It's crowded in our small house, Mrs. Teacher. Here in school there are big windows and a wooden

Floor, the maps, and pictures and blackboard, the stories,

The dreams…

I don't want to go home, Mrs. Teacher. Please tell me a story."

[He stands there on one foot like a water bird, warming the Other at his calf.]

"I will tell you a story, my child. I will tell you a true

Story about a beautiful Princess who became Queen of Poland

As a child. She was only eleven years old when the heavy

Crown was placed on her head.

Though betrothed to handsome Prince William of Austria,

She renounced him in sorrow and tears, to marry the pagan

And wild Prince of Lithuania; for such was the advice and

Wish of her people.

The Queen was only thirteen, but her heart and her mind

Were clear and strong and pure, like crystal. She brought

Christ to the pagan Lithuania, she made the brute Prince

Jagiello a king. By uniting the two countries in one Kingdom,

She tried to give it more strength and power to resist

Mighty Germans, then called Teutons.

She built churches, monasteries, hospitals and was kind

To the poor. Though she lived five centuries ago when only

Kings, scholars and the rich could read and write, she ordered

All her jewels and robes to be sold, the money to be divided

Into equal parts — one half to the University of Krakow to

Enlarge and improve it for all who wished to learn, the other

One half to the poor. All this she did in her short life.

She never asked God for anything, for anything except a child.

But the little baby was born and soon died, and the Queen

> *Died, too. They say it was a childbirth fever, but maybe it*
> *Was of sorrow; of too much burden on her shoulders, of a*
> *Broken heart. She died young, because those whom Gods love*
> *Die young..."*
>
> "Go home, child... It's still snowing..."

The next morning Sister Teresa brought clean linen and tea. She looked at Sophie, put the cup quietly on the table, the linen on the chair. She took a little mirror from her pocket and held it to Sophie's mouth. There was no trace of moisture on it.

Sister Teresa held a cross that hung from the end of her large Rosary, and knelt in a short prayer. Then she left to notify the priest.

In the corridor she passed an orderly.

"As soon as Father applies the last rites, Number 12 will be ready for the morgue," she said.

So, it was in late November that Sophie died.

Mother had gone to see her twice each week all these months, but she refused to take the girls with her.

"It's not safe for young people to come to the TB Ward," she said.

That was partly the reason, but most of all she did not want her daughters to see the appalling change in Sophie.

One day the Sister of Charity would not let mother in. "Your daughter does not want to see anyone. She is very weak, and I would not upset her."

Mother stood at the half-open door: Sophie's eyes were closed. She looked at the wisp of a body under the blankets, at the wax-colored, ghostly thin face. Was *that* her child, the one she had brought into the world, nursed and taken care of?

She closed the door gently. That was the last time she saw her daughter alive.

The next day Irene was told that Sophie had died. She was given a new black dress with a white lace collar, and Helena had sewn a black crepe band to the sleeve of her coat.

It was a cold, foggy day when they buried Sophie. The gate of the hospital's chapel was ajar. Irene saw her aunts, uncle and cousins waiting at the entrance. It was a bitter, penetrating cold, and the black figures gathered at the chapel seemed to Irene to be shriveled with cold and sorrow.

Irene looked around: Henryk was not there. He knew that Sophie had died from Aunt Juta; besides, he must have read the death notice in the newspapers. She could forgive him for turning his back on mother and his sisters, she could forgive him for hurting those who loved him so, but she could not forgive him for failing to attend Sophie's funeral. Then she noticed an open coffin high on the black catafalque. In the coffin lay a horrifying skeleton, clad in a bridal-like white chiffon dress. The damp cold had molded the silk, revealing the ugly thinness of human bones. From a little, bird-like head protruded a sharp, thin nose.

Irene wanted to scream and run. Instead, she stood and watched with stony eyes, bewitched by the sight of the cruelty and ugliness of death... Sophie, the girl with the face of a Madonna — where are you?!

The priest came, spoke and sang in Latin, and the smell of incense filled the air. The attendants closed and sealed the coffin, put it down with a heavy thud on the marble floor, took it out and placed it on the hearse. A man with a cross stood in front of it with the priest. The white horses, clad in black and silver, nervously shaking their heads as if trying to rid themselves of the fancy headgear, started to pull.

The family followed. They faced more than an hour's walk through half the city to the cemetery. The air was frosty, but the snow on the streets was melting into slush. Mother was crying... crying. She could not see the hard lumps of snow under her feet and a few times faltered in her walk. Uncle and his son were holding her arms. Irene and her sisters walked behind them.

"One, two, one, two, slush, slush," went the galoshes in the snow. "One, two, one, two, slush, slush..."

The rhythm of the funeral hearse moving slowly and of the feet walking in front of her and behind her reminded Irene of the poet Wyspiański's words: *

> « *Keep rowing, keep rowing, Old Man Charon,*
> *Through the endless waters of the River Styx...* »

---

* From S. Wyspiański's *Noc Listopadowa* (1904)

It started to snow. Big, light flakes were falling on Irene's face, stinging her skin. Some of them settled on her eyelashes; they seemed so enormous when she blinked, but soon they melted into tiny drops of water. Then, other flakes would come and sit on her shoulders like tiny elves. She watched the flakes on her sleeves, too: delicate, transparent stars, all different, melting in front of her eyes. But those that fell into the street disappeared immediately into the brown slush.

"One, two, one, two, slush, slush…"

The endless brick wall of the cemetery, with its three wrought iron gates, drew near. Along the wall stood the flower and wreath vendors, stamping their feet to keep warm.

"Ah, good! Another funeral is coming!"

The usual agitation: men turning flower pots to show the potted chrysanthemums to advantage, shaking off snow from the pine and spruce wreaths. Those with carts getting ready to wheel them to the gate where the hearse would be stopping.

"Second gate!"

The race of the carts from the first to the second gate began. Who comes first makes business first. Little carts, rattling with flower pots on snowy, bumpy ground. Chariot races. Only in the place of proud and speedy stallions, miserable men in bulky clothes stumbling on icy, slippery snow. Behind them, women and children with wreaths on their shoulders. Who comes first makes business first. They push and swear, fighting for the best places. Anything to make a few pennies.

Not that they expect the family of the deceased to buy the flowers. The coffin is usually smothered with them. It is the friends of the deceased who buy the greens. After the funeral they will stop to visit their families' graves. It is such a long trip to the cemetery that once there, they will remove the fallen leaves, clean up, and leave some flowers — a token of remembrance.

How many millennia old is that custom? Whether it was food, wine, flowers or paper money, the reason was always the same: be on good terms with the unknown gods, and be generous, so maybe the wheel of fate will not strike you down too soon.

The twentieth century was not much of a change from the past. To remember deceased relatives was only an excuse, a disguise for an ancient custom to flourish: to bribe the angry gods against the horror of death. Otherwise, why should people care about the "dust that goes to dust"? And so they go, in an endless procession with wreaths and flowers, embellishing graves, thinking of the departed, trying to push away that frightening feeling of the inevitable: soon you will be here, too, all alone in eternity.

Irene was now with the others, following the men who were carrying the coffin. She knew the way well, and she knew all the other graves in the main alley. Some of them were very large, even with chapels, and some had life-size sculptures of angels or of the deceased. Most had stone and marble structures above the vaults, with the family name engraved on a frontal plate made of marble, and a wrought iron fence and gate. Others were in the form of an obelisk, attached to which were names and porcelain miniatures of the deceased.

They were at that moment passing the grave of a young woman. Her lifelike statue in marble caught all the slender charm of a beautiful girl. With one arm on a broken column, in a high-collared, corseted dress, with snow covering her shoulders like an ermine cape, she seemed to be waiting for a carriage to take her to a ball.

Now they were passing a bronze statue of a boy in a school uniform. Every time Irene came here, she stopped by and said a prayer for him. He reminded her of Tomasz in the family pictures. The last time that she was here was All Saints Day, when the beautiful old trees and shrubbery were dressed in all the splendor of autumn. The day was warm, the sky showing patches of aquamarine among the reds and golds of the leaves. The boy had greeted her with his eternal smile, his eyes looking into something that she could not see. But today, white frost clung to the bronze statue. The red-berried shrub that had lovingly protected the boy had shed its last golden leaves and its scarlet berries, like a woman in sorrow tossing her head with tresses undone on the ground. The snow clung to the lines of his face, covering his unseeing eyes and his lips. Today, the boy in the school uniform did not smile.

« Keep rowing, keep rowing, Old Man Charon,
Through the endless waters of the River Styx... »

The funeral procession stopped.

The large marble top with brass handles was removed. The cold darkness of the grave was gaping at them.

CHAPTER SIXTEEN — Narcissus

Irene's interest in the theater had become dormant since her return from Moscow. At school she had to memorize poems — especially in Polish and French — yet now she memorized them more or less like all the other students did: because she had to. She had lost that *feeling* for poetry, for words expressing deeds, moods and emotions. Selling a book to buy French pastry with the money, roaming the public parks after school, having little fights with her friends and then making up, this seemed to be all that mattered.

Occasionally she went to the theater; either school-organized mass attendance to the classic plays of Polish and foreign repertoires, or else she went with her sisters. But the seats were always somewhere far in the balcony. You could hear well and see the stage adequately, but you could never see the actor's face and never felt "in contact" with the play. It was all very theatrical, remote, unexciting. A few theaters in Warsaw played a delightful repertoire of French comedies and new "modernistic" plays like those of Pirandello, but Irene never got a chance to go there — unless those theaters also put on a classic like *Cyrano de Bergerac* or some play by Beaumarchais.

"Why," she thought, "why did I use to be thrilled with anything that had to do with the stage — singing, dancing, reciting poems — and now it all seems strange, almost alien to me?"

One day the teacher of Polish literature decided to spend an hour with her students, reading aloud a scene from a symbolic play, constructed in the manner of a Greek tragedy and based on the fall of Troy. The play symbolized the annihilation of Poland in the eighteenth century: the so-called "first partition of Poland." The teacher called out at random the names of students who were to read various parts: King

Priam, Paris, Cassandra, Hector, and so on. Irene was given the part of Cassandra. It was a big part, ending in a long monologue in which Cassandra predicts the fall of Troy and death and doom for the people, just like in the tragedy itself.

The girls were reading their parts in a monotonous, dull tone of voice. Then Irene's part came: a young maiden in a trance, seeing what no one else could see. The quiet, sad voice changes into a tragic moan, the words come out of Cassandra's throat at times quickly, plaintively, as if there was no time to lose in saving her beloved city. At other times the words are pronounced slowly, as if every word opened a painful wound. The voice, deep and subdued at times, then rises and rises to a crescendo to bring out all the tragedy and impotence of a clairvoyant trying to communicate with people ignorant of fate and of their inescapable doom...

When Irene finished the monologue, there was quiet in the classroom. No one stirred or turned a page. The teacher, staring in amazement at Irene, cleared her throat. Luckily, the recess bell rang, and everyone got up from her seat.

"I made a fool out of myself," thought Irene, feeling blood pounding in her temples.

She knew then that she was stage struck.

From then on, she went through all the poetry books and plays in the house, memorizing everything that was in accord with her interests and moods. How sorry she was now that she had sold those books for sweets! They seemed to her like lost babies that you cannot bring back from the grave. Like in Moscow, she would again stand in front of the mirror, watching critically all kinds of expressions on her face. She now felt a great need to be close to the stage, close to the actors. But how could this be accomplished?

As in Pauline's life, as in Henryk's, fate played an inconspicuous trick once again. As they would say in a mystery story: it was *The Case of One Missing Match*.

As there was no man in the house since Henryk left, the girls got used to running around stark naked in the morning. They did not have any bathrobes, and the simplest thing to do was to run into the bathroom, take a sponge bath and get back to their rooms to do their morning exercises in front of an open window. It did not seem to bother them at all that in the wintertime the bathroom, with no heating of any kind, was very cold. But they had been conditioned from early childhood not to mind near-freezing temperatures. As of late, they were profiting from one luxury: gas pipes were installed, and a simple two-plate iron gas stove was placed on top of the kitchen's coal stove. No more smoke in the house! Plenty of hot water at any time of the day or night — a sheer delight!

That particular Sunday the girls, one after another, dashed in and out of the bathroom, and after a few minutes of Swedish exercises, got dressed and sat down to breakfast. When the doorbell rang, Helena got up, and casually munching on a piece of bread, opened the door. It was their next-door neighbor, who also lived in a "built-up" apartment except theirs was smaller, consisting of two rooms and a kitchen.

They all knew each other by sight, often riding the elevator together. As Poles have no word for "hello" in their vocabulary, and people of the upper classes do not talk to strangers, their entire social intercourse for years consisted of polite half-smiles and half-nods of the head.

The neighbor was always meticulously well-groomed and dressed. In spite of her age, which must have been about the same as mother's, she wore cobweb stockings and high heels. Her fur collar emanated a discreet fragrance of Parisian perfume, and she wore a touch of makeup — just enough to improve her looks, but not enough to be in bad taste. All in all, she was definitely a very distinguished, elegant lady, but entirely different from the type mother was. For years, mother wore black and gray clothes, with a touch of white, like a dickey or jabot around her neck. Her coats and hats were always very conservative, not like her neighbor's, who did not hesitate to wear a lilac-colored velvet hat with a veil to match.

The neighbor, standing at the door, was dressed in a well cut, elegant housecoat. "Excuse me for intruding," she said. "It's perfectly silly of me, but I ran out of matches, and I can't light my cigarette or make my coffee on the gas stove. Do you think that you could spare a match or two?" She was holding a cigarette in her hand.

"But of course," Helena replied. She came back shortly with a box of matches. "Since you are here, and we are having morning coffee, would you like to join us?"

"Oh, I am not dressed, and I hate to bother you,"

"No bother at all," insisted Helena, leading the neighbor into the dining room. "Please meet my mother and my sisters."

They all introduced themselves, even though they knew their last names from the plates downstairs that hung near the mailboxes.

"My name doesn't mean anything to you, but I am the mother of _____ and mother-in-law of _____."

She mentioned the most popular and talented names in the acting profession. Her daughter was an actress, and her son-in-law was also a director and owner of the most progressive, modern and sophisticated theater in Warsaw! They never played as a team, though, and there were rumors about their rather stormy marital life. Whether the reason was jealousy on both sides, or the typical differ-ences about directing, casting and choosing the right repertoire, it was hard to tell.

Now, their close relative was sitting right there, sipping coffee and talking about all the actors, producers, directors and playwrights in a casual way, calling most of these people by their first names! It was exciting! It was incredible! She apparently enjoyed herself, having breakfast in a friendly circle of avidly interested young girls, instead of having coffee alone. She told them a few anecdotes and theatrical jokes, all in a reserved way. Then she asked the girls about their lives, visibly interested in what they had to say, especially about Helena's training in medicine.

"You don't know it, but she has been dreaming since childhood of becoming an actress," said Helena. By "she" Helena meant Irene, in whose direction she waved her hand.

The woman looked at the young girl with special interest. Irene blushed.

"Really?" she asked. "I could fix you up with a meeting with my son-in-law, but I know in advance what he will tell you. How old are you?"

"Fifteen."

"You see? What he will tell you is to finish school first, then go through the College of Drama, and study hard. Talent, in his opinion, is only one of an actor's tools. If one wants to become a great actor or actress, that is. Do you know that after so many years on stage, he still practices his speech, tone and voice intensity every day? He will tell you that you have to study the history of culture to know all about the old myths and religious cults on which the ancient Greek tragedies were based. To learn about the Italian *la Commedia dell'arte* and the medieval Passions, from which sprung European comedy and drama and which reached their peak in Elizabethan theater. He will tell you to study the world's drama to see how the same theme, the same story or myth has been used and reused by different writers throughout the centuries in different ways, forms and manners. He will tell you to study costumology, so that you do not accept a costume designer's sketches in complete ignorance, but talk them over and ask for changes, if necessary. Of course, I am talking about period costumes. There is nothing more distressing than seeing an opera singer or actress dressed not as a Greek, Egyptian or Spanish heroine, but looking as if a madman had wrapped her hastily in torn-down velvet curtains and silk drapes."

Everybody laughed.

"Studying old prints and pictures," she continued, "you will learn not only how women dressed, but you will get the feeling of how women stood, sat down and moved, in different periods. But heavens! I talk too much. I have to go; your heads must be spinning!" she exclaimed.

"On the contrary; it was all so interesting," Irene's mother assured her, "and Irene must have learned enormously about what she can expect, I mean how much work it takes to become an actress."

"Would you like maybe free tickets to the theater?" asked the woman. I can have two tickets for you a few times a month, including the Opera."

"Would we like it?! How can you ask such a thing?" cried Irene.

Everybody joined Irene in an enthusiastic chorus.

"Then you will hear from me soon," she continued, bidding them goodbye. "Oh, by the way," she turned to Irene in the hall, "how would you like to meet my daughter? She is coming soon to have dinner with me. Maybe you could come after dinner and recite something for her. Would you like to have her opinion?"

"I... I would be very grateful and honored to meet such a great actress," stammered Irene, blushing to the roots of her hair.

"Good. I will let you know what day it is."

After the neighbor's visit, Irene's head was in the clouds. She was excited about the promised tickets, and she had stage fright just thinking about meeting the actress. "What shall I wear, how will I arrange my hair (certainly not plaited in a tress!), what should I choose to recite?"

Besides these problems, many new problems sprung up around her — growing, crowding her — making her feel as though she were struggling like a helpless, ignorant explorer in the jungle. Up to now, she had thought that *vocation* was all that counts in acting. Vocation plus talent, of course. But who would doubt that you had talent if you wanted to be an actress so much?

Now she heard that the greatest actor — after years of a most successful career — is still *improving* his voice, his diction. She heard the woman say how much and how many different subjects — besides acting — you have to take in the College of Drama before you can *start* being an actress. Until now, she was so sure that the first time she appeared on stage, *everyone would simply die* with enthusiasm and adoration for her looks, her voice, her style of acting. Now, she was not sure at all; in fact, overconfidence was entirely replaced by doubts.

"But," she told herself over and over again to regain confidence, "the class and the teacher were impressed with my Cassandra, and I did not have a chance to study that role at all."

The day finally came when Irene was notified by the neighbor to please come over at about seven o'clock. After hours of doubts about what to wear, she decided to stay in navy blue — her white-collared school dress was of that color. She combed her long, ashen blond hair and held it together with a narrow black ribbon.

As a poem, she chose a long monologue of Mary Magdalene: coming to anoint Christ's face, and seeing boundless compassion, understanding and love in his eyes, she confesses all her sins and cleanses her soul of guilt.

When Irene arrived, the actress was sitting on the sofa in a pose of graceful informality. She did not rise to meet Irene, and her mother, after a few words of introduction, tactfully withdrew to another room. The girl stood in the middle of the room, her heart pounding. The only light came from a table lamp covered with a thick, beige silk shade; it was rather dark in the room. The actress asked Irene to sit down.

"No, thank you, I would rather stand up," she replied.

They exchanged words of polite generalities, which the actress used to appraise Irene's voice, her looks and personality, while skillfully pretending not to pay much attention to her.

"How beautiful she is," thought Irene.

Actually, the actress was not what you would call a beauty. It was the strange combination of a childlike innocence in her large, dark eyes, the small, delicate features and a sensual, generous mouth that gave her face a sex-appealish look. As if on stage, she spoke slowly now, as if halting on purpose for a split second before each word. It made those who listened hang, so to speak, to every word, to concentrate much more on what she was saying than one would with the average person. Her voice, neither high nor low in pitch, had a special quality of intimacy, softness; it was almost caressing, yet at the same time it gave the impression of regal distance. These qualities, almost impossible to exist in the human voice at the same time, were nevertheless present in her voice and made her so unique on the stage. It was as if she were a child and a full, sensual woman at the same time; as if she were listening to you attentively, yet at the same time she was an ancient priestess in a trance, as if she were warm, human and kind, yet distant, indifferent and elusive.

"What a beautiful girl," she thought, looking at Irene standing there in the rosy shadows of diffused light, her eyes shiny, her cheeks flushed from emotion. "Would you like to recite something for me?" she asked softly, folding her hands on one of the armchairs.

For months, every time Irene recited that long poem about Mary Magdalene, she thought that it was the greatest performance in the world. Now, she was feeling miserable; she knew that what she was doing was an imperfect, crude piece of acting. She finished the piece, and the silence in the room seemed to crush her shrunken ego into nothingness.

"Well," said the actress finally, "let's start first with the positive aspects of your performance. You have a low, melodious and naturally well-set voice, and that is a great asset. You will not have to worry about getting hoarse after opening night in a role demanding great use of the voice. Your pronunciation, that is your diction, is very good, too, and you don't join the last syllable of one word with the first of the next one, as — unfortunately — even many good actors do. But I think that you could still use some practice on diction, like musicians have to practice scales. It will give you a purity of speech, even when the role demands very rapid speech under great stress and strain."

"As to your looks, you are very young, but one can see — and you are no doubt aware of it — that you are a very good-looking girl. But don't think that it will be of great help to you. On the contrary, quite often it might be an obstacle. The actress of average looks playing fairly well is more appreciated by the public than the beautiful one acting equally well. You might easily be accused of not 'acting,' but 'using your looks.' You will have to work harder, because more will be expected of you. Do you see what I mean?"

"Yes, I do."

"Now, to the criticism. You chose a very difficult part. First, because it is in verse, second because it is a monologue, on which even experienced, talented actors often stumble. Third, you have to be a grown woman, to have gone through the pain of love and losing love, to have known what sin is, and to have known the need for repentance to understand Mary Magdalene."

"Do you have a sense of rhythm, do you have a good ear for music?" she asked suddenly.

"Yes, I appreciate music very much, and I think that I have a good sense of rhythm."

"Good. Then you won't have to worry about playing parts written in verse. All you need to have is a sense of rhythmic flow of poetry and forget that it is in verse. There are many good actors who are impossible to watch in so-called 'Shakespearean' plays — which means any great plays — be it Schiller, Rostand and so on. These actors fall into a sing-song mannerism the minute the part is in verse. Up and down, up and down go their monologues; if you happen to know their lines, you will know in advance how they will say them. Beware of falling into this kind of mannerism because once you acquire it, it will be very hard to get rid of."

"Now, please forget *all* that I have just told you for a while. Remember only one thing: you are a woman whose body has been abused by sin, whose soul is tormented with guilt. You have come to tell it all to someone full of understanding, compassion and love. Now, tell me that poem once more."

Irene stood and listened. The ribbon, which was sliding slowly down her shiny hair, fell to the floor. The long hair covered her arms and chest. She fell on her knees and began: *

> *"Do not look at me, I beg of you,*
> *for my soul is in torment and fear!*
> *I come with an amphora full of fragrant oils,*
> *to anoint your tired feet..."*

---

* From *Magdalena* (1903) by Kazimiera Zawistowska.

From then on, the girls went to the theater a few nights every month, including the opera. The seats were always in the middle of the first few rows. You could see the actors' faces well, and even notice the "private" reactions on their faces when one was stealing the show from the other, or forgot his lines for a second. You could hear the prompter's whisper, and all this gave Irene the feeling of familiarity and close contact with the stage. Seeing so many plays also enriched her literary background. School required much reading: European literature and plays, and the memorizing of poetry, but all of it was limited to the most important writers — Molière, Beaumarchais, Ibsen, Shakespeare and famous Polish playwrights. There was no time for the latest avant-garde of talented German, Italian and French writers. The gap in Irene's education was now successfully filled in the most interesting and exciting way... theater-going.

Since meeting the actress, Irene — remembering every word of her advice — started to study "the professional way." Now, just to recite a poem fairly well, and then hear the comment "how wonderful" or the clapping hands of relatives, was not enough. Now, every poem was torn apart bit by bit, analyzed for determining the correct emotional approach, for taking a breath at the right moment, for control of voice and diction. Irene would experiment to see whether a tragic scene could leave a listener more impressed if she raised her voice, or rather lowered it almost to a whisper.

The flow of her talent was just as strong and powerful as before, but it was no longer undirected. If before it could be compared to a raft floating and bouncing in the open sea, it was now a sailboat operated by skillful hands, headed along a chosen course.

When a few months later the neighbor dropped in and said: "My daughter talked of you to her husband and told me that you could come to his office anytime this week. He does not start rehearsals until next week. Would you like to meet him?"... Irene thought that she was ready to conquer the world right away.

She borrowed a dress and high heels from Helena; it was a nice blue French dress with a white appliqué, a copy of a Parisian original. Irene was sixteen now, but the high heels and the hair pinned up around her head made her look older. It was summer, so school did not interfere with her morning appointment. Going to the theatre building in the morning was unusual in itself. Somehow one always thinks that these buildings don't exist until it is time to open the gates and let the public in. Taking the stage entrance was another adventure. The simple, dark stone staircase was so different from the highly ornamented Opera staircase, or other "public" entrances at theatres.

She climbed to the second floor. She was visualizing herself in the cozy, private atmosphere of a lavishly furnished office with discreet drapes, half-pulled at the window. She, alone with the most handsome, desirable, popular actor in existence! Naturally, he would fall in love with her beauty and talent instantly, and would beg her not to finish her last year of school or go to the College of Drama. He will offer her a part in his coming play, and she will be an instant hit!

What she saw as she entered the door was a huge room, rather dusty and drab, with many uncurtained windows. On one side stood a desk, and there were a few hard wooden chairs here and there along the walls. The actor-director was there, but he was not sitting. He was standing in front of his desk, talking to a few men. There were several other men and women in the room, walking in and out, talking to each other, and apparently waiting for a chance to have a word with the actor. Irene told the nearest man that she had an appointment with the director, at which he unexcitedly told her to sit down and wait.

In her bright-colored dress and unfamiliar hairdo, she felt terribly out of place, almost foolish. Everything was so different from what she had expected! Everything, that is, except the actor. He was just as handsome, charming and full of personality as he was on stage. The unique timbre of his voice, soft and caressing, was always the same whether he was talking to the stage hands or to the costume designer, to the actress or to the artist whose stage setting he was discussing.

Sitting there for a long time, Irene watched what was going on around her. The atmosphere of that "new" kind of world, which she was hoping would someday be *her* kind of world, was exciting and absorbing. Yet, after a while she became aware of an unexplainable but explicit "something" that was bothering her in the entire setting. After a while, it bothered her more and more... what was it? "There it is. Now I know," she thought. "He was *le Roi Solei* — the king surrounded by his court — all dependent on the grace, favor and kindness of a capricious benefactor. The young actors and actresses, like disciples, were standing here and there, waiting for a bit of attention."

It was obvious that all this could have been avoided if the director had an office in one of the small rooms available on the same floor, and talked with each person privately.

It was also obvious, at least to Irene, that he chose this setting because it suited his narcissistic ego. She understood that he was not *as natural* and charming on stage as he was in life, that it was the other way around: he was as *unnaturally natural* in life as he was on stage: every turn of the head, every word and gesture was carefully planned for the people in the room, as if they were on stage.

"Do all these people let themselves be fooled, or do they *pretend to believe* in his natural charm and simplicity because they depend on his favors?" Irene wondered. "Do they really believe in his magic superiority?" These people around him talked and behaved… with a kind of nauseating servility.

The man to whom Irene had spoken on first entering the room brought her presence to the attention of the Director at the proper moment. He knew that she was there, anyway. Sitting a few feet away from him in her blue and white dress, good-looking as she was, she was hard to miss. Yet he behaved for about forty minutes as if she did not exist at all. Then, at a time he thought "right" for the scene, he came over and started talking to her. Irene got up, prepared to recite something for him. "It is going to be awkward with all these people coming and going, and talking," she thought, "but I had better get used to being in public."

By then, all of her stage fright and trepidation in meeting this great actor was gone. She was not only cool and composed, but foolishly enough found herself possessed by a superiority complex… Talking to her in his velvety voice, he held both of her hands in his; a sort of Romeo and Juliet scene, but of course all this looked so *spontaneously* natural to onlookers.

"My wife and mother-in-law spoke to me about you very favorably," he began.

It was exactly as the neighbor had said a few months ago: he asked her how old she was, and advised her that after she got her baccalaureate she should enter the College of Drama and "study hard." That was all. He did not ask her to recite anything, which did not disappoint Irene but rather relieved her.

Going down the same flight of stairs, she thought angrily: "Why did he bother to ask me to come at all? Was his interest mildly stirred by the talk of a girl that his wife mentioned, or was it because he thought that I would fill in nicely as one more member of his court for a day?"

She decided that it must have been the latter. In an instant, she remembered how years ago mother received beautiful long-stemmed roses for her "name day," and Emily, the maid, had exclaimed:

"Gosh, they are beautiful. They look just like they are artificial!"

"With *him*," thought Irene, "it's the other way around: he is so beautifully artificial, he looks real! If I ever succeed in becoming an actress, I swear never to be in private life anything but *me* — Irene. And when I act, I will think only about the role, about the human being who I am on stage, and not which side of my profile looks better in public. And when I breathe, I will take a breath when I *need* to, not when I am *supposed* to."

She understood that for the time being there was nothing else for her to do but study, to mature, to analyze human emotions, and above all… to analyze her own emotions toward other people and events.

CHAPTER SEVENTEEN — Mrs. Doctor

Alone in the house, Helena was finishing her coffee. Irene was at school, and Janka had just left for her office. Helena glanced at her watch: it was a few minutes after eight. She still had to do the dishes before leaving for the Children's Clinic where she worked every morning. In the afternoon she shared an office with an obstetrician in a newly organized "Care for Mother and Baby" clinic. It was a project started by the new government, which for the first time brought free medical care and drugs to workers and their families. As a pediatrician she was in charge of the children, and her colleague the mothers.

The office was on Wolska Street, in the heart of the Wola district slums, where crooks, thieves, and unskilled and underpaid or unemployed workers lived. Besides the Jewish section, Wola was another part of the city with its own language and way of life.

Stolen goods from other parts of the city and suburbs were sold openly on the "market" and peddled in the streets. When one walked into the Wola district, it was like entering another world, with its own laws and morals... or in this case, the lack of them.

It was in these surroundings that Helena worked every afternoon. Usually, it was not safe for young women from "outside" to walk the streets of Wola alone. However, the laws of the slums, while peculiar, were strict. News, any news, traveled fast. The very first day, everyone knew that the young, attractive woman who got off the trolley car was "Mrs. Doctor from the Clinic." Not only she was not bothered by anyone, but was treated more reverently than perhaps even a priest. The people of Wola were bitter and cynical, but they knew how to be grateful.

Helena and Andrzej, the obstetrician, had their hands full at the clinic. Untidy women looking twice their age waited with sickly-looking children, waiting, always waiting. Their sicknesses? Mostly malnutrition, rickets, unending colds, skin disease. You prescribe cod liver oil and iron for a child who lives on potatoes; you prescribe a bath and ointment for a child who has never seen a piece of soap in his life. You tell the mother to keep the child warm in an unheated flat. You tell her: "your child should drink milk," knowing that she cannot afford it. You give a woman your own money to buy milk — so she can give a child medicine with milk. Maybe she will get the milk, but maybe the money will be spent on vodka. Liquor and sex — the two spices of the drab, hopeless life of the pauper. Children are born every year, every ten months, in dirt, squalor, drunken abuse and cold. Many die, some live.

"Attending to the sick should give me a sense of accomplishment," thought Helena, "yet working in Wola gives me only a sense of frustration, of hopeless struggle — like trying to empty the ocean with a bucket. Andrzej has the same feelings; when he takes me home, we always talk about it. Andrzej. He is in love with me. Am I in love with him? No. He attracts me in a certain way; his serious face, his searching gloomy eyes. We work together, talk about common medical problems, but..."

The doorbell rang. A long, penetrating, insistent sound, as if the person pressing it wanted to be sure it was heard.

Helena opened the door.

A small, pale woman with dark, shiny eyes stood at the door. She walked in without being asked, and somehow Helena did not find it strange to let her in. They stood in the hall, facing each other, the woman's eyes searching Helena's face. Helena wondered why the woman's face was so deathly white and why her hands, clutching a small black bag were trembling so. The few seconds it took for them to stare at each other seemed endless.

"What can I do for you?" asked Helena in a detached yet attentive way, like doctors do a dozen times a day.

"I am Andrzej's wife," the woman said, almost in a whisper.

"Oh?"

"You took him away from me. He loves you. I lost him. I have nothing in the whole world but him, and I lost him."

She spoke rapidly, in a monotonous quiet voice. Except for her burning eyes and nervous hands, one would think that she was talking about some unimportant matter.

"I *never* tried to take your husband away from you. We work together, that's all."

"Yes, but after work you walk, you go to the café together; I saw you… I've seen you many times. Yes, I spied on you. He hardly speaks to me. He comes late, he, he… has not touched me for months." She lowered her eyes. "Do you love him?"

"No. I loved someone else. I don't think that I will ever be able to love again."

"Then, why do you stay with him after work?"

"Do you know what it is to work in Wola? Do you know how I feel advising a mother to provide sunshine and good food for her child who lives in a dark cellar on a heap of dirty rags? To order medicine to be taken with milk, when they never *see* milk. Do you know how your husband feels examining women who have never seen a doctor in their lives, who have never taken a bath? Who had to attend to their own childbirths because they were too poor to afford a midwife, too stupid or apathetic to arrange for the help of a neighbor? Women, who because of frequent childbearing, neglect, disease and lack of care have their uteruses half torn out of their bodies, dangling between their thighs? How it feels to attend to emaciated, hungry children, too weak even to cry?"

"If both of us had not gone through the hardening period in medical school, dissecting cadavers and watching operations, we would be sick many times every day. Do you know that after work, leaving Wola, after taking a walk, when we sit in a café smoking a cigarette, our hands still tremble?"

"He never told me that…"

"Did you ask him? Did you show any interest in his work? Did you encourage him to talk about it? Or were you concerned only that he was late for dinner?"

The woman struggled with the clasp of her handbag. She opened it and took out a small revolver.

"I came here to kill you. I feel ashamed. Even if you told me that you love him and will take him away from me, I could not kill you… He belongs to you."

"No one *belongs* to anybody. Meet him halfway, and very likely he will… he will walk with *you* after work. I will ask for a transfer from Wola Clinic. He won't see me again."

Andrzej's wife put the pistol back into her bag. The noise of the clasp snapping shut seemed to both of them unusually loud in the stillness of the hall.

"This will sound hollow," she said, "but it *is* a real privilege to have met you. Thank you."

"You will forgive me, but I have to be at the Children's Clinic at nine o'clock," said Helena, opening the door.

CHAPTER EIGHTEEN — Do You Remember…?

School was over for the day, and the girls spilled out by twos and threes, waving goodbyes. Some of them went home, others decided to go to the Botanical Gardens, where in mid-May, amongst the rare shrubbery, bloomed French lilac bushes, pruned and tended in such a way that they produced flowered stems several feet long. The many colors and hues, of single and double type blossoms, were not only a riot of color but a symphony of fragrance. Some had more of a bitter-almond perfume, others a sweeter and more delicate aroma. Irene usually walked from one bush to another, burying her face in the cool freshness of the flowers like a butterfly tasting the nectar of many blossoms.

"Aren't you coming with us, Irene?" called one of the girls. "I thought you were a flower lover."

"I can't. I have the first fitting of my suit today at the tailor's," answered Irene, not without show-offish pride.

She crossed the street and turned left toward the square where she was to take one of the cross streets going toward the Vistula River. It was one of the happiest days of her life; she felt grownup and carefree. She was seventeen; in a few weeks she would receive her baccalaureate from the girls' school. The day was beautiful, and she was getting her first custom-made *tailleur*. Was not all of this enough to make you feel happy?

Stefa, who bought the wool fabric for the suit, told Irene to meet her after school at a given address. There were many tailors in Warsaw, as all women except servants or the really poor had their coats and suits made to order. Not all tailors, of course, were equally expensive, though all were quite good. The address of the tailor's or dressmaker's establishment had much to do with the price that they charged. Turning from the center of the city toward the Vistula, Irene knew that the tailor would not be expensive.

The years of struggle and unhappiness were over. Stefa, who had married a successful lawyer two years before, had a large apartment in the city and a country estate. She traveled abroad often, and spent her winters in Zakopane. Mother stayed mostly with Stefa, taking charge of the servants while she was away, or keeping her company at the estate when she was there. Irene was now sharing the family apartment with Janka and Helena. How their family of eight had shrunk to just three so quickly! They each had their own bedroom, and they could afford to hire a maid, as Helena's practice had expanded and Janka was working in a bank. Mother's pension was enough to cover Irene's expenses.

The only thorn in this rosy picture was that Henryk never made the slightest move toward reconciliation. From Aunt Juta they heard that he had quit engineering and switched to business administration, which had evening courses. The girls never talked of Henryk, and tried not to think about him. It was still an open wound, so it was best to leave it alone.

Going down the street, thinking of many unimportant things, Irene became more and more aware of *something happening*—was it within her, or around her? Something *was* happening, what was it? Pleasant or not? Disturbing? She had a feeling that it was unusual and disturbing, but not unpleasant. The streets in Warsaw are flat, lined with three to five-story houses; some of the streets are wider, some narrower, but *flat*. Now, this street was definitely *going downhill*. It was not too wide, with small houses two stories high, some with gardens. When was the last time that she walked on a street like this? She stopped at the number Stefa had given her. The wall... the iron gate. She pushed it, and it swung open: the yard with fruit trees and lilac bushes in bloom... old-fashioned lilacs... purple and white...

Suddenly, like a tidal wave, like a rushing avalanche, a powerful feeling of remembrance swept in and enveloped her. Their place in Moscow, their *pereulok* going down toward Taganka Square! There was so much suffering associated with that final year in Moscow, so much unhappiness, that Irene never, never thought about Russia. It was gone, like a bad nightmare, like a sea monster that you don't care to approach.

Standing in this empty courtyard, looking at this simple garden, Irene suddenly realized that there was nothing to be afraid of anymore; that memories, however painful, can be very precious and beautiful. That in time you forget the intensity and the bitterness of the pain. That the facts and events become transformed into some-thing everlasting: the feelings and impressions become interwoven with your memory, your soul. You cannot create a priceless tapestry without puncturing the cloth with a needle thousands and thousands of times, but when the work is finished you see the object of art, not the needle that tore through the cloth.

What now remained in Irene's mind of Russia, in her heart, was not the memory of cold, hunger and unhappiness, but of a family living together, of devoted and hard-working parents, of seasons coming and going… the sudden rush of spring after a long winter, the summer dachas, the white nights… the childhood antics and games with Adela… the *tserkov* bells ringing all day at Easter: « *Christos voskrese, voistinu voskrese!* »

Irene felt a quiet softness and purity within her, like the quiet and softness of the garden in bloom around her.

"Read this," said Stefa, showing Irene a paragraph in the newspaper.

Irene was sitting at the tailor's waiting for the fitting to start. In the paper was an announcement of the annual graduation at the Conservatory of Music. The names of the graduates were printed — among them, Magdalena's name. She was to play in a difficult concerto for two pianos at the grand Philharmonic Concert Hall, where all the graduates were given a chance to perform once. After that, they were on their own.

"She certainly messed up Henry's life, but not her own," said Stefa.

"Are you going to the concert?"

"Certainly not. I could not stand the sight of her. You know me. I don't wish anybody evil, but as far as Magdalena's success goes, I certainly do not wish her my best."

"I don't know why," said Irene, looking out the window, "but somehow I can't hate her. And I wish I could go to hear her play. Nobody can play like Magdalena…"

After the fitting, Irene walked part of the way back with Stefa. Then, they parted, each heading to her home. Crossing Marszał-kowska Street, Irene bumped into a passing young woman. Mumbling "excuse me," something made her head turn and look at the woman. She, too, turned her head.

"Adela!"

"Irene!"

"You would not believe it, but I was just thinking about you!"

"I have thought of you a thousand times!"

"Is it not strange we looked up, is it not strange we recognized each other? You are so grown up!"

"You, too, Irene. Gosh, you are beautiful! Can you come in for a while to my office? I work in here."

"Work? Did you finish school already?"

"I quit school two years ago."

"Why? When did you come back from Russia?"

"We came just a few months after you left. My father simply disappeared one day. We never found out if he had been arrested or whether he had just run away to hide with Rachela. They both disappeared the same day. My mother sold the furniture and silver, and came here with Halina and me."

"Why did you leave school?"

"We had to stay with relatives. Can you imagine the three of us cooped up in one room? You know my mother — always half ill and complaining. The relatives meant well, but they were mingling and interfering with everything. Every time I ate a ham sandwich, my aunt practically fainted — they eat kosher food, you know. Besides, remember what a little devil I used to be as a child? Well, my sister Halina became even worse. And listening to all those family squab-bles and my mother's complaints, I thought that I would go out of my mind. I quit school, took business courses — you know, typing, filing, bookkeeping — and here I am."

"I can't believe it! You little brat, supporting the whole family! It makes me feel so immature! I am finishing school next month."

"You are lucky. But I can't complain. We now have our own apartment: nobody sticks their nose into my ham sandwich, and Halina is much better."

"Where do you live?"

"On Złota Street."

"Next street to ours! To think that we've been living so near and haven't bumped into each other sooner."

"Well, I work in the morning until one o'clock, then I go home, help Mother with dinner, see Halina after school, help her with homework, then come back to work here. It's a wholesale business office, so hours aren't important, as long as a certain amount of work gets done daily."

"I am to start working in September. I have been promised a job at the Foreign Ministry. It's very difficult to get in there; you have to have the highest recommendations because the work is top secret: coded papers, *notes verbales*, and so on. But Stefa and Helen know a few influential people who will recommend me; one of them is a Minister of the Cabinet.* I'm practicing typing in French like mad."

"Are you not planning to enter University?"

"No, I want to pass the exams at the School of Drama at the Conservatory. The classes start late in the afternoon, so I can hold a job and study, too. The professors and actors on the staff of the School have mornings free for teaching at the University or for rehearsals."

"But, of course! I remember now, you were always dancing and singing. I thought you would be a ballerina or opera singer!"

"I want to be an actress more than anything in the world. Not because of wanting to be a celebrity, for money, popularity or any-thing like that. I just have powerful feelings that I have to share with others in the best way that I know how… it's hard to explain… I feel like a priestess in an ancient Greek temple…"

"You are a lucky one. But don't think that I am a complete moron just because I quit school. I read about ten books a month: Polish, French, German, English, American, Italian, Scandinavian — mostly in translation, of course. And not only fiction. I also read philosophy, astronomy and archeology. Right now I'm struggling with Bertrand Russell."

"You see, I am a greater moron than you are! I haven't read any of his works yet. I thought that I was pretty smart reading Nietzsche."

---

* The individual was Norbert Barlicki, future husband of Helena. He was Deputy Minister of Interior in the government of Jędrzej Moraczewski (1918-19). Also, it was through his efforts that Stefa had obtained placement at the Belvedere Palace and Janka a position with a bank in Warsaw. See *Bibliography*.

"I realize that I'll never be able to make up for my lack of tutoring in advanced science and mathematics. I *am* a moron. How about your family, what are they doing?"

"I lost my father. Jadwiga and Sophie died, too."

"Oh! It's hard to believe that they are gone — especially Sophie."

"Yes — especially Sophie. Stefa and Henry both got married. Helen is a doctor and Janka works in a bank."

There was a short pause while the two friends looked into each other's eyes, as if they were trying to relive their lost childhood.

Suddenly, Irene tousled Adela's short-cropped hair.

"You cut your hair! You lucky! I am going to cut mine and buy myself a lipstick as soon as I get out of that silly school!"

"Do you remember how we first met at the Tserkov Square?"

"Do you remember how we were laughing like mad when…?"

"Do you remember…?"

"Do you remember…?"

CHAPTER NINETEEN — Who Is Going to… ?

"Thank God I am through for the day," thought Henryk wearily, putting on his overcoat and hat and wrapping a muffler carefully around his neck.

It was Saturday, and like any weekday, Henryk had to stay in the office until four. Then he usually stopped at a small cheap cafeteria for a simple dinner, and after that he had to rush to be on time for classes at the Business School.*

Today he decided to skip the lectures. He felt completely exhausted; he was walking around with a bad case of the grippe, and trying to keep his temperature down, he had to take dozens of aspirins. They made him sweat, day and night.

"That's why I feel so wobbly," he thought. "I sweat too much."

Instead of stopping at the cafeteria, he decided to see Uncle Sigismund in his office.

"Maybe he will give me something better than aspirin."

Aunt Juta and her husband were the only members of the family with whom Magdalena decided not to break off relations (probably because she thought it would be handy to have a doctor you did not have to pay any fee for). From Aunt Juta mother and the girls got skimpy information about what was happening with Henryk. Once, Aunt Juta tried, during one of Magdalena's visits, to mention Henryk's relatives, but Magdalena cut her off abruptly: "We are not interested."

Uncle Sigismund examined Henryk carefully.

---

* *Wyższa Szkoła Handlowa*

"You can't neglect colds like that, Henry. Two, three times a year you come and expect me to perform miracles, while actually there is nothing much to do but to stay in bed when the fever starts, instead of walking around with it to aggravate things. If you don't take care of yourself, you will be heading toward the same trouble Sophie was in."

Henryk decided to go straight home after leaving Uncle's office. "I will cook something myself at home," he decided.

He opened the apartment door with a key, hung his coat on a rack in the small entrance hall. The beds in their only room were not made. The floor and the furniture were dusty. Magdalena was supposed to clean on Sundays, but she hated housework, and it was always Henryk who had to do it. On Saturdays the apartment reached its peak of shabby, dusty abandonment.

He came into the kitchen. The sink was full of dishes; on the stove stood a few pots and pans that could stand some washing, too. On the small table was a half a loaf of bread, a piece of Swiss cheese and a messy butter dish, filled with half-melted butter. Henryk lit the gas stove, put on the tea kettle, washed one of the pots, and cooked some oatmeal cereal — the only thing in the cupboard. He made some tea and sat down at the table, pushing things to all sides to make room for the dish of cereal and the glass of tea.

Through all these years he never allowed himself to think about mother, his sisters, or the home that he had left. But somewhere, deep down in his flesh and soul was a feeling of longing for the family with whom he had grown up. Coming home to an empty, untidy apartment, he *felt* (though he did not *think* about it) the need for an orderly home, for a table set neatly with a clean, shiny tablecloth, for a linen wardrobe where you could reach for a clean shirt or towel, for the young voices of his sisters, for mother's attentive voice when she would ask what he had done that day at the Polytechnique...

Strange, for all these years since he had left home, he only thought of Magdalena's feelings about the rift; never did he stop to think how it affected his mother and sisters. Now, like a blind man who suddenly can see, he could see his relationship with his mother from a better perspective. It was a cruel, senseless, selfish act to abandon an aging widow who was struggling financially with the responsibility of bringing up his sisters. He, the only man in the family... instead of giving moral if not financial support, had discarded her like an unwanted object at a public dump.

"It's too late now," he thought. "It's too late now, after four years, to try to build a bridge between us. *To build a bridge.*"

"Who is going to take care of you when you are sick? ...who is going to... who is going...?"

That sentence had stuck in his mind since he left Uncle's office. Henryk sipped his tea. He took a box of aspirin tablets from his pocket, picked out two and swallowed them with his last sip of tea.

"Who is going to...?"

Where was this sentence from? In a book, or in a play he had seen? Oh, yes, mother had said it the last time he saw her. That was long ago. That was when he was dreaming of building bridges and dams, such beautiful, graceful, powerful bridges and dams that no one had ever built before... Now, he was employed by the Bureau of Taxation. When he finishes business school, he can expect a promotion. Someday — if he lives that long — he will even become a Director of the Bureau: how exciting! The salary is not high, but what prestige! And if you are dishonest, you can make a lot of money on the side. All these big companies, industrialists, approaching you for tax reductions and exemptions... it will all be in your hands... just one signature... gifts, lavish gifts for you and Magdalena. It could all be yours one day — if you are still alive...

"Except," thought Henryk, "I am not a crook."

He went into the bedroom, undressed and threw himself on the bed.

"How good that it is Sunday tomorrow, and I don't have to go to that wretched office," he thought, falling asleep.

CHAPTER TWENTY — Silence in the House

About a year after the rift with Henryk's family, Magdalena's father died. As uprooted as her mother had felt years ago when she had to move from the family estate, she now simply fell to pieces.

"I am sorry, but you can't expect any financial help from me any more, Magdalena," she told her daughter after the funeral. "Your father was a state employee for too short a time to leave any rights for a widow's pension. Henry has to take care of you, 'my dear little flower.' After all, he has a full-time job, has he not? I will sell the furniture, move into a small flat, and by selling a piece of old silver or jewelry now and then, I will manage somehow. All I can do for you is to pay your Conservatory fee."

Henryk's salary was not adequate to cover all expenses: rent, food, clothes and laundry. Magdalena had to work. The only thing that she could do was to look around for students to whom she could give music lessons. Every afternoon after classes at the Conservatory, she had to run from one house to another, climbing countless steps and facing, for an hour at a time, apathetic, hostile or mischievous children.

There was no one less suited to be a teacher of music than Magdalena. Impatient, high-strung, a perfectionist, she could not stand ill-prepared or careless children making the same mistakes over and over. After a few lessons, if she knew that the child had no gift for music, but stuck to it "because mother said so," she would drop the student immediately.

From those who showed talent and interest in music, she expected such a degree of perfection, and hours of practice, that they soon dreaded each coming lesson instead of looking forward to it. She seldom gave a word of encouragement, for the most part sat tight-lipped, and quite often would humiliate the student.

"If you expect to bang on the keys in this manner, you'd better concentrate on chopping onions in the kitchen," she would say suddenly — when the child was sure that he was doing well.

Some children — maybe with masochistic tendencies — stuck to Magdalena's teaching through thick and thin. Others could not stand the tension and asked their parents to please change the teacher. Now and then, Magdalena would be told politely that "we are sorry, but for the time being we have to stop music lessons."

"Ah, what do I care," thought Magdalena. "As soon as I graduate from the Conservatory, I am going to play what I want and when I want. I am going to be a concert pianist and nothing else. Never, never again will I have to listen to these brats murdering music."

The years passed. Nothing mattered to Magdalena except reaching the day when she would hold the diploma in her hand, the day that she would for the first time sit down at the piano on stage and play at Philharmonic Hall — in front of that endless sea of heads. All the hard work, the perseverance and sacrifice, all this was for one purpose only: to reach that goal.

These were dreadful, discouraging years... the shabby apartment, a tired, overworked and unhappy husband, the lack of family life — it will all soon be forgotten, cast away. Their once violently strong sexual attraction had changed after a few years into lukewarm, sporadic marital lovemaking. Either she was too tired or had a dreadful migraine, or he was feverish, coughing and sneezing, or both were dead tired and worn out... And love? There was no time for love and affection, it seemed. But it all did not matter much. Nothing mattered much... except Magdalena's music.

More and more, Magdalena was getting those dreadful migraines. There were days when she had to take eight, even ten headache powders to get through the day of studies and lessons. At night she would be unable to sleep, and the next day she had to drink countless cups of coffee to stay awake. The following day, headache powders again...

PART III — CHAPTER TWENTY

The time of graduation was drawing nearer and nearer; only a few weeks until her concert at Philharmonic Hall. Now, suddenly, instead of looking forward to it, Magdalena felt panic clutching at her heart; not just simple "stage fright" or "butterflies in the stomach," but panic. She tried to control it.

"You know that you are not only the best student graduating this year, but the best they have had in many years. What are you afraid of? You know that you have prepared your part of the piano concerto to perfection. What are you afraid of?!!!"

But she could not sleep for a moment at night. Night after night, night after night. She went to see Uncle Sigismund. He gave her some sedatives. A single dose did not work, and a double dose knocked her out for the night and half the next day. Sometimes, she did not even know what she was doing.

"I have to be in good physical shape, and mental shape, at the concert," she thought desperately.

That afternoon, she went to her student's home for a lesson. It was her most gifted student, the only one for whom she cared. At the end of the lesson, the child's mother appeared.

"I am sorry, but for the time being we have decided to stop the lessons."

"She is lying, she is lying! She has already hired someone else," thought Magdalena bitterly.

The woman paid her for the last few lessons, and Magdalena left. Outside it was one of those freak days in late May; cloudy with an icy wind, making all the green fluffiness of the trees and shrubs appear to be shivering with cold.

"I suppose I will go home," thought Magdalena.

Home. Was it ever really *home?* No. A room, a hall and a kitchen, but not a home. She walked in, did not even notice Henryk's gabardine coat and hat on the rack, and went straight into the kitchen. The familiar disorder. Usually she would put off the cleaning until the next day. She was very careful about her delicate hands and always tried to push the dirtiest work off on Henryk. But today, she did not care. Anyway, she knew that Henryk had the grippe, and coming home later from Business School, he would go straight to bed and stay there all Sunday to get better. He was starting his final exams the next week.

SILENCE IN THE HOUSE

She was still in anger at her pupil's mother for having dismissed her, and she was angry at herself for living in that constant state of panic about the coming concert. She was mad at everybody and everything.

She threw herself with frantic fury into cleaning the kitchen. Dishes were washed and put away, the table wiped clean, the floor swept. There were a few odds and ends on the floor and window sill that should have been put away long ago into the hall closet: Henryk's galoshes were among them, as he wouldn't need them until next fall.

Magdalena opened the wardrobe, put the boots on the bottom, and tried to find room on the upper shelf for the other things that she was holding. Between the upper and lower shelves hung some clothes: her old suit and Henryk's officer's uniform... the rusty stain of blood, the tear from a Bolshevik bullet as a memento of war. Pushing things aside on the shelf, she touched Henryk's service revolver. The leather of the holster was dry and stiff from the lack of use and care. She pulled out the gun: it was heavy and had a thick barrel. She walked into the kitchen, sat down, and put the gun on the table, staring at the tops of the trees behind the window.

"It's very windy today," she thought absent-mindedly.

Her hands, usually steady and strong — with an amazing "masculine touch," as her professors would say — were now weak and trembling.

"You will never be able to get out on that stage and play, and you know it," she suddenly said aloud with disgust and contempt in her voice, as if she was talking to one of her pupils.

When was it that something had snapped within her, breaking into pieces that precious inner being that should be whole?

Was it the day that her family had to abandon their beloved home and estate, fleeing from the Bolsheviks?

Was her boisterous energy, wit and sense of humor — during those days when she went to live with Irene's family — caused by the excitement of meeting Henryk? Or was it a front to cover an unhealed wound?

Or was the burden of genius simply too heavy for her body, for her imperfect soul?

Or maybe she finally understood that life is something more than building the shell of a snail around you, that you have to love and to give, not hate and destroy, and not being able to change her nature...

In the next room Henryk, sweating from the aspirin, was dreaming… dreaming that it was a hot summer day. He was a little boy and was watching a peasant load the cart with hay. His sisters, little children also, were running around, picking some flowers at the roadside. The cart was now filled high, high up with hay.

"Can I have a ride?" cried Henry. The peasant nodded and pulled him up by the arm. Henry slid down a few times, grabbing big clumps of hay and finally made it to the top. The cart began to move, and Henry, on the very top, swayed with every movement.

How good it was to swim in that deliciously smelling sea of hay! His little sisters were following the cart, throwing flowers at him, which he was trying to catch and throw back at them. Just like in the *bataille de fleurs* on the French Riviera.

Suddenly the peasant whipped the horse with full force. "It sounded like a gunshot," thought Henry in his dream. "I wish he would do it again!"

But the dream became blurry, distorted and faded away.

There was silence in the house.

ENDNOTE

ENDNOTE

Irene began her acting career in 1930. Shortly afterward, she married actor Tadeusz Frenkiel, son of the famed actor Mieczysław Frenkiel, but the liaison lasted only a few years. She married a second time in 1936, eventually arriving with her family in New York in 1940 after a prolonged odyssey, never to return to her homeland. After the age of fifty, her health began to deteriorate. She died in a nursing facility in Hawthorne, New York in 1993 at the age of 87, leaving nine grandchildren.

Father's death was on 20 February 1920. He was 65 years old. According to Helena, his unexpected death was a total financial catastrophe for the family.

Tomasz rests in peace, having died on 27 September 1909 at the age of 17. A year after his death, Father had his body exhumed from its initial burial place and interred at a new family gravesite.

Sofie's death was on 6 November 1924 of tuberculosis at the age of 26. Henryk and Stefa were also treated for the disease.

Henryk never reconciled with the family. He moved to Katowice in the south of Poland after WW II, where he spent the remainder of his life. Information on the circumstances of his wife's death is lacking.

Stefa married lawyer-activist Antoni Chmurski. She survived the war in Warsaw, together with her husband and son. She died in 1988 at the age of 87.

Janka (who had the nickname of "busybody", according to Helena) married a director of the bank where she was employed. She survived the war in Warsaw with her husband and two children. She died in 1981 at the age of 78.

Mother was shot in 1944 during the Warsaw uprising. She was 78 years old. Mother, Helena, Stefa and Janka had been mutually supportive in Warsaw during those dark days.

Camilla (Zofia Podkowińska) became a noted professor of archeology in Warsaw. She was an activist for Jewish rights, leading to her incarceration at the Ravensbrück and Königsberg (Neumark) concentration camps during the years 1944-45. She was much affected by those years, but resumed her career in archeology after the war. She died in 1975 at the age of 80. Her brother, Władek had died in 1920 in the defense of Warsaw at the age of 24. Her mother, "Aunt Juta" (Jósefa), died in 1941.

ENDNOTE

Helena found a benefactor in Norbert Barlicki, who also served as a father figure to Stefa, Janka and Irene, and whom she eventually married. In a testament written shortly before her death, Helena expresses her devotion to her husband. She had a distinguished career in the field of pediatrics, being the recipient of many awards. She barely survived WW II, working without pay in the children's hospital in the Wola district when it was liquidated by the Germans in 1944. She never abandoned her children, even to the day that they were summarily shot in their beds (the words that Helena would hear were *"alles Banditen, alles Partisanen — auch Kinder"*). After the war, she became a highly respected director of a pediatric center in Wrocław where she died in 1980 at the age of 85.

Jadwiga returned to Warsaw from Moscow in 1924 with Vlodek and Tadyo, at variance with Irene's account. Vlodek became employed as a manager in the Polish armaments industry. Jadwiga died after a prolonged illness on 19 June 1926 at the age of 38 and is interred in Warsaw. Tadyo went on to marry and have children.

It appears that the episode involving Jadwiga and Vlodek at the Lubyanka prison refers not to them, but rather to Helena and her husband, Norbert Barlicki. Norbert was arrested by the Gestapo on 3 July 1940 and held in Pawiak Prison in Warsaw, while Helena desperately tried to get information on his whereabouts. Eventually, hearing that he was to be transferred to Auschwitz, she went to the prison before dawn, hoping to see him and to give him a package with some warm clothes. She risked her own life by trying to enlist the aid of an individual having contacts with the Gestapo, only to be deceived. She tried to sell her belongings in the hope that money might somehow help. But it was all for naught. She never saw him again. He managed to smuggle out a note to her "on a shred of newspaper". On it were written only the words: "Remember that you are my Only Love".

And so, the records state that on the 6th of August 1941, near a town with the name of Oświęcim, in the south of Poland, not far from Krakow, an individual known to Irene by the name of Norbert Barlicki died. He was 61.

# ILLUSTRATIONS

PLATE 1. Father and Mother: Aleksander Tarnowicz and Zofia Grochowska Tarnowicz.

PLATE 2. Aniela ("Irene") at age 13.

PLATE 3. The Tarnowicz children, *ca.* 1901. *From L to R*: Henryk, Tomasz, Helena, Sophie, Jadwiga and Stefa. Janka and Aniela ("Irene") are yet to be born. [*A. Wyrobisz*]

PLATE 4. Father and Mother, *ca.* 1886. [*A. Wyrobisz*]

PLATE 5. Aunt Helena, one of Father's sisters. [*J. Chmurski*]

PLATE 6. Aniela's mother, Zofia (*right*) with three of her sisters (*L to R:* Maria, Domicella, Stefania). [*J. Chmurski*]

PLATE 7. Jadwiga (*top, 2nd L*) with schoolmates. [*J. Chmurski*]

PLATE 8. Jadwiga in Moscow, *ca.* 1915. [*B. Wasiljew*]

PLATE 9. "Mrs. Teacher." Sophie, Sister of the Red Cross… the girl with the face of a Madonna. [*J. Chmurski*]

PLATE 10. Henryk, lieutenant in the Polish Army. [*J. Chmurski*]

PLATE 11. Stefa, in her teens and Janka, about twenty years old. [*J. Chmurski and A. Wyrobisz*]

PLATE 12. "Camilla", student of archeology, *ca.* 1918. (Zofia Podkowińska). [*Polskie Towarzystwo Archiwalne*]

PLATE 13. Stefa (*middle row, 1st R*), Moscow Gymnasium, *ca.* 1917. [*J. Chmurski*]

PLATES 14 & 15. At the Tretyakov Gallery, Moscow.

Above: Ivan the Terrible with slain son. [*I. Repin*]

Below: "Life Is Everywhere." [*N. Yaroshenko*]

PLATE 16. "Mrs. Doctor." Helena, who became director of a regional pediatric center in Wrocław. With husband, Norbert Barlicki. [*J. Chmurski*]

PLATE 17. Political activist husband of Helena, Norbert Barlicki. Commemorative stamp issued September 10th 1982 in series "Activists in Polish Labor Movement." [*Poczta Polska*]

PLATE 18. Spała, 1886. The tsar's palace on the Pilica River.

PLATE 19. Aniela Tarnowiczówna, the actress.

PLATE 20. Aniela with her mentor, the noted actor-director Aleksander Zelwerowicz, 1930. [*Instytut Sztuki*]

PLATE 21. Aniela as Gwinona in *Lilla Weneda*, 1934. [*Juliusz Słowacki Theater, Krakow*]

PLATE 22. Aniela as Gaby and Roman Hierowski as Sasza, in *Rycerz kameliowy* in 1934. [*Narodowe Archiwum Cyfrowe*]

PLATE 23. Aniela's flight from Poland with her family in 1939. The numbers correspond to dates. Thus, they were in Lódz on Sept. 1-4, etc. They barely crossed the border at Zaleszczyki on Sept. 16th. [*map: Holocaust Museum, Washington, D.C.*]

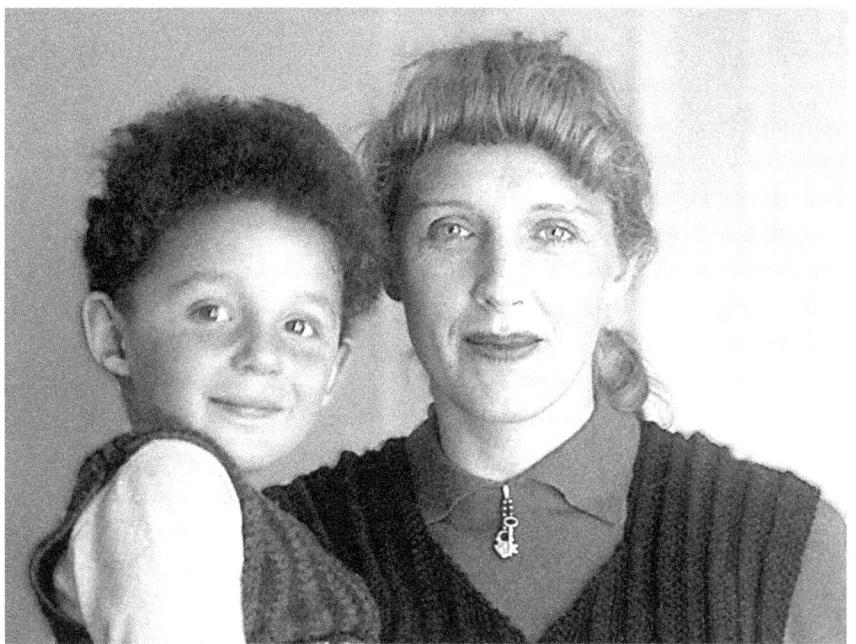

PLATE 24. Aniela with eldest child, displaced to the USA, 1940.

PLATE 25. Aniela interviewed in Rye, New York by a local newspaper, 1953. [*The Daily Item*]

PLATE 26. Aniela at eighty.

-541-

"Wait here, please. I will see what we can do."

She left for what seemed to mother an eternity. It seemed to the girls, sitting outside, an eternity, too. Irene was getting numb with cold, Sophie felt weaker, dreaming about a bed into which she could sink her fatigued body.

Finally the woman came back, accompanied by a nurse.

"We managed to move an extra bed into one of the larger rooms," she said. "You can bring your daughter in."

Afterwards, leaving Sophie behind in her room, they sat outside on the bench - mother and daughter - and ate some leftover, stale sandwiches.

"I feel as if a big stone has been removed from my chest," said mother. "The air is so fresh here, Sophie must get well. Come, Irene. We will have some hot tea at the station. We have to take a train back soon."

They walked all the way to the station - a long way.

Just when they were about to reach the station, the clouds dispersed and suddenly the tops of the mountains appeared in black contours on the gray sky. There he was - Giewont - the sleeping knight, felled by death, yet powerful and defiant, tearing with his proud face at the sky, at infinity, unconquered even by death.

"How beautiful, how beautiful he is...Oh mother, even death could be beautiful!"

"What made her think of death?", wondered mother.

A big, soft cloud drifted in an enveloped the tops of the mountains; it covered the face of the sleeping knight, like a merciful hand pulling up a sheet over a dead man's face.

PLATE 27. A page from the manuscript... *A big, soft cloud drifted in and enveloped the tops of the mountains. It covered the face of the sleeping knight, like a merciful hand pulling up a sheet over a dead man's face.*

SOURCES OF ILLUSTRATIONS
&
BIBLIOGRAPHY

SOURCES OF ILLUSTRATIONS

Plate

3-11,13,16 Tarnowicz family photographs from Jacek Chmurski, Andrzej Wyrobisz and Bohdan Wasiljew.

4 Aleksander and Zofia Grochowska Tarnowicz, probably at the time of their marriage (1886), from Andrzej Wyrobisz.

12 Polskie Towarzystwo Archiwalne.

14,15 Tretyakov Galkery, Moscow.

17 Commemorative issue, Polish Postal Service.

18 Spała, imperial residence in rustic style, built for Alexander III in 1884. Contemporary photogravure.

20 Aniela Tarnowicz in the role of Monika, with Aleksander Zelwerowicz as Dr. Butrym, in *Miłość Czy Pięść* by K. Dunin-Markiewicz, Teatr Lutnia, Vilnius, 1930. From the collection of Instytut Sztuki, Polish Academy of the Sciences, Warsaw.

21 Aniela in the role of Gwinona, with Władysław Woźnik as Lech, in *Lilla Weneda* by J. Słowacki, Juliusz Słowacki Theater, Krakow, 1934. From the archives of the theater.

22 Aniela in the role of Gaby and Roman Hierowski as Sasza, in *Rycerz kameliowy* by Rita Rey, Juliusz Słowacki Theater, Krakow, 1934. Narodowe Archiwum Cyfrowe.

23 Adapted from map: the United States Holocaust Memorial Museum, Washington, D.C.

24 Aniela with son, Artur. South Orange, New Jersey, *ca.* December 1940.

25 *The Daily Item*, Port Chester, New York, March 14th 1953.

others Collections of A. Benis.

page

xviii, 66 Adapted from maps: Google Inc.

168 Giewont: photomontage by A. Benis.

cover

front image: Vladimir Drovalen

back Collection of A. Benis.

inquiries: abenis2000[at]gmail.com

BIBLIOGRAPHY

Tarnowicz-Barlicka, Helena, *Testament to Norbert Barlicki (1880-1941)*, English translation, A.M. Benis, New York, KDP electronic and paperback editions (2018).

www.ingramcontent.com/pod-product-compliance
Lightning Source LLC
Chambersburg PA
CBHW031614160426
43196CB00006B/128